# Become a
# Recognized
# AUTHORITY
# In Your Field

## In 60 Days or Less

Robert W. Bly

**ALPHA**

A member of Penguin Group (USA) Inc.

*To a good friend and great writer, Robert Lerose.*

## Copyright © 2002 by Robert W. Bly

International Standard Book Number: 0-02-864283-X
Library of Congress Catalog Card Number: 2001095860

05   04        8   7   6   5   4

Interpretation of the printing code: The rightmost number of the first series of numbers is the year of the book's printing; the rightmost number of the second series of numbers is the number of the book's printing. For example, a printing code of 02-1 shows that the first printing occurred in 2002.

*Printed in the United States of America*

**Publisher:** Marie Butler-Knight
**Product Manager:** Phil Kitchel
**Managing Editor:** Jennifer Chisholm
**Acquisitions Editor:** Mike Sanders
**Development Editor:** Tom Stevens
**Senior Production Editor:** Christy Wagner
**Copy Editor:** Cari Luna
**Cover Designer:** Doug Wilkins
**Book Designer:** Trina Wurst
**Creative Director:** Robin Lasek
**Indexer:** Brad Herriman
**Layout/Proofreading:** Gloria Schurick

# Contents

**Preface**

1 What Is a Guru?     1

Defining "Guru"     2

Do People Like or Hate Gurus?     6

Are Gurus B.S. Artists?     8

Benefits of Becoming a Guru     11

Who Qualifies for Guruship?     13

*Case Study*
Roger Parker Reinvents Himself as a Guru     17

Why Our Society Is Enamored of Gurus     19

2 How to Join the Guru Elite     21

Philosophy     21

Guru vs. Mini-Guru     22

Attitude     23

    The Guru Attitude     24

Ethics     25

Methodology     26

Knowledge Base     27

Market Niche     28

The Invented Term Strategy vs. the
Fit-a-Category Strategy     30

Action Plan     32

    The Sixty-Day "Become a Guru" Action Plan
    at a Glance     33

The Four Phases of Guru Development     35

The Rule of Seven     36

*Case Study*
Jeff Davidson                                           38

To Sum It All Up                                       41

3    Articles                                          43

The Secret of the Trade Journal Trade                  43

What Magazine Should You Write For?                    44

The Type of Article You Should Write                   45

Get to Know the Publication                            47

Making the Initial Contact                             48

Exclusivity                                            53

Length and Deadline                                    55

Writing Articles for the Web                           57

4    Books                                             63

Why Every Guru or Would-Be Guru Should
Write a Book                                           65

Which Publishing Option Is Best for
the Wanna-Be Guru?                                     67

Selling Your Book Idea to a Major
Publishing House                                       69

Agents and Publishers                                  77

Writing Your Book                                      78

Self-Publishing                                        78

E-Books                                                81

5    Information Products                              83

What Are "Information Products"?                       84

Reasons Why Gurus Should Produce
Information Products                                    86

Tips for Producing Specific Types of
Information Products                                    87

Tip Sheets                                         87

Booklets and Pamphlets                             87

Special Reports                                    88

Monographs                                         88

Resource Guides                                          89

Manuals                                                  89

Books                                                    89

Audio Tapes                                              90

Audio Albums                                             90

Power Packs                                              91

Video Tapes                                              91

Paid-Subscription Newsletter                             91

Software                                                 92

How to Design a Catalog Featuring Your
Information Products                                      92

How to Sell Your Products Profitably to Clients
and Prospects                                            93

How to Use Direct Marketing to Boost Your
Product Sales                                            94

Narrow the Focus                                         94

Seize a Subject                                          95

Plan the "Back End" Before You Start Marketing           95

Test Your Concept with Classified Ads                    96

The Importance of the "Bounce-Back" Catalog              96

Create Low-, Medium-, and High-Priced
Products                                                 97

Let Your Buyers Tell You What Products They
Want You to Create                                       97

Be the Quality Source                                    98

Using Small Ads to Sell Information Products             98

6   Newsletters and E-Zines                              105

The Company Newsletter                                   106

Size and Frequency                                       107

Building Your Subscriber List                            108

Promoting the Newsletter                                 110

Designing Your Company Newsletter                        111

Charging a Fee for Your Newsletter                       113

Writing Your Newsletter 114

What Will It Cost? 118

Paid Subscription Newsletters 120

E-Zines 122

7   Speaking 125

Why Gurus Give Speeches 125

Finding Speaking Opportunities 127

Be Selective When Accepting Speaking Invitations 129

Negotiating Your "Promotional Deal" 130

Planning an Effective Presentation 133

The Three Parts of a Speech 136

Ending Your Talk 137

Length and Timing 138

Handouts 139

Getting People to Take Your Handout Home
with Them 141

The PowerPoint Question 143

8   Seminars 147

Why Every Guru and Would-Be Guru Should
Consider Giving Seminars 149

Option One: Free Tutorial Seminar 151

Option Two: Promotional or "Product" Seminar 152

Option Three: Self-Sponsored Fee-Paid Public
Seminar 154

Option Four: Seminar Sponsored by a Seminar
Company 155

Option Five: Speech or Presentation at an
Association Meeting or Industry Event 156

Option Six: Teaching a College or Adult
Education Course 156

Will Seminars Work for *You?* 158

Setting the Seminar Fee 159

Fees and Scheduling                                        160

Choosing a Seminar Title                                   161

Obtaining the Mailing List                                 162

Controlling Costs                                          164

Self-Promotion at the Seminar                              165

9  Public Relations                                        169

How PR Works                                               169

Develop a Hook                                             170

Letters to the Editors                                     173

Press Releases                                             174

Pitch Letters                                              182

Syndicated Columns                                         183

Radio Talk Shows                                           192

TV Appearances                                             193

10  The Internet                                           197

Do You Need a Web Site?                                    197

What's in a (Domain) Name?                                 198

Guru-Focused vs. Topic-Focused Web Sites                   199

Building Your E-List                                       202

E-Mail Promotion to Your Web Site Visitors                 203

Publishing on Your Web Site: The E-Zine                    205

Publishing on Your Web Site: Articles                      205

Publishing on Your Web Site: Reports and E-Books           207

Your Online Bookstore                                      208

You Ought to Be in Pictures (and Audios
and Videos)                                                209

Online Polls and Surveys                                   210

Building a Community of Interest on Your Site              212

Third-Party Endorsement Postings                           215

Networking Online (and Offline, Too)                       216

Search Engines                                             218

| 11 | Profiting from Your Guru Status | 223 |
|---|---|---|
| | Referrals | 223 |
| | Repeat Orders | 225 |
| | Resales | 227 |
| | Investing Your Guru Income | 228 |
| | How to Calculate Your Earning Potential | 228 |
| | Financial Planning for Self-Employed Professionals | 229 |
| | Be a Saver, Not a Spender | 231 |
| | Invest for Return | 232 |
| | Be Frugal | 235 |
| | Time vs. Money | 237 |
| | Retirement Plans and Other Retirement Investments for Self-Employed Professionals | 240 |
| | Tax Deductions | 240 |
| | Health Insurance Is the Number-One Financial Problem of Self-Employment | 243 |
| | Life Insurance—How Much Do You Need? What Type Is Best? | 244 |
| | Disability Insurance | 245 |
| | **Appendixes** | |
| A | Bibliography | 247 |
| B | Recommended Vendors | 253 |
| C | Sample Documents | 263 |
| | Index | 287 |

# Introduction

So many small-business people struggle—titanically—to keep the cash register ringing and the work flowing. They network, send out mailings, make cold calls, and stay up nights worrying whether they'll get enough work to pay the bills. "An entrepreneur," someone once said, "is someone who will work 80 hours a week for himself to avoid working 40 hours a week for someone else." In exchange for freedom from commuting and a boss, entrepreneurs put up with uncertainty, anxiety, unsteady work, and uneven cash flow.

But a few don't. These seemingly blessed entrepreneurs—freelancers, self-employed professionals, small business owners—always seem to have all the business they can handle ... and then some. Potential customers line up to buy from them, often waiting months until they can be serviced. So strong is the customers' desire to buy from these particular sellers that they'll wait and wait—and pay top dollar—even though other sellers are available now, are eager to take the business, and charge much less.

Why are some entrepreneurs busy and in demand virtually all the time, while others struggle to get by? Because they have established themselves as leaders in their field—the top plumber, photographer, architect, accountant, lawyer, doctor, consultant, manufacturer, e-business strategist, Java programmer, builder, or service provider in their market or industry. They are, in short, *gurus*—considered so knowledgeable and expert in their field that customers flock to them, while their competitors wonder why and must settle for picking up the leftovers.

*Become a Recognized Authority in Your Field in 60 Days or Less* is written to give you a tremendous edge over your competitors by showing you how to quickly become the preeminent, in-demand guru in your field. In this book you will learn:

- What a guru is and the advantages of being one
- Simple steps you can take to rapidly establish yourself as a leading authority in your field
- Why, once you are a guru, you will never have to ask people to buy from you. And you'll never have to make a cold call again
- Maintaining and increasing your status as a superstar in your field—and letting even more and more people know about it
- How to use your newfound guru status to build your business and increase your personal wealth

I do have a favor to ask. When you become the guru in your field, why not share with readers of the next edition of this book your story about how you did it? You will receive full credit, of course. Simply e-mail your response to rwbly@bly.com.

## Acknowledgments

Thanks to Bob Diforio, my agent, for finding a home for this book; and Mike Sanders, my editor, for giving me the opportunity to write it.

Thanks also to the gurus and experts who allowed me to reprint their advice and stories in this book: Ilise Benun, Fran Capo, Jeff Davidson, Roger C. Parker, Dottie Walters, Joe Vitale, and all the others quoted throughout these pages.

## Trademarks

All terms mentioned in this book that are known to be or are suspected of being trademarks or service marks have been appropriately capitalized. Alpha Books and Penguin Group (USA) Inc. cannot attest to the accuracy of this information. Use of a term in this book should not be regarded as affecting the validity of any trademark or service mark.

*Chapter 1*

# What Is a Guru?

The average professional speaker gets $3,500 for a speech and has to market like crazy to get the engagements. But Tom Peters has more requests than he can handle for speeches at $30,000 a pop. *Why?*

There are thousands of attorneys with better track records than Alan Dershowitz, but when the media wants to interview an expert for an opinion on a hot case, he's the one they call. *Why?*

The world is filled with clinical researchers, family counselors, and psychotherapists, but ask people to name a sex expert, and 99 out of 100 will answer without hesitation, "Dr. Ruth Westheimer." *Why?*

The answer: These people are gurus—recognized authorities in their fields. Because of their guru status, they enjoy greater visibility and reputation than their peers, not to mention more success, income, and wealth.

But they are gurus not because they are more talented or successful, or because their performance and track record are superior. (Lots of attorneys have won more cases than Dershowitz.) Instead, they gained their guru status through self-promotion and publicity. That is, they are gurus not because they are great at what they do, but because they are great at *selling and marketing* themselves and what they do.

*Become a Recognized Authority in Your Field in 60 Days or Less* is the first book to show the average practitioner in any field how, through a deliberate plan of self-promotion, they, too, can quickly elevate themselves to guru status—and enjoy the success, money, fame, and other benefits that go with the position. By becoming a guru, you set yourself above your competitors, become the preferred source of advice and service in your market, and eliminate the need to make cold calls and do the selling ordinary vendors do.

If you have ever looked at the gurus in your field and thought, "How did they become gurus? Why do the media and the public fawn over them? I know more than they do, and I'm better than they are," now you can join their elite ranks—and have others envy and wonder about you in the same way. And they will never be able to match your newfound expert status, unless you take pity on them and give them this book.

## Defining "Guru"

Management consultant Peter Drucker once observed that people use the word "guru" because "charlatan" is too difficult to spell. But what is a guru? And does positioning yourself as a guru somehow imply a degree of phoniness or even outright fraud?

A guru, simply put, is a person widely recognized as a leading expert in his or her field. There are degrees, of course. Are you a recognized expert in a narrow niche or a broad area of knowledge? Are you the number-one expert in this field, or one of several top authorities?

In today's Information Age, there is so much knowledge out there that no one can credibly master it all. People simply can't keep up with all they need to know. As Stephen King points out in his book *Secret Windows* (New York: Book of the Month Club, 2000, p. 358), "When you stack up the years we are allowed against all there is to read, time is very short indeed."

Therefore, by defining a niche specialty, you can slice off a segment of the world's knowledge that you can realistically hope to master—and then convince others of this mastery. No one is considered a guru in a field as broad as science, for instance, but the late Carl Sagan became the guru in the specialty field of planetary astronomy.

The narrower your niche, the greater your chances of becoming the pre-eminent guru in it. The broader your discipline, the more competition you will have. But that's okay. In many fields—management consulting, for instance—there's a big enough pie for several gurus to share the spotlight. Ken Blanchard, Tom Peters, Stephen Covey, and Peter Drucker are all in the top tier of management gurus, and you can probably come up with a few other names.

Some of the people occupying the top guru slots in a particular field change frequently (see the following table). Remember when re-engineering was hot? Now, what was the re-engineering guy's name again? You get the idea. In other cases, gurus maintain their leadership positions over long periods of time; Drucker and Peters come instantly to mind.

Eric Yaverbaum, president of New York public relations firm Jericho Communications, has another name for the guru—"the go-to guy"—because the guru is the individual the media goes to when they need a quote for a story relating to his field of expertise. During the O. J. Simpson trial and other major court cases, you saw attorney Alan Dershowitz on TV almost nightly, because he has become the top guru and the go-to guy in law.

## A Partial List of Today's Top Gurus

| Topic | Representative Guru |
| --- | --- |
| Advertising | Jerry Delefamina |
| Careers | Joyce Lain Kennedy |

*continues*

## A Partial List of Today's Top Gurus  *(continued)*

| Topic | Representative Guru |
| --- | --- |
| Change | Rosabeth Moss Kanter |
| Commercial real estate | Donald Trump |
| Competitive intelligence | Alan Dutka |
| Competitive strategy | Michael Porter |
| Computer programming | Tom DeMarco |
| Conservative politics | Rush Limbaugh |
| Consulting | Herman Holtz (recently deceased) |
| Consumer trends | Faith Popcorn |
| Cooking | Emeril Lagasse |
| Creativity | Edward DeBono |
| Desktop publishing | Roger Parker |
| Dieting | Dr. Robert Atkins |
| Digital media | Nicholas Negroponte |
| Digital prepress | Frank Romano |
| Direct response advertising | Joseph Sugarman |
| Employee motivation | Bob Nelson |
| English language usage | William Safire |
| Entertaining | Martha Stewart |
| Etiquette | Letitia Baldridge |
| Excellence | Tom Peters |
| Fads | Ken Hakuta |
| Fashion | Dr. Blackwell |
| Film | Roger Ebert |
| Flow | Mihaly Csikszentmihalyi |
| Future | Alvin Toffler |
| Home improvement | Norm Abrams |
| Information overload | Richard Saul Wurman |
| Information technology | James Martin |
| Interior design | Christopher Lowell |

| Topic | Representative Guru |
| --- | --- |
| Investments | Louis Rukeyser |
| Juicing | Jay "The Juiceman" Kordich |
| Law | Alan Dershowitz |
| Leadership | Warren Bennis |
| Management | Peter Drucker |
| Manufacturing | Richard Schonberger |
| Medicinal herbs | James Duke |
| Negotiation | Gerald Nierenberg |
| Networking (computer) | Bob Metcalfe |
| One-minute management | Ken Blanchard |
| One-to-one customer relationships | Don Peppers |
| Online marketing | Dan Janal |
| Options trading | Ken Roberts |
| Organization | Stephanie Winston |
| Parenting | T. Barry Brazelton |
| Permission marketing | Seth Godin |
| Personal advice | Ann Landers |
| Personal computing | Bill Gates |
| Personal effectiveness | Stephen Covey |
| Personal finance | Jane Bryant-Quinn |
| Personal power | Tony Robbins |
| Physics | Stephen Hawkins |
| Positioning | Jack Trout |
| Product naming | Naseem Javed |
| Psychology of persuasion | Robert B. Cialdini |
| Public relations | Regis McKenna |
| Quality | Philip Crosby |
| Re-engineering | Michael Hammer |
| Relationships | Dr. Phil McGraw |

*continues*

## A Partial List of Today's Top Gurus  *(continued)*

| Topic | Representative Guru |
|---|---|
| Retail marketing | Murray Raphel |
| Self-publishing | Dan Poynter |
| Self-transformation | Deepak Chopra |
| Selling | Tom Hopkins |
| Service marketing | Harry Beckwith |
| Sex | Dr. Ruth Westheimer |
| Shark cartilage | Dr. William Lane |
| Stocks | Warren Buffett |
| Success | Og Mandino |
| Technology | Geoffrey Moore |
| Time management | Alex Mackenzie |
| Travel | Stephen Birnbaum |
| Visual communication | Edward Tufte |
| Web usability | Jakob Nielsen |
| Weight loss | Richard Simmons |
| Wild animals | Steve Irwin |

## Do People Like or Hate Gurus?

Gurus are not loved by everyone. I have found that there are three schools of thought concerning gurus, and the population seems to be split almost $1/3$-$1/3$-$1/3$ into these three camps.

The first camp is people who worship, idolize, or at least respect or look up to gurus. They are impressed by the best-selling books. They buy the audio tape albums and listen in their car. They attend seminars or rallies. They are fans.

They think the guru's ideas are revolutionary, even earth shattering. They become evangelists for the guru, spreading the word and repeating the guru's ideas and concepts to anyone who will listen. If they are managers, they buy the guru's book in quantity and force everyone in their department to read it and follow the ideas.

Many in this camp go further, seeking out the gurus for consultation for their businesses or in their private lives. By attracting this huge following—and even in a small niche market, having one third of the market wanting to buy from or hire you can ensure prosperity and success—the guru makes a stellar living his competition can only envy.

The second camp is guru-neutral. They are aware of the gurus, may even acknowledge their status, but don't care much one way or the other. While they don't buy the best-selling books or attend the seminars, they may read articles by or about the guru, or log onto the guru's free Web site. They find the advice offered perhaps sensible and useful, but nothing earth-shattering, and they frankly don't see what the fuss is about. The fact that the guru is probably getting rich off this seemingly obvious advice doesn't matter to them much, either.

The third camp consists of the doubters, skeptics, cynics, and curmudgeons. They actively dislike the whole notion of gurus, and may intensely resent individual gurus. They refer to gurus as fakes, phonies, and "bullshit artists." They show the gurus no respect and even open contempt.

Many articles and several books, such as John Micklethwait's and Adrian Wooldridge's *The Witch Doctors* (Times Books, 1996), have been written with the sole purpose of debunking and criticizing the guru industry. The book quotes Rupert Murdoch who, when asked whether there is any management guru he followed or admired, said: "Guru? You find a gem here or there. But most of it's fairly obvious, you know. You go to Doubleday's business section and you see all these wonderful titles and you spend $300 and then you throw them all away." A colleague of the authors' hopes they don't miss the obvious thing: "That it's 99 percent B.S. And everybody knows that."

"The echoes of punditry are everywhere," writes Emelie Rutherford in a guru-negative article in *CIO* magazine (April 1, 2001, p. 131). "We business folk eat this stuff up." According to Rutherford, American business spends $20 billion annually to get advice from gurus, $750 million alone on business books.

The disdain of some people for gurus borders on hatred. "I hate motivational speakers," a manager at Panasonic told me. "They make me sick." Despite the inherent dislike of large numbers of people for gurus, the mathematics of guruship is in the guru's favor. Even if only one third of your market loves you, you've captured a market share astronomically higher than 99.9 percent of the service providers who are your competitors.

Motivational speaker Rob Gilbert teaches a formula in his seminars: SWL + SWL = SW. It stands for "Some will like me (my product, my service). Some won't like me (my product, my service). So what?"

Although no one likes rejection, most adults in business are aware of the SWL + SWL = SW formula, even if they've never heard it stated. They know that not everyone has to like you or buy your product for you to be successful. The gurus simply manipulate the formula in their favor by greatly increasing the SWL (some will like) portion in their favor, which happens automatically once they attain guru status. It's like playing poker with five aces in your hand.

## Are Gurus B.S. Artists?

In her *CIO* article, Emelie Rutherford is highly sarcastic about guruship, stopping short of calling gurus frauds. Rutherford writes: "'I could never be a guru,' you say. 'I think and speak too clearly. I'd be embarrassed to charge all that money just to talk to people. I'm too young. I work for a living.' Well, keep thinking like that and you won't be."

Is there any validity to Rutherford's charge that gurus are phonies who are somehow pulling the wool over their readers' and listeners' eyes? It depends on the expectations you have of the guru ... and what the guru wants you to think about him.

If a guru is promoting himself as having invented a new discipline or having discovered new methods, this claim is likely overstating the truth. The fact is, there are very few things totally new in the world. Revolutionary ideas are extremely rare and infrequent. Be suspicious of anyone who says he has one. More likely, the individual has dressed up an old idea, or put a new label on an old box.

There's an old saying, "Experts don't know more than other people; their information is just better organized." To me, this is a more accurate definition of what the gurus have to offer: A mastery of an existing discipline (not creating a new one) which the guru communicates in a clear, understandable, and useful manner to a well-defined target audience.

Your typical guru doesn't often have wholly original methods. But he had taken what is known in a field and synthesized it into a clear process or system that people like, can understand, and find useful. This clarity of thought and simplicity of explanation is what people find appealing.

Many gurus are not content to stop here, but invent their own terminology or deliberately convey the impression that they have not merely synthesized known data, but have in fact invented something altogether new. They believe, and perhaps rightly so, that this approach impresses clients more and further establishes their position as one who delivers unique value in their field.

The reality, however, is that a guru's mastery of a given subject or discipline typically comes from a combination of experience, education, self-study, and research. It is not usually the result of brilliant thinking or extraordinary creativity.

For instance, an executive recently told me about the difficulty her company was having marketing their product. I immediately gave her a solution which, when they tried it, solved their problem within a few weeks. "How are you able to come up with these ideas so quickly and easily?" she asked me in amazement.

The truth, which I told her, is anything but amazing. Writing direct marketing copy and solving direct marketing problems is all I do. I do it 5 days a week, 12 hours a day. And I have been doing it without interruption for over 20 years. For me not to be at least competent at it, I'd have to be pretty stupid. And like most people who have established at least minor guru status in a field, I am at least average in intelligence.

Although she was facing her particular problem for the first time and was therefore stymied, it was not unique; in fact, it is a common problem. I have seen it literally dozens of times in my consulting career. All I did was give her a recommendation based on what I had seen work dozens of times before. Therefore, I knew the likelihood that it would work for her company was strong, and the probability of my advice being successful was extremely high.

No brilliance on my part. Simply learning through repetition. By concentrating on a niche specialty, you see the same problems over and over, and eventually gain a repertoire of solutions for solving 90 percent of the situations any client is likely to encounter. The guru isn't smarter than the client. He just has more and broader experience, makes a study of the particular field, and has his information better organized.

You do not have to posture and make your skills and ideas seem brilliant and original to attain guru status. An opposite approach, and one which has worked quite well for many experts, is to be humble and honest about what you do and its limitations.

For instance, fundraising guru Jerry Huntsinger went out of his way to let clients know he had no special abilities or talents. All he could do, maintained Huntsinger in advertisements for his copywriting services, was write a fundraising letter "a little bit better than you can." And that, he said, was because he did nothing but write such letters all day long.

"The more you tell the client you are not a guru, not a rainmaker, the more credible you are," says superstar stockbroker Andrew Lanyi.

## Benefits of Becoming a Guru

Volumes have been written about selling and marketing, especially for entrepreneurs, small businesses, and self-employed professionals. But there is one marketing strategy that, if you master it, eliminates the need to do any other type of selling or marketing ever: becoming a guru.

Why can becoming a guru in your field virtually ensure you a long-term sustainable marketing advantage over your competitors?

We live in the Information Age, an era in which we are bombarded by data and drowning in information yet starved for knowledge. Although information is more plentiful and available than at any time in history (thanks largely to the Internet), people are overwhelmed by information overload and unable to process it all. Increasingly, we look to experts who seem to have a handle on this information (or at least on a segment of it in a narrow field) and can help us make sense of the data and guide us in our actions.

By becoming a guru, you position yourself as the information expert in a particular topic or subject. Therefore people needing help with this topic or subject turn to you first. As Alexander White observes in his book *Trading for a Living* (John Wiley & Sons), "The public wants gurus, and new gurus will come."

When you become a guru in your field, therefore, here's how you benefit:

1. You create an immediate overwhelming demand for the products or services you sell. If one third of a market of a million people are favorably predisposed to buy from gurus, the guru in that market has 333,333 prospects vying for his attention.

2. Since the demand for your services far outstrips the supply (most gurus can handle far fewer than 333,333 consulting assignments and speaking engagements), there's no need to get out and hustle for new business: You have prospects coming to you instead of you having to go to them. This eliminates the need to do most types of conventional marketing, such as advertising or cold calling.

3. Since you do not have to spend time marketing or selling yourself, you can spend more of your time on billable work. So your income increases.

4. Another benefit of demand outweighing supply is that you no longer have to negotiate your fees. With so many people vying for so few slots available on your schedule, you have the luxury of taking only those who can pay your full fee and turning away all other inquiries. Your prices go up and your revenue increases even more.

5.  The greater your guru status, the less likely clients are to question your work, advice, or judgment. This can be a double-edged sword. On the one hand, it frees you to give straightforward advice regardless of whether the client agrees or is pleased by it. And it eliminates the headache of clients who argue with or challenge you. On the other hand, you risk getting arrogant to the point where you close yourself off to what may be valuable client input (no one, including gurus, can possibly know everything).

6.  Having the demand for your services far outstrip the supply gives you the luxury of being selective. You can select only the assignments that interest you, and work only with the clients you like. Not only will you enjoy work more, but your success rate will likely be higher, since you are doing work you are good at for people you like (and who like you).

## Who Qualifies for Guruship?

Perhaps not everyone is qualified to be a guru, but more of us are than you might think.

Everyone lives a unique life, and therefore acquires unique knowledge, skills, and expertise that others can benefit from. The recognition of this core knowledge and the deliberate development of it is the first step on the path to achieving guru status.

"You possess a lot more knowledge than you suspect," writes Gary North in his newsletter *Remnant Review* (March 23, 2001, p. 11). "I have found that successful specialists often think, with respect to their specialized knowledge, 'everyone knows that.' The fact is, hardly anyone knows it. In many, many cases, the specialist's knowledge is valuable to those who don't possess it—far more than the possessors imagine."

It's difficult to be a white collar professional today, or even a blue collar professional, without possessing specialized knowledge or skill. A first cousin of mine wanted to get into the seminar business but didn't know what topic he could speak on with authority. He was working at the time as a concierge in a hotel. What was he eminently qualified to speak on as an expert? Why, customer service, of course.

Just about every company needs to improve customer service, but I suggested he focus on the hospitality industry, because his work experience would give him firsthand knowledge that generic customer service speakers could not easily duplicate.

Speaker Wally Bock defines a market niche as a combination of a topic (customer service, selling, marketing, management) with an industry (hospitality, pharmaceuticals, high-tech, food service). Therefore your market niche might be customer service in the hospitality industry, pharmaceutical sales, high-tech marketing, or food service management. You ideally want a niche narrow enough for you to master yet broad enough to appeal to a large, reachable market.

Some gurus can master broad areas. John Gray, with his *Men Are from Mars, Woman Are from Venus,* covers the whole of male/female relationship, excluding perhaps only gay couples. But most of us will mix and match our experience to create a sharply defined niche where we can hope to stake a claim. For instance, if you can teach managers the principles of effective business writing and you speak Japanese, your niche can be teaching business writing to executives in Panasonic, Sony, and other Japanese-run companies.

You can use the *Skills, Interests, Aptitudes, and Experiences Inventory Worksheet* to take a quick inventory of your skills, interests, aptitudes, and experience. Then juggle the elements until you find a niche you are comfortable with. Write down as many possible niches as you can come up with. Later on, you can focus on the ones you want to.

Notice I said ones plural, not one singular. Can you have more than one niche? Yes, and many gurus do, operating in multiple niche markets. There are pros and cons to doing so, of course.

The main advantage of focusing only in one main area is the ability to devote all your resources—time, money, and energy—to building your guru reputation in that field. Since every activity is in your core area of expertise, no experience is wasted, and everything you learn builds your base of knowledge. And for most gurus, knowledge and time are what they are selling.

The main disadvantage of focusing only in one main area is that, if that industry is in decline or the market is soft, your business can fall off.

The way some businesspeople prevent this is to have several specialties. If you operate in two or three different niches, you can stay busy and profitable even if one is slowing or in decline.

What is the maximum number of niches in which you can be a credible expert or guru? Dan Poynter, author of *The Self-Publishing Manual,* says three, and he gives himself as an example: He is an expert in self-publishing, parachuting, and being an expert witness. Freelance writer Richard Armstrong similarly worked in three niche markets: speech writing, political fund-raising, and circulation promotion. I also have three areas of copywriting in which I specialize: high-tech, business-to-business, and direct mail.

You may envy the guru who seemingly owns a niche and stands head and shoulders above the competition. But if it is her only niche, she is vulnerable. A single-topic guru is like a unicycle rider: If the tire goes flat, the cycle stops. A multidiscipline guru is like an 18-wheeler: The truck keeps going even if one or two of the tires blow out.

## Skills, Interests, Aptitudes, and Experiences Inventory

**Education**

College major: _____

Vocational training: _____

Specialized training: _____

Favorite/best subjects: _____

**Work Experience**

Jobs: _____

Titles: _____

Responsibilities: _____

Projects completed: _____

Results achieved: _____

Favorite/best tasks: _____

**Industry Experience**

Industries in which you've been employed:

_____

Industries in which you've had clients or customers:

_____

**Skills**

Business skills: _____

Office/computer skills: _____

Technical skills: _____

Foreign languages: _____

Computer languages: _____

**Aptitudes**

Hobbies: _____

Interests: _____

Community activities: _____

Areas of interest: _____

## *Case Study*
## Roger Parker Reinvents Himself as a Guru

What happens if the niche in which you've established yourself dries up or goes away? If you have multiple niches, the others can pick up the slack. Otherwise, you may have to "reinvent" yourself in mid-career, choosing a new area in which to establish yourself as a guru.

My friend Roger C. Parker is a good example. Here is his story, in his own words:

> I was fired a week before the American bicentennial because I had the wrong last name—that is, I was working for a family business and I was not a member of the family.
>
> Vowing I would never be fired again, I became a self-employed consultant specializing in marketing for audio retailers. To develop my visibility in the field, I wrote a free monthly column for an industry trade publication in exchange for a quarter-page ad.
>
> About ten years later, it became obvious that the industry was going down the tubes, replaced by mail order and discount stores. So I needed to find a new field.
>
> I wanted to get in on the ground floor of "the next big thing." Living in Seattle in the mid-1980s, I saw that desktop publishing, spearheaded by Aldus PageMaker, was it. Desktop publishing promised to make every writer a designer. The problem, of course, is that most writers don't possess polished design and typesetting skills.
>
> I wanted to establish myself as a guru in desktop publishing by writing a book on the topic, but I had no track record with which to approach the major publishers. Instead, I approached the Aldus Corporation and offered to write a simple little book for them, *The Aldus Guide to Basic Design.* Once they published my 72-page book, it was easy to approach a "real" publisher.
>
> Indeed, one approached me, and the result, *Looking Good in Print,* was an instant hit and remains in print to this day. (*The New York Times* called it "The one book to buy when you're buying only one.") The book changed my life by helping me become a successful consultant, speaker, and trainer.

The moral is that your success is based on your long-term credibility, and whether you attain that credibility is based on that first book. If you want to attain success as a consultant or speaker, you must be published by a major publisher. And then you must follow up that book with a stream of magazine (and now Web) articles.

The long-term credibility can revolutionize your career. With this credibility established (and I'll show you how to do this in the rest of the book), the objections and resistance prospects you typically have when buying a service or product vanish when it comes to hiring you. Instead of presenting themselves as wary suspects, leads come eager to hire you and ready to close. The effort required to convert an inquiry from potential client to closed sale shrinks from colossal (typical for your competitors) to minimal or none (for you).

For instance, I had one client hire me to do several jobs. I had no idea he had read any of my books or heard some of my talks—or this had been an influence in hiring me—until he sent me the following e-mail after my latest job for him:

> By the way, Bob, I started reading your books years ago. My bookcase is full of them. The most tattered is *The Copywriter's Handbook* and your articles from *Direct Marketing* magazine. The principles you outlined in those books and articles I admired long before I accepted my present position here. I have quite a library of copywriting books, but I haven't found many that outline the savvy concepts the way you have.
>
> Little did I know that I would some day be in a position to use your services for a company I worked for. But once I heard you speak at the Newsletter and Electronic Publishers Association conference, I knew that it was time to ask for your help!

Best of all, when you have long-term credibility in your niche market, the inquiries come to your door unbidden, through the mail, phone, e-mail, and fax. You no longer have to go out and get people interested in you. They come to you, rather than you going to them—a position most of your competitors will envy and never achieve.

## Why Our Society Is Enamored of Gurus

Earlier in this chapter I said that probably one third of Americans resent gurus, one third are indifferent to them, and one third love gurus. Why does the latter group feel the way they do?

There are a lot of reasons, but I think the main one is that in our busy, fast-paced, technological, and increasingly pressured and complex society, people feel a little lost and overwhelmed.

There is so much to do, so much to know. And we can't do it all ourselves. That's why we turn to the experts—for help, advice, and answers. Kids misbehaving? Ask a child psychologist what to do. Want to retire? Call a financial planner.

When we turn to outside experts, we give up our autonomy and become somewhat dependent on them. This scares us. We want to be sure we are spending our time and money wisely, and putting our faith in the right people.

This is why the gurus are so in demand. By building an incredibly strong long-term credibility, they have convinced us that they can indeed help us, that their advice is on target, and their answers are correct. We trust them because they have done the things that create trust.

The rest of this book tells you the things you need to do to build this long-term trust in your niche market for yourself. Do them. Follow the plan laid out in this book. If you do, you will attain guru status in your field, and enjoy the benefits—happiness, satisfaction, wealth, job security, respect, even adulation—that come with it. ■

# Chapter 2

# How to Join the
# Guru Elite

Gurus are not born, they are "manufactured" through self-marketing and promotion. This chapter outlines the philosophy, attitude, and action plan you must implement to elevate yourself to guru status.

## Philosophy

The philosophy behind *Become a Recognized Authority in Your Field* is one of acceptance. Specifically, accepting the fact that we live in a guru-oriented society, there will be gurus in virtually every field of knowledge, and that since there's going to be a guru or gurus in your field, you might as well be one of them.

Whether you think the adulation many people lavish upon gurus and celebrities is justified is, frankly, irrelevant. That gurus and celebrities are looked up to is simply the reality of life, and this is a book about dealing with reality and being successful in the world as it is, not as you or others wish it would be. Recognizing that the business world is guru-driven—and that guru status can be yours if you work at it—is the first step to becoming recognized as a leading expert in your field.

"See yourself as a brand and learn techniques to distinguish yourself from others," writes Roz Usheroff in *Speakers Gold*

(April 2000, p. 1). "Developing brand distinction builds your reputation and opens the door to future promotions, opportunities, and options."

## Guru vs. Mini-Guru

You should decide whether your goal is to be a guru or a mini-guru. I define a guru as the recognized expert in a particular field that is fairly large in size and broad in scope. John Gray, as the leading authority on male/female relationships, certainly qualifies as a guru. So does Peter Drucker, the leading authority on management.

A mini-guru is one of several recognized leading experts in a particular field, not necessarily *the* leading expert. And the mini-guru operates in a niche that is smaller in size and narrower in scope than the full-scale guru's arena.

My colleague Travis McFee is a mini-guru in the field of practice-building for dentists. Why do I put Travis, who knows an incredible amount about his subject, in the mini category? Two reasons. First, he is not alone; there are a number of speakers, authors, and consultants who teach dentists how to build lucrative practices. In fact, there is a speaker's bureau that handles only dental speakers! Second, interest in dental marketing is limited to about 100,000 dentists in the United States, compared with Peter Drucker's management advice being of interest to virtually every white-collar worker in America.

I definitely fall into the category of mini-guru—probably *very* mini—but that is good enough for me. My specialty, as I've mentioned, is direct mail copywriting. There are hundreds of direct mail copywriters and consultants, but by applying the method outlined shortly in this chapter, I was able to break out somewhat and position myself in the top tier.

Does this mean I am smarter or better than the hundreds who are relatively unknown or at least not as widely known as I am? No. It does mean I have a consistent flow of prospects ready and eager to hire me for work I want to do, at the full fees I want to charge—without me having to prospect, market, cold call, sell, negotiate, network, or do many of the other things my competitors do to keep the workflow steady.

Does being a mini-guru, even at what is admittedly a very modest level, make a big difference in my life? Absolutely. A survey from *Creative Business,* an industry publication, indicates that the average freelance copywriter grosses around $50,000 a year. I make that much about every six to seven weeks. I am not super-rich, but I have become a self-made multimillionaire in a field—freelance writing—where most practitioners struggle to get by.

I spend my time doing what I love—writing—and not schmoozing clients, going to meetings, or networking. We have a materially comfortable, financially secure, pleasant life, all made possible by the fact that I have achieved the status of a mini-guru in a specific niche market.

That's what I wanted, although I didn't realize it when I started. If it's what you want, too, the good news is that it is within your grasp and achievable sooner than you might think.

## Attitude

Ironically, even though I am the author of this book about becoming a guru, I am by nature a cynic, crab, and curmudgeon. I fall into the one third of the population who are skeptical and distrustful of gurus.

Do I dismiss all gurus? Not at all. The ones I like—and there are quite a few—I really like. I buy their books, eagerly mooch free content off their Web sites, subscribe to their e-zines and newsletters, attend their seminars, even hire some of them to consult with me on my business. It's just that, all else being equal, a guru has to quickly prove to me that there is substance behind the style, that he's not just smoke and mirrors. I prefer solid, authentic experts to the trendy and overblown any day of the week.

Having established that, how did I reconcile my inherent distrust of gurus with my own desire to become a mini-guru in my narrow-niche field of direct mail copywriting? The following list is the attitude I have. As you read this list, can you share this attitude? Do you feel comfortable thinking and saying these thoughts? If you do, you will be well-positioned to pursue your own attainment or guru status in an unconflicted manner.

## The Guru Attitude

1. I don't think the current societal obsession with gurus is right or wrong, good or bad. I just accept it as a fact.

2. I am a realist. I live in the world as it is. I might in my heart of hearts wish to change the world, but I don't think that is realistically going to happen. The best I can do is work within the system and create a successful life for me, my family, and my clients within those confines.

3. The system is difficult and a struggle if you are one of the pack, although a quality service provider or merchant with a sincere desire to help customers can succeed very nicely. The system readily gives wealth and success to those who are considered gurus by their customers and prospects.

4. Although I am not the smartest person in my field, the most educated, the most successful, or even the most talented, I'm at least as good as most people who are considered gurus in my field, and probably better than many. They are gurus not because of talent or achievement, but

because they have done things to position themselves as gurus. I would like to get in on this action.

5.  There is no mystery to what I have to do to position myself as a guru. It involves a simple list of tasks, shown in the following Action Plan. Most of the tasks are not that difficult, and even the most challenging are easily within my abilities and resources to complete. If I do what it takes to become a guru, I *will* become a guru, at least to some degree that is an improvement over my current position.

6.  When I begin to attain guru status, rewards and kudos will come my way. I will not agonize over the fairness of this fact or question it unduly. I will accept the success, money, fame, and praise; after all, I deserve it as much as anyone else. Someone is going to be the guru in my field. It might as well be me.

## Ethics

"But if I know being a guru is largely a matter of self-promotion and marketing, isn't it wrong for me to pursue that?" you may ask. "Won't I, in essence, be pulling the wool over people's eyes?"

I resolve this dilemma by being the only kind of guru I can personally like and admire myself: an ethical guru.

Some gurus are merely hype—all self-promotion, with no substance to back it up. They deliver little or no value. They either know this, or else they are so self-deluded by their own PR that they can no longer see it clearly. I dislike these phonies, so I refuse to be one even if it would make me much richer than I am.

That's my choice. You might be thinking, "Hey, if I can make up the next management theory trend and make $50,000 a speech even if it's totally B.S., that's what I want to do." Fine. Do it and go in peace.

Other gurus—the kind I like and emulate—are the real thing. Yes, they've positioned themselves as gurus. But they have the knowledge, experience, and credentials to back it up. They may be selling sizzle, but they're cooking good steak.

Don Libey—direct marketer, futurist, catalog expert, and valued friend—is a good example. Don, though a brilliant author and successful speaker, is not in the top celebrity tier of futurists. His books are from a small press, not the major New York publishers. He does not have the fame of the big-name futurists, such as John Naisbitt or Faith Popcorn.

Don focuses on the niche market of the direct response industry, and specifically within that, on catalog marketing. And there his knowledge is unequaled. He has a long history as a successful catalog marketer, consultant, and investment banker specializing in catalog acquisitions. He even wrote an entire book on square-inch analysis, which is a method of determining the profitability of each item in a catalog.

If I owned a catalog company and wanted guidance on the future of my business, Don is the only person I would call; I wouldn't even think of giving Faith Popcorn a ring, as good as she may be as a general futurist. Don owns the catalog niche and no one can take it away from him.

Confucius said, "The superior man understands what is right. The inferior man understands what will sell." My position as a guru is to do both well. Do what is right—master your niche and offer unique value your competitors cannot. But also do what will sell—take the steps, outlined in the following sections, to secure your position as a guru in your domain.

## Methodology

Alan Kay, a Disney fellow at Walt Disney Imagineering Research and Development, sums up the methodology used in becoming a guru as follows: "You make progress by giving your ideas away; businesspeople haven't learned this yet."*

As the following plan outlines in detail, *the basic method of becoming a guru is to research and gain through experience, organize, and disseminate information on your topic frequently and in a variety of formats to your target market.*

To distill this to its simplest level: If you want to position yourself as a marketing consultant to audio retailers, write how-to marketing articles for their trade publication, as Roger Parker did (recall his story from Chapter 1, "What Is a Guru?").

But that's just phase one. To truly establish yourself as a guru and set yourself ahead of the pack, you have to conduct an ongoing program of self-promotion in which information dissemination is the primary vehicle.

You can and should do a lot of other things to market and promote yourself, of course—for instance, running ads, networking, making cold calls, or sending out direct mail. But, while these generate leads, they don't do much to build your reputation. That goal is reached through the program outlined in the following sections.

## Knowledge Base

"The great mistake of most small-business people is to imagine that their detailed knowledge of their niche market is widely dispersed," writes Gary North in *Remnant Review* (April 20, 2001, p. 5). "On the contrary, hardly anyone knows it. They are owners of a capital asset that others do not possess and have no easy way of possessing it."

Chances are you already have substantial knowledge in one or more specialized areas, or else you probably wouldn't be reading a book on how to parlay your expertise into guru status.

*CIO, *June 1, 2001, p. 32*

The knowledge you have gained will serve as the base of your guruship, but experience alone is not enough. You have to augment your knowledge base with further research and study.

The guru should have solid knowledge of his topic, but need not possess earth-shattering new data, breakthrough methodology, or unique secrets. To establish yourself as a guru, the main requisite is to present what you know—the latest thinking, proven principles, best practices—in a clear, interesting, accessible fashion.

I am not an academic, but I consider myself a scholar or at least a student of my topic, direct mail. I attend workshops and conferences, subscribe to industry periodicals, study the direct mail that crosses my desk each day, read numerous books on direct marketing, and regularly exchange results on what's working with clients, colleagues, and competitors.

Therefore, when I offer myself as a leading expert to clients, I do it with a clear conscience, knowing I have done everything in my power to make that claim legitimate. Am I the undisputed best direct mail copywriter in the world? No. But I constantly strive to be the best direct mail copywriter I can be, which is all anyone can ask.

Surprisingly, most people don't do that—they don't try to be the best. A. L. Williams, the life insurance magnate, once said, "You beat 90 percent of the people just by being good. Beating the other 10 percent is a dog fight." Even if you do not reach the level of "guru-hood" you think you deserve, simply striving for excellence in a world where most do not will set you far ahead of 90 percent of the pack.

## Market Niche

You want to be a guru, but of what? You need to have a clear picture of both your subject and your market.

Gurus find their niches in one of two ways: on purpose or by accident.

In Chapter 1, we explored the idea of a niche being a cross between a topic (quality, design for manufacturability, management) and an industry (automotive, plastics, paints and coatings). For instance, there are marketing consultants galore. But I met a consultant who specialized in the niche of marketing for car washes.

He knew marketing and had a business background, but he had also owned and operated a couple of successful car washes. He had found a niche where he could be credible and successful, and not have to compete with all the marketing generalists out there. With thought, you can probably find two to three or more niches in which you can stake a guru claim.

Other people, like self-promotion guru Ilise Benun, fall into a niche largely by accident. Says Ilise:

> I was fired from the second (and last) real job I ever had. I had been working for a year and a half in the New York office of a family-owned, Kenyan safari company. I was hired thanks to my best friend, but ours had always been a rocky friendship and working together, I know now, wasn't a great idea.

> One Friday in April 1988, I was called into the conference room by the Big Boss—in reality, a small, silent type not given to emotional outbursts. He sat down at the table, handed me an envelope and said, "Thank you very much." At first I didn't understand what was happening. He couldn't possibly be firing me, but he was, and when I finally got it through my head, I was livid! "I will never work for anyone again," I vowed to anyone who'd listen.

> Indeed I had no plan, so I got busy trying to figure out what to do. In terms of my skills and talents, my degree in Spanish seemed useless because I didn't want to work for the UN. However, I was the most organized person I knew (still am), and all of my artsy friends were completely and utterly disorganized (though they aren't so much anymore). So I came up with the fancy and (I thought) original title of Professional Organizer and got busy telling everyone

what I did. (In other words, I started networking!) Before long, I had a few clients willing to pay $15 an hour to have me sit with them and pick through their mountains of clutter, one piece at a time.

It was strangely therapeutic, though very slow going, and little by little, I began to notice a pattern: buried under each person's pile, there was inevitably one piece of paper representing some little self-promotion task they were neglecting. Once we'd unearthed that phone message or note from someone asking for information, I'd say, "Let's write them a letter describing your work," or "Why don't we send them those slides?" I didn't know from marketing, but to me, it seemed like nothing more than common sense. It didn't take me long to realize that the clutter was not the problem, but merely the obstacle people used to protect themselves from the responsibility of self-promotion.

Over the course of the next few years, I evolved from Professional Organizer to Self-Promotion Specialist, learning from my own mistakes and those of my clients, practicing what I preached—and "preaching" by running my little self-promotion empire out here in Hoboken, New Jersey.

Ilise is now a successful speaker, author, and consultant in the field of self-promotion. She publishes an excellent newsletter on the topic, *The Art of Self Promotion.* You can learn more about her at www.artofselfpromotion.com.

## The Invented Term Strategy vs. the Fit-a-Category Strategy

One other decision you must make is whether to establish yourself as a guru within an existing specialty or niche or create your own.

The first option is to become known in a known industry or subject: quality control, objection-oriented analysis, database marketing, sales, customer service, interpersonal skills, time management, or stress reduction.

The advantage of this first option is that, since everyone recognizes and understands the topic, they can easily understand what you do. And, there is a built-in demand for gurus—a huge, ready market of people who want help with quality, time management, or whatever.

The disadvantage is that, since you are not the first person to be attracted to the field and desire to make it your specialty, you have competition. You share your guru status with other specialists. The clients have more gurus to choose from. When both you and your competitors want the client's money, and the client knows this, they gain a buyer's advantage and can negotiate better pricing, terms, and conditions from you.

The second option is to invent a category or niche in which you will become the preeminent specialist. Usually this invention is cosmetic or semantic rather than actual.

"By inventing words, your ideas will seem fresh whether they are or not," writes Emelie Rutherford in *CIO* (April 1, 2001, p. 133). People invent a new buzzword, theory, or jargon, then claim ownership of it. Examples include Michael Hammer's "re-engineering" and Tom Peters' "liberation management."

I once had a meeting with the business partner of a guru in the negotiating field. He told me, "Our success is due to the fact that we invented negotiating as a topic." I asked him to explain. He answered:

> The guru began his career as a lawyer. One day he woke up and said, "What I really do is negotiate all day; it just happens to be in the area of law."
>
> He realized that negotiation, which lawyers have to become skilled at, is central to almost every facet of life. Based on this realization—that everything is negotiation and lawyers are negotiation specialists—he changed his focus from law practice to teaching corporate managers to use negotiation skills to get what they want in business.

The advantage of inventing your own niche is that, if the concept, term, theory, or buzzword catches on, you "own" the category. You are by default the leading guru in the field. You "own" your niche.

The disadvantage or risk is the likely possibility that the buzzword you invent does not catch on, and that people do not understand what it means. If you promote yourself as the guru in "hyper-communication," and no one knows what it means or wants it, you gain no advantage.

While I recognize the "invent-a-term" strategy as extremely powerful, I have avoided it for two reasons that may or may not hinder your pursuit of it.

First, my mind doesn't work that way. I am good at packaging information and working within a known field, but I am not a pioneer or revolutionary thinker. In all my life, I have had neither a brilliant original concept nor a nifty jargon to go with it.

Second, the invent-a-term gurus are happy to invent and use buzzwords, which opposes my plain-speaking nature.

When a buzzword or new jargon becomes part of the language and culture, the inventor benefits enormously. But until it does, he is speaking in doublespeak whenever he uses his jargon in lectures and writing. Even after the buzzword is accepted, it often does not communicate its concept as clearly as a plain English phrase would do.

I prefer clear writing, clear thinking, and plain speaking. And I think a plain-speaking approach conveys a sense of credibility, trust, and integrity to your audience.

"Never use jargon words like *reconceptualize, demassification, attitudinally,*" writes David Ogilvy in *The Unpublished Ogilvy* (New York: Crown Publishers). "They are the hallmarks of a pretentious ass."

## Action Plan

This book gives you a complete plan for rapidly establishing yourself as a leading expert, or guru, in your field.

The plan is outlined here. The detailed instructions for accomplishing each task are given in upcoming chapters.

## The Sixty-Day "Become a Guru" Action Plan at a Glance

1. **Writing articles.** Writing articles for publication is the quickest and easiest way, and usually the first step, in building your guru reputation. In Chapter 3, "Articles," you will discover how to come up with article ideas, write a winning query letter, research and write a successful article, get it published, use the reprints in self-promotion, and get people to respond to your articles and buy your products and services.

2. **Writing books.** Writing one or more books is crucial to attaining guru status. In an article in *CIO* magazine about the top 10 gurus in Information Technology, every one of the 10 had written at least one book. In Chapter 4, "Books," I show you how to write a book on your area of expertise and get it published by a major publishing house. We'll also discuss self-publishing, books on demand, and e-books.

3. **Producing and selling information products.** Gurus are focal points of information on a specific topic, and they enhance their reputations as experts by producing and marketing "information products" on these topics. Chapter 5, "Information Products," describes what these products are and how to create and market them. It includes audiotapes, videos, CD-ROMs, software, directories, resource guides, special reports, market research, booklets, pamphlets, and more.

4. **Publish a newsletter or e-zine.** A powerful technique for building your reputation with a defined audience over a period of time is to regularly send them a newsletter,

which can either be free or paid subscription. Chapter 6, "Newsletters and E-Zines," shows you how to produce, distribute, and market traditional print newsletters as well as electronic newsletters delivered via the Internet (e-zines).

5. **Make speeches.** Giving keynote speeches at meetings and conventions quickly establishes your reputation as an expert. Chapter 7, "Speaking," shows how to get these invitations and deliver a memorable talk that positions you as an expert in your topic.

6. **Give seminars.** Virtually every guru gives seminars, both to reach new prospects and to as solidify his or her position as a leading expert. Speeches are short talks, typically an hour long. Seminars, in comparison, are more comprehensive presentations ranging from a half-day to three days. Chapter 8, "Seminars," outlines the various types of seminars, the pros and cons of each, and how to use them effectively to promote yourself, your company, and your services or products.

7. **Conduct a public relations campaign.** Get the print and broadcast media—newspapers, magazines, radio, TV—to interview you and feature you in stories relating to your area of expertise. Covered in Chapter 9, "Public Relations."

8. **Use the Internet.** Another central component of establishing yourself as a guru is building a Web presence, the centerpiece of which is a Web site that is both an information resource and community of interest on a subject relating to your core expertise. Chapter 10, "The Internet," shows how to map out and create a Web site for yourself as a guru, and covers other Web marketing techniques including e-mail marketing, banner ads, forums, chat rooms, communities of interest, online content, and discussion groups.

9. **Achieve critical mass.** Critical mass is the point where the business pay-off from the tasks completed in your guru action plan sustains long-term results beyond each short-term promotion. This is discussed in the next section.

10. **Maintain guru status.** As a guru, you can't rest on your laurels. The world is changing constantly, and the leader in any field must change with it or be left far behind. You must work continually to maintain your guru status, or you may lose it.

## The Four Phases of Guru Development

There are four phases in the process of developing your reputation as a guru: the start-up phase, growth phase, critical mass phase, and maintenance phase.

In the start-up phase, you begin implementing the guru action plan. At this stage, any interest generated in you and your services is specifically linked to each promotion. You write an article; you get a few phone calls. You give a speech; a few potential clients give you their business cards after the presentation and express interest in learning more about who you are and what you do. If you stop promoting yourself—no new seminars, no new client newsletters, no new books—people forget about you, and the inquiries stop flowing. You have not yet built up awareness or your reputation to the point where people think of you even if you are not running some type of promotion.

In stage two, the growth phase, you still run a series of promotions as outlined in the guru action plan, but now you see synergy between the various efforts. You give a speech and someone in the audience, in post-lecture conversation, compliments you on your latest book. Or a prospect you are referred to takes your call because he reads your column in his industry journal and is impressed by what you write. The individual tasks in the action plan begin to feed one another. You get a synergy in which the total impression is greater than the sum of the individual communications.

Stage three is the critical mass phase. In nuclear physics, critical mass is the point where a nuclear reaction becomes self-sustaining; the reaction does not have to be fueled but continues to generate tremendous energy on its own.

In self-promotion, I define "critical mass" as the point where your name is out in the marketplace so much, so often, that people are continually aware of who you are and what you do. You are getting a steady flow of inquiries that would continue even if you stopped promoting yourself for a time. People have heard of you and know who you are. When they contact you, they are predisposed to buy your services and do not have to be "sold" on doing so. Your lead volume is high and you get numerous leads that you cannot trace to a particular promotion; people just seem to hear about you and call you.

But just because you could stop promoting yourself doesn't mean you should; the critical mass must be maintained or it will, over time, cool down to a noncritical level. If that happens, you'll slide back to phase two. Phase four is maintenance: doing a level of promotion required to keep you at critical mass. This level is not as high as required in phase one or two, but it's not zero either.

You can't totally rest on your laurels. Competition and a changing environment necessitate that you make a deliberate effort to maintain your leading edge status.

## The Rule of Seven

How often must you market yourself to achieve guru status? How much exposure do you need?

A good rule of thumb is the Rule of Seven. First stated by marketing consultant Jeffrey Lant, the Rule of Seven says you should reach your target market seven times within an 18-month period.

Although somewhat arbitrary, the Rule of Seven is a good starting point. The following table indicates how the frequency of action tasks should be adjusted based upon which phase of the guru development process you are in.

At the beginning, in the start-up phase, you typically spend a lot of your time marketing, and launch a barrage of promotions one after the next in a relatively short period of time. Making a splash with a flurry of frequent self-promotion gets attention and makes your name stand out.

Since you're just starting out, an added benefit of this phase is that all this activity produces materials you can reprint as sales literature for yourself or your firm. After a few months of heavy marketing activity, you'll begin to build a collection of promotional materials—reprints of bylined articles, seminar announcements, press clippings, reviews, audiocassettes, videos.

When a prospect inquires about your services, sending him a selection of these materials in addition to your sales brochure helps establish credibility. These materials should also go in press kits; when the media sees you have already gained major press for yourself, they will be more likely to give you additional coverage.

## Frequency of Guru Action Plan Tasks Based on Phase in Development

| Phase | Frequency of Self-Promotion |
|---|---|
| Start-up | Four to six times within three to six months |
| Development | Every other month |
| Critical mass | Quarterly |
| Maintenance | Two to three times per year |

## *Case Study*
## Jeff Davidson

Jeff Davidson has established himself as an expert in balancing work and personal life. Like many gurus, he discovered the guru action plan on his own, almost by accident, starting with writing articles:

> Years ago, as an employee of a small consulting firm in Connecticut, I approached my boss during a slow period in the work week and asked what I could do to help the firm. He suggested writing an article, an activity that would never have occurred to me, a B– student in English composition with no thought of writing.

> After several false starts, I hit on a simple formula to help me through my first piece. The title of the article was "Ten Tips on Survival for Small Business." The concept was simple. I came up with 10 different tips that would be the start of a paragraph or two. I would then add opening and closing paragraphs and that would be my whole article. The article was easy to write. I later found, when you attach a number to your title, such as "Eight Ways" to do something, you finish the article with less struggle, even if you don't come up with eight ways. (You might only reach six.)

> I mailed my manuscript out to a publication that sat on it for five months and then rejected it. I then mailed it to another magazine, *The New Englander,* which sat on it for four months. One day, without advance notice or word of any kind, a package arrived. It was thick. I opened it and found that my article, "Ten Tips on Survival for Small Business," had been published in the current issue.

> It was the last article in the issue—the least of my concerns. The graphics and artwork that they had done were wonderful, and the article made an attractive reprint. I was so excited to have my name in print that I probably photocopied that article 500 times and sent it to everyone I knew.

> Although the magazine paid me nothing, I learned a priceless lesson. Up until then, I thought that only superstars and the privileged classes got their names in print. When I discovered portable dictation equipment a couple of years later, I began dictating articles at the pace of about one a month, increasing within a year to one per week.

Much later, I wrote an article entitled, "How to Build a Law Practice," following a consulting engagement I had with a Washington, D.C., law firm. The article essentially followed a "14 tips" format, although I didn't use that title. I sent the article to *Case and Comment* in Rochester, New York, which accepted it for publication.

About a year later I was going through my files and came across the article. It dawned on me that with little time and effort I could convert that article to "How to Build a Medical Practice." In the previous year I'd worked with a couple of doctors and dentists and was now familiar with their terminology and the differences required to restructure my earlier article. I reworked "How to Build a Law Practice" 14 times, including versions for dentists, real estate agents, insurance agents, accountants, graphic artists, consultants, and others.

Around the time I started to get articles published, I also began public speaking. I can vividly recall the first time I ever spoke to a group professionally. I was speaking to about 75 entrepreneurs at the Hartford District Office of the Small Business Administration. At the time I was working for a management consulting firm that provided marketing and management assistance to small and medium-sized businesses. One of our marketing activities to gain exposure for the firm was to serve as seminar leaders at SBA-sponsored workshops.

Although I had only been with the company six months, this Tuesday in May was to be my public speaking initiation. The presentation was to last 30 minutes. I was prepared and qualified, having offered the same type of advice to individuals on a one-to-one basis for two years.

When I got in front of the group, everything changed. The words were coming out and what I was saying had impact, but my stomach was doing somersaults. By the end of the session, a feather could have knocked me over. I was lightheaded, dizzy, exhilarated, and glad I was finished.

In the months that followed, the presentation became easier and easier to give. I think it was after the sixth time that the butterflies left and my feet were firmly planted. A funny thing happened by the next year—I actually started looking forward to speaking before groups. All of the things that I had read about the nervous energy that never dissipates didn't seem to apply. In succeeding years I was better prepared to communicate on the job, impressing bosses and co-workers with the names of groups I had spoken to, and acquired confidence that spilled over into other areas of my career.

I began writing books and unleashed several that topped 50,000 sales, such as *Marketing Your Consulting and Professional Services* (Wiley), *The Complete Idiot's Guide to Managing Your Time* (Alpha Books), *The Complete Idiot's Guide to Managing Stress* (Alpha Books), and *The Joy of Simple Living* (Rodale). All the while I kept an eye out for PR opportunities.

My friend Robert Bookman lives in Chevy Chase, Maryland, and frequently reads the *Washington Post* "Style Plus" column. He noticed that one of the staff writers, Don Oldenburg, wrote on topics that were particularly intriguing. My friend began a professional, somewhat aggressive, letter-writing campaign to influence Oldenburg to write about Bookman's team productivity programs. In a matter of weeks a major article appeared in the *Washington Post* featuring Bookman's team productivity program. However, the story doesn't end there.

A few weeks after the article appeared, my friend suggested that I contact Don Oldenburg to do a story on me, concerning the value of promoting yourself to get ahead in your career. Robert was nice enough to write Don Oldenburg to let him know that I would be making contact. I called Oldenburg, followed up with a package of career marketing materials, and followed that up with another call.

Several months went by before he interviewed me. And several more weeks went by before the article was published. Soon enough, however, there it was, splashed across the Style Plus section of the *Washington Post*—an article entitled "Putting Your Best Self Forward," which reflected my 90-minute interview.

Even better, Oldenburg was a member of the Washington Post Syndicated Writer's Group, and the article appeared in hundreds of other papers across the country. Since the article prominently mentioned my first book, sales picked up nationally and, within its first year, the book was in its third printing.

After more than 10 years as a part-time speaker, on January 1, 1994, I made the decision to be a full-time professional speaker. In seven years, I've been fortunate to have had some dramatic results both for my audiences and for my career. A feature article on speakers contained this about me:

> "Years ago, Davidson figured out that there were socioeconomic common denominators as to why everyone was feeling increasing time pressure and stress. Using a combination of stories and anecdotes, startling statistics, which he can recall with near encyclopedic mastery, and a strong affinity for each of his audiences, Davidson enthralls his audiences from the first minute on, initially captivating their minds and then their hearts. He has been a repeat and/or long-term multiple presenter at the World Bank, IBM, America Online, Internal Revenue Service, and Farmer's Insurance, to name a few."

## To Sum It All Up

- The world loves a guru. Become a guru and you have the world (or at least a hefty portion of it) at your fingertips.

- You have almost everything you need to become a guru in your field already inside you. The rest you can get through research and study.

- You build your reputation as an expert in your field by giving your knowledge away in a variety of forums—articles, books, seminars, speeches, newsletters, e-zines, Web sites, and information products.

- Be a practitioner in the field in which you seek guru status. Learn by doing and through research, writing, and teaching your subject. ■

*Chapter 3*

# Articles

Writing articles for publication is the quickest and easiest way, and usually the first step, to build your guru reputation. This chapter shows how to come up with article ideas, write a winning query letter, research and write a successful article, get it published, use the reprints in self-promotion, and get people to respond to your articles and buy your products and service.

## The Secret of the Trade Journal Trade

Most articles in consumer magazines you buy on the newsstand are written either by staff journalists or freelance writers.

In trade journals, about half the articles are written by staff journalists, and a small fraction by freelance writers. The rest are written by practitioners in the field.

Unlike the freelance writers who write for consumer magazines to make a living, practitioners who contribute to an industry journal are usually not paid. Then why do they write the article? To promote themselves, their company, or their product or service.

Just one article in a trade journal or consumer magazine can bring a company hundreds of leads and thousands of dollars in sales. And with more than 6,000 magazines from which to choose, it's a safe bet there's at least one that could accommodate a story from your company.

Yet while nearly all business people know the value of placing trade journal stories, they don't always know how to approach an editor. What's the best way to pitch an idea? Should you present more than one idea at a time? Is it wise to present the same story to more than one editor? Should you call or write first?

Following are some tips that answer those questions, and more. They can give you an edge in placing an article in the right journal for your company and reaping the rewards of increased recognition.

## What Magazine Should You Write For?

Chances are that you already know which journals you'd like to approach. The magazines that cross your desk every week are strong candidates, because they're likely to deal with you and your competition. Also, check out what magazines people in your target niche market are reading. Those are the periodicals in which you want to be published.

If you have an idea for an article that is outside your industry, or if you're just not sure which magazine would be most appropriate, here are two excellent resources: *Bacon's Publicity Checker,* from Bacon's Publishing Co., Chicago; and *Writer's Market,* from Writer's Digest Books, Cincinnati.

*Bacon's* is the bible of the public relations industry. It lists thousands of magazines and newsletters according to business or industry category, and also provides an alphabetical index. Besides giving the basics of magazine titles, addresses, phone numbers and editor's names, *Bacon's* notes circulation and the types of articles published by each journal.

*Writer's Market,* by comparison, lists fewer publications, but describes their editorial requirements in far greater detail.

Since *Writer's Market* is published primarily to help freelance writers find suitable markets for their work, it is more helpful than *Bacon's* when it comes to finding a home for a full-length feature story.

If you are not familiar with a magazine that sounds as if it may be appropriate for your article, be sure to read a few issues before contacting an editor there.

Many trade journals will send a sample issue and set of editorial guidelines to prospective authors upon request. These can provide valuable clues as to style, format, and appropriate topics. They often tell how to contact the magazine, give hints on writing an article, describe the manuscript review process and discuss any payment/reprint arrangements.

## The Type of Article You Should Write

Although your objective is to promote yourself, your firm, or your product or service, you should not write an article that is a blatant self-promotion. Editors will usually not publish such articles, and if one should get published, readers will not want to read it.

Readers read articles to learn how to run their businesses more profitably or do their jobs better. That's what your article must tell them. The article should be pure information, advice, how-to, strategy, or ideas—useful and immediately actionable, or else conceptual and thought-provoking.

Some gurus in training ask me, "My information is basically just a repackaging of known information in my field? Won't editors reject it because it's not new?"

No. People read articles for reinforcement more than anything else. If your article tells them something they already know and believe, they'll think, "Hey, I agree with this author a hundred percent. He really knows his stuff!" Which is exactly what you want.

If you actually present one or two new ideas in your article, that's a bonus. But it's not necessary. Do not feel pressure to invent something new when writing an article for publication. Remember, guruship can wholly be achieved just by repackaging and clearly presenting existing information, without creating a brand-new idea or concept.

The "advertisement" for you, your company, or your product or your service in the article is your byline and the brief bio of you that runs with the piece. The bio should give your name, company, a brief description of your product or service, and a way for the reader to contact you.

In the pre-Internet days, this would sometimes be a problem. I would want the editors to include my phone number in my article bio, but some would hesitate, thinking it too self-promotional.

I handled this by trading my services as an article writer for ad space in the publication. "I get X dollars to write an article," I told the editor, naming some arbitrary fee. "I will waive my usual fee in exchange for a free ad in your publication." The size of the ad I asked for was what one could have bought for twice my article-writing fee; if I said I got $500 for an article, I wanted a $1,000 ad."

Then the closer: I told the editor he didn't even have to give me the ad as long as he ran my phone number with my bio in the article.

The Internet has solved this problem. When you write your brief bio for your article, include your Web site. Doing so means the reader can always find you on the Web and contact you from there. For instance:

Robert Bly is a freelance direct marketing copywriter and the author of *The Complete Idiot's Guide to Direct Marketing* (Alpha Books). Bob's clients include AT&T, IBM, Network Solutions, and Haht Software. He can be reached at www.bly.com.

Why will editors gladly list your Web site address when they were so reluctant to list phone numbers earlier? A phone number was viewed as blatant self-promotion, which editors don't like to think they are aiding. But a Web site is more than a contact vehicle; it's a resource that gives readers even more useful information.

## Get to Know the Publication

The quickest way to turn off an editor is to offer an idea that has nothing to do with his or her magazine. "My pet peeve with people calling or writing to pitch an idea is that they often haven't studied the magazine," says Rick Dunn, editor of *Plant Engineering*. "If they haven't read several issues and gotten a handle on who we are and who our audience is, they won't be able to pitch an idea effectively."

"There's no substitute for knowing the audience and the various departments within a magazine," adds Jim Russo, editor of *Packaging*. "I'm more impressed by someone who has an idea for a particular section than by someone who obviously doesn't know anything about our format."

Every magazine is different in some way from its competitors and from other magazines in general. Tone, style, content, and the quality of a journal's writing and illustrations should all be studied to increase your chances of making a "sale."

Offer an editor the type of article that the magazine seems to prefer—frequency and length are good indicators of preferred subjects—and the odds are more in your favor. For instance, don't propose a "10 tips" article to the *Harvard Business Review;* you can see by reviewing an issue that their articles are much more in-depth.

Companies can easily increase their chances for coverage by requesting a magazine's editorial calendar and scanning it for planned articles that might mesh with their products or activities.

"If people respond to our editorial calendar with ideas for specific issues, great!" says Mr. Dunn. "Or if they can provide background for a story we want to do, they'll have an edge in getting into the magazine."

You may even want to suggest feature story ideas for next year's calendar. The trick is to do that tactfully. "Don't come across as pushy or demanding," warns Mr. Dunn. "Stay away from saying things like, 'This is important to your readers' or 'You should run this story.' If someone knows our business better than we do, we'll hire him or we'll go back to school."

However, if you spot a new trend in say, packaging food in plastic containers vs. glass jars, and you can provide statistics and information to back up your claim, go ahead and contact the appropriate editor. He or she will probably appreciate your interest and effort.

## Making the Initial Contact

Should you call or should you write? Most editors won't object to either method of pitching an idea, but they usually have a preference for one or the other. It's simply a matter of personal choice and time constraints. If you don't know how a particular editor feels on the subject, call and ask. An appropriate opening might be: "This is Joe Jones from XYZ Corp. and I have a story idea you might be interested in. Do you have a few minutes right now, or should we set up a time to discuss it later in the week?"

An editor who prefers a letter or written outline will no doubt take this opportunity to tell you so. Editors who prefer a quick description over the phone will appreciate your respect for their time, whether they take the call or ask you to phone back later.

Some editors, such as Mr. Russo, favor a phone call to zero in on an idea. "If I know someone and have confidence in their work, I'll often say go ahead and submit an article. Otherwise, I like to see an outline first," he says.

Mark Rosenzweig, editor at *Chemical Engineering,* agrees. "With a phone call, I can tell someone right away he's on the right track. But a letter summarizing the idea is okay, too. In any case, if I like an idea, I'll then request a detailed outline describing the proposed article."

A written query with a detailed outline appeals to Mr. Dunn because, he says, "A phone call is all right, but I can't make an editorial decision until I see a query letter."

At *Modern Materials Handling,* Assistant Editor Barbara Spencer suggests writers send in a letter of introduction, followed by a phone call a week or two later. "We look for someone who knows his field and products, and the letter helps us gauge that expertise," she explains. "But call the magazine first and find out which editor handles the type of article you have in mind."

That's good advice for dealing with any journal. A two-minute phone call to find the right editor, get the correct spelling of his or her name, and check the address where the query letter should be sent can save time and aggravation later.

All letters should be addressed to a specific editor. A letter that begins "Dear Editor" not only could end up in the wrong hands, but it's also unlikely to impress the editor with the writer's research abilities.

Follow-up calls are almost always a good idea, too. The editor's reaction to your call will determine whether you should call again later. If an editor flat out rejects an idea, accept the verdict gracefully and try another publication.

If you're told an idea has "merit" but needs further explanation or a different approach, you may be able to get a go-ahead by answering the editor's questions or suggesting a new angle over the phone.

On the other hand, you may need to supply more information in writing and call again a couple of weeks later. Of course, if the editor gives you a go ahead, great. You've cleared the major hurdle to getting an article in print.

What if you have more than one great story idea you want to pitch? Most editors are willing to listen to two or even three at once, but don't overdo it. Each idea should be fully developed ahead of time, not "pulled out of a hat" in desperation if an original idea is turned down. A good tack is to ask editors what kind of stories or applications they're looking for. Perhaps you'll find out they're interested in new ways to use one of your company products, or how a new government regulation is affecting your industry's production operations. They may well have an interest in something that ties in with your company and which you are qualified to write about.

Mentioning certain elements in your initial query—whether over the phone or in writing—can sway an editor toward accepting your proposal. For instance, many magazines seek practical information that shows their readers how to save money, time, labor or improve on-the-job performances. Statistics, benefits, examples, and how-to tips can strengthen your case substantially.

Specifics are what sell a story: You're much more likely to grab an editor's attention if you say, "Our newly developed Dry Scrubber pollution control device saved the Smithson Paper Plant $4,400 a day in fuel costs" than if you say, "Our new product can save paper plants a lot of money." Then go on to explain just how the company has saved money. And be prepared to back up your claim with documented facts.

"If someone tells us something is more efficient than something else, we want to know how much more efficient," says Mr. Russo. "Superlatives should be backed up with percentages and explanations."

The more help your idea promises readers, the more likely it is to interest an editor. "We're interested in articles that help our readers solve specific problems," says Mr. Dunn. "We want technical, engineering-oriented but down-to-earth articles that address common problems. A good question to ask before coming to us is, 'Will this provide readers with information they can apply to their jobs?'"

Put yourself in the readers' shoes, analyze their problems, and you will have a better perception of what kind of articles an editor wants. If you happen to read the magazine regularly, you may well have a head start in coming up with useful ideas. Also, any knowledge and technical expertise you have will help you "sell yourself" to an editor as an authoritative source.

"We prefer bylines by technical experts or plant engineers, since that is our audience," Mr. Dunn says. "If they've got a good subject, we'll go as far as necessary to accommodate them."

Adds Ms. Spencer: "We value technical ability above writing ability. Know your field and its products; if you are 'visible' in your field for giving speeches or being active in a professional organization, so much the better."

But don't despair if you are not a technical whiz or industry "name": Plenty of trade journal authors, including legions of public relations executives, aren't either. They are published because they take the time to study a subject they want to write about. That doesn't mean they acquire nearly the amount of knowledge a technical expert would have; they are simply able to delve into a subject enough to write clearly, concisely, and logically about it. For many trade journals, that's all that's required.

Take *Packaging*. Says Mr. Russo, "We have both outstanding journalists and excellent technical people on staff, so we can consider articles that are short on either end." What counts for him and scores of other editors is the newsworthiness of an article.

"I'm particularly interested in new ways of doing things, whether someone has found a better way to package products, or new and significant developments that are practical."

Mr. Rosenzweig looks for "heavy duty nuts and bolts articles, not puff or promotional pieces. Title or position isn't that important to us. It's whether there's any 'meat' in an idea," he says.

Impartiality is another "must" with many editors. Remember, they're not there to praise your company's products—although being published can be as good as if they were; they're there to give readers an objective overview of what's going on in their industry. This can be a particular sticking point in dealing with public relations personnel, although most editors recognize the "one-hand-feeds-the other" usefulness of such contacts.

"We're certainly not prejudiced against articles from PR firms," says Mr. Rosenzweig. "We just generally have to make more revisions to eliminate their tendency toward one-sidedness. We want all the disadvantages spelled out, as well as the advantages."

Adds Mr. Dunn: "If an article is about storage methods, we want to see all 15 methods discussed, not just the ones used by the writer's company or client."

Still, the fact that public relations people are generally eager to give editors information and can be trusted to produce articles on target and on time helps endear them to many editors. "We don't have to chase after them," explains Mr. Dunn. "They understand our role a little better than most people, they know how we operate, and they tend to give us good service."

So follow the public relations agencies' example and make yourself available to editors when they call, follow their guidelines, and deliver written copy as promised. You'll put yourself in good stead with people who are in a position to exert considerable influence on your company's fortunes.

Some magazines will kill a feature story simply for lack of photos or illustrations. Many others weigh heavily the availability of appropriate graphics. Those visual "extras" can be a deciding factor in choosing one story idea over another. Even though the larger journals may have illustrators on staff to produce high-quality finished drawings, they often work from original sketches supplied by an author.

You can get a good idea of how important visuals are to a particular magazine, before you make your pitch, by scanning a couple of issues. Note whether photos or drawings are used. If photos, are they black-and-white or color? Is at least one illustration used with every story of one page or more? If so, you should be prepared to provide the same. Otherwise, your article may move to the reject pile, regardless of its other merits.

Professional photographs, while nice, are not necessary for most trade journals. Straightforward, good-quality 35mm color slides satisfy most trade editors. Some magazines will also take black-and-white glossies or color prints. The editor will be happy to tell you what's acceptable.

## Exclusivity

Never submit the same idea, or story, to more than one competing magazine at a time. Only if the idea is rejected should you approach another editor. This is one point nearly all editors agree on: They want exclusive material, especially for feature articles.

If a story is particularly timely or newsworthy, and has run in a magazine not directly competing with the one you're approaching, you may be able to get around the problem by working with the editor to expand or rewrite the piece. But be up-front about it or you will risk losing an editor's confidence and goodwill.

"I'd like everything to be exclusive," says Mr. Russo. "That increases its value to us and can sway us toward acceptance if it's a 'borderline' story." Offering "world exclusives" can also make an article more appealing to an editor. That means you promise not to submit the article to any other magazine, even if it's in a completely different field. Whether you are willing to do that depends on how much you want a story in a particular magazine. You may decide you'd rather try to get more mileage out of a story by submitting it to a number of unrelated magazines or newspapers.

As Mr. Dunn points out: "Exclusivity is a quality consideration for a feature article. Editors don't want their readers to pick up their magazine and see something that they've already read elsewhere." Often the exceptions to this rule are column items or case histories—for example, a problem/solution/result story describing how a particular customer successfully used a company's product. However, even those items should not be submitted to a magazine that competes with one that has already accepted them.

Submitting unsolicited manuscripts is always a risky proposition—again, with the exception of case histories and short new pieces. Some editors never want to see an unsolicited manuscript; others are willing to review them and may even publish a few. *Chemical Engineering* falls into that category.

"We get hundreds of unsolicited manuscripts every year, but we have the resources to do a heavy amount of rewriting for the ones we use," says Mr. Rosenzweig.

On the other hand, Ms. Spencer says she never uses unsolicited feature manuscripts, and Mr. Russo can't remember the last time his magazine used an unsolicited piece as a major story.

What it boils down to is this: Most editors prefer to be asked about story ideas before an author writes the article. It saves them the substantial amount of time required to read a lengthy manuscript to determine whether the subject is right for the magazine. And it saves the author the time and trouble of researching and writing an article that might never get accepted anywhere.

Even if you have a manuscript already in hand, by submitting it "blind" you may lead an editor to suspect you're submitting it to nine other magazines at the same time. That's not what an editor wants to hear. It's far better to query first, then send the story only if the editor expresses interest.

## Length and Deadline

Once you've got your idea accepted, which is always tentative until final review of the manuscript, you'll need to know any length and deadline requirements. If the editor doesn't volunteer this information, by all means ask. The answers may help avoid misunderstandings later.

As a rule, be generous with length. Include everything you think is relevant, and don't skimp on examples. Editors would rather cut material than have to request more.

A few magazines, such as *Chemical Engineering,* are very flexible on length. "We run articles anywhere from three paragraphs to 40 to 50 pages long," says Mr. Rosenweig. Most other magazines give authors more specific limits. Check with your editor for the specific range.

I like to write articles that are either 800 or 1,500 words in length, but no longer. The reason: The average magazine article has about 800 words per page. Therefore, an 800-word article can be reprinted on one side of a sheet of paper, while a 1,500 word article can be reprinted in two sides of an 8½ by 11 inch sheet of paper.

There's something convenient and reader-friendly about a single-sheet reprint. It is easy to run off on your office copier and it makes a nice hand-out to give away at your speeches. If you write an article longer than 1,500 words, you need to reprint on more than one sheet of paper.

Deadlines, too, can vary considerably among journals. Some don't like to impose any deadlines at all, especially if they work far enough ahead that they're not pressed for material. But if the article is intended for publication in a special issue, the editors will probably want the finished manuscript in hand at least two months prior to publication. That allows time for final revisions, assembling photos or illustrations, and production.

*Chemical Engineering,* for example, has a one-year lead time on many of the articles it assigns. In at least one case, the magazine waited for six years before receiving a promised manuscript. Not surprisingly, the editor had completely forgotten about the story.

Some magazines may send a follow-up letter to remind delinquent authors about expected articles, but, as Mr. Dunn says, "We won't chase after someone. If we don't hear from a writer in about six months, we figure the article is never going to materialize."

Don't put an editor's patience to the test. You may gain a reputation as being undependable, which can hurt your future chances of getting ink.

By winning an editor's friendship, or at least his or her respect, you may find yourself in the pleasant position of being asked for information about your company in the future. At the least, you'll find a receptive audience for your story ideas.

So how do you develop this kind of rapport? Stay tuned to the editor's needs by keeping up with information in their field, as well as your own; staying up to date with any changes in format or content of their publications; heeding their suggestions; being considerate of their time; and, above all, delivering articles as promised. "The best way to cultivate an editor's friendship is to produce results," advises Mr. Dunn, "because the people who are sincerely interested in helping us out are the ones we go back to."

## Writing Articles for the Web

The Internet has created a fresh new demand for articles, known as "content" on the Web, by the ton. Should you write articles for Web-only publication? Should you allow Web sites to post your existing articles?

Right now, the Web is not as targeted or as organized as the print world. Controlled circulation magazines are audited to verify readership. Therefore, you know your article or ad is reaching your target market.

A "controlled circulation" magazine is one that readers are given free, if they meet certain qualifications indicating they are members of the audience the publisher wants to reach. Most industry publications are controlled.

Paid circulation magazines also do extensive research to target the right subscribers in their subscription promotions and demonstrate to advertisers that they have attracted the right audience. So you can be fairly sure your article is giving you exposure to the right people.

Web sites are currently not audited; magazine circulation is. Therefore, the audience at any particular Web site is less clear and well defined.

My strategy at this point is to target your articles for primary publication in the right print magazines—those with a subscriber base made up of your target audience. Once the articles are published, post them on your Web site, and also get them posted on as many other sites as possible.

Does this mean you should not write original articles for Web publication only? You may if you wish, but be careful. Writing articles takes time and effort. I expend the time and effort only if I am fairly certain of reaching a large portion of my target audience with my message. With a magazine, I get that assurance. With a Web site I never heard of, I don't.

Because of the low cost of putting up a Web site today, everyone is doing it, including a lot of amateurs. While it's easy to put up a site, generating traffic is not so easy, and many of these sites are visited by almost no one. The problem is, since Web site traffic isn't verified by audit as is magazine readership, you have no idea whose site can give you a lot of exposure and whose site is a waste of your time and effort.

Therefore, I would be extremely reticent to write an original article for a Web site I hadn't heard of. You can make exceptions for Web sites you know have large volumes of traffic or are leaders in their field.

Allowing Web sites to reprint my existing articles, however, is another story. This is something I agree to ready. Let me explain why.

When I started my freelance copywriting business in the early 1980s, my self-promotion strategy was to write articles for the leading trade publications in direct marketing and business-to-business marketing, my specialties. During the 1980s and early 1990s, I had dozens of how-to articles on copywriting and marketing in such magazines as *Direct Marketing* and *Business Marketing*.

In the later 1990s and 2000s, I figured I was about done with articles. I had reached the critical mass stage where leads came to me steadily and in greater volume than I could handle, without me doing any promotions.

But a funny thing happened. I started getting even more inquiries from people telling me that they had read those old articles—some almost 20 years old—on Web sites I had never heard of. My articles were getting a second life, and I was getting a big promotional boost out of them, with no action taken on my part.

Sometimes people would e-mail me and ask permission to post an article on their site. I always said yes. My only condition was that they run the byline and bio that originally appeared with the article, and include my own Web site URL.

My philosophy is to always grant permission whenever anyone asks to post any of my articles on any Web site. I don't ask questions or make requests or conditions. The more strings you attach, the less likely someone is to use your article. And I am aiming for wide distribution of my articles on the Web (I will tell you why in a second).

Other times my articles would simply appear on Web sites without my permission. I never question, complain, or ask people to remove them. I'm happy they are there. They should have asked permission, but since I would have said yes anyway, I don't make an issue of the fact that they technically are violating my copyright. (I own the rights to all my articles; they are not in the public domain.)

To make it even easier for any Web site owner to use my articles, I have posted a selection of them on my own Web site and added the option to download any article as a Word file. When someone e-mails me to ask permission to post a particular article on their site, I say yes. I also invite them to review the other articles on my site and use any they wish. The result is that I get a bigger presence on their site than I would have.

My goal is wide distribution of my current inventory of articles on the Web, as long as it involves no additional time or effort on my part. If someone wants to post an article of mine on their site, I say "yes" without investigating who they are or spending time thinking about whether I should allow them. I just click REPLY to their e-mail, type "go ahead," and click SEND. It takes two seconds of my time.

My feeling is that the articles are already written. The work is done. The more exposure they get, the better for me. If many people outside my target market see them, it doesn't help or hurt me much either way.

But people in your target market also look at general Web sites; they don't restrict their Web browsing just to a few industry-specific sites. You never know when potential clients may be surfing the Web and come across your article in an odd place. If that happens even once—and it has happened to me many times—you benefit greatly. I have had people who read one of my old magazine articles, posted on Web sites I never heard of, hire me to write direct mail packages for them or give seminars to their employees, both at nice fees.

Notice that I do not proactively go out and ask Web sites to use my articles. You can, but I think it's not worth it. Your time is precious. Untargeted Web sites are unproven. If my articles get picked up without an investment of my valuable time, I'm thrilled.

But I do not think it would be worth my time to actively pursue Web publication. As the Web becomes better established, I may change my mind.

Are there any exceptions to this rule? If your industry has one or two sites that are clearly the preeminent Web presence in the field, I might approach them to see if they use or need articles. For example, www.clickz.com is the preeminent site on Web marketing, and my colleague Nick Usborne gets a lot of exposure being the online columnist on Web copywriting there. But that's the only exception I would make right now. ■

## Chapter 4

# Books

Writing one or more books is crucial to attaining guru status. In an article in *CIO* magazine about the top ten gurus in Information Technology, every one of the ten had written at least one book. In this chapter I share my experience, gained in writing 50 published books, to show the reader how to write a book on your area of expertise and get it published.

In their book *The Witch Doctors* (Times Books), John Mickelthwait and Adrian Wooldridge note that for many gurus "books are largely a form of advertising." About 50,000 books are published in the United States each year. That means 1,000 new books come out every week of the year.

That's good news and bad news. The bad news is there are too many books published, and therefore too many books competing for the reader's attention. The good news is that publishers need authors to write those 1,000 books each week. One of those authors might as well be you.

What percentage of these books become best-sellers? If we assume there are 10 nonfiction best-sellers on the Sunday *New York Times* best-seller list each week, and multiply by 50 weeks per year, you get 500 best-sellers. Out of 50,000 books published during the year, that means only 1 percent become best-sellers.

Writing a best-seller can instantly establish your guru status and make you wealthy from the royalties and speaking fees alone. But, as we will see in a moment, even if your book has modest sales, having a book published is an important accomplishment in your guru action plan.

You may ask, "With 50,000 books published a year, the bookstores are already full of titles on every conceivable subject under the sun. The last thing the world needs is another book. So why should I bother writing one?"

Aside from the promotional value a book brings to your career, the book you write will also bring unique value to your readers. Even if you write on a topic others have written about before, your experiences and perspective are unique. "It is in the totality of experience reckoned with, filed, and forgotten, that each man is truly different from all others in the world," observes Ray Bradbury in *Zen and the Art of Writing* (Santa Barbara, CA: Capra Press).

No one has done exactly what you have, or lived the exact life you have lived. The uniqueness you have as a professional and a human being brings uniqueness to your book, which is what makes it worth reading even though there have been many others on the topic before.

Perhaps much of the content of your book is similar to other books on the topic. Perhaps even 99 percent of the content is the same. But in the anecdotes you tell, and the techniques you share, you will give your readers ideas and examples they haven't thought of before.

And as far as professional advice goes, books are an incredible bargain. The reader might have to pay you $2,000 for a day's consultation or $250 to attend your workshop. But your book is a bargain at only $10 or $20. If reading the 99 percent of your book that repeats what he already knows reinforces the reader's knowledge and understanding of these subjects, he has gotten his money's worth. If reading the 1 percent that is original gives him an idea or two he hadn't thought of before, it can pay back his investment in your book a hundred fold or more. Not a bad bargain when you think of it that way.

## Why Every Guru or Would-Be Guru Should Write a Book

I tell virtually every self-employed professional, as well as many small-business owners, who ask me for advice on how to promote themselves to define their niche specialty, write a book about it, and get it published.

While I have done every strategy outlined in this book, nothing has been as helpful in establishing my own career and generating a steady flow of business than the many books I have written on my specialties of direct marketing, business communication, and more recently, Internet marketing.

Here are just a few of the ways you can benefit from writing your own book and having it published:

1. In writing a book on a subject, you are forced to do additional research to flesh out gaps in your knowledge. Your knowledge therefore increases, making you a better authority to your clients.

2. Writing a book also requires you to organize your material in logical sequence. Doing so increases clarity of presentation in all your communications, including individual consultations with clients.

3. A book can serve as the basis for a profitable seminar or workshop. The chapters of the book become modules of the seminar.

4. Potential clients reading your book will call you to inquire about the services you offer, and will be predisposed to hire you.

5. Associations will ask you to speak at their conferences for handsome fees if you are the author of a book that interests their members.

6. Listing yourself as the author of a book is an impressive credential on your Web site, brochure, and other marketing materials. It increases your status.

7. You can give copies of your book to potential clients to familiarize them with your methodology and convince them that you are an expert in your field.

8. You may be called upon to serve as an expert witness on your topic in court cases, at a handsome day rate.

9. Editors will ask you to contribute articles to their publications.

10. The media will want to interview you as an expert in your field. This can lead to appearances as a guest on radio and TV shows.

Whenever I want to establish credibility in a new niche market, one of the first things I do is secure a contract to write a book about it. For instance, when Internet marketing was becoming popular, I worried that my lack of experience in this new field could harm my freelance copywriting business over the long run—especially if the rise in Internet marketing caused traditional marketing to decline.

I specialize in writing direct mail packages. A few clients began asking me to write Internet direct mail: e-mail marketing campaigns. I liked this niche segment of Internet marketing for several reasons. Internet direct mail was similar in many ways to print direct mail, something I knew well. And it has less competition than Web site development, which was already overcrowded.

I immediately wrote a proposal for a book on Internet direct mail and sent it to one of my publishers, NTC Business Books, who gave me a contract to write the book. During the next six months, I wrote e-mail marketing campaigns for clients. I read everything I could get my hands on about e-mail marketing. I also interviewed numerous e-mail marketing experts and users about what was working for them to research the book. And of course I wrote the book.

The result? I gained enormous expertise in e-mail marketing. I now knew how to do it and was doing it, at nice fees, for both new and existing clients. The interviews I had done, which I would not have gotten had I not been writing the book, showed me techniques that increased the effectiveness of my e-mail campaigns. And when the book was published, it cemented my reputation as a leading copywriter in the e-mail marketing field. Many factors contributed, but the book was certainly the catalyst and driving force that gained me early entry into this new niche market.

## Which Publishing Option Is Best for the Wanna-Be Guru?

Thanks to the Internet and such advantages as digital printing on demand, the options for publishing your books are more varied than ever. They include:

- Publishing your book with a major publishing house
- Publishing your book with a small press
- Self-publishing
- Publishing your book as an e-book

Different choices are right for different people at different times. However, for most people seeking credibility, the best route is to place your manuscript with one of the major publishing houses. Examples include Pearson, John Wiley, McGraw-Hill, Prentice Hall, and Doubleday, to name a few.

Why do I recommend this option? Simply because to build credibility and attain guru status, you have to impress others. And people are most impressed by authors who are published by traditional publishing houses. They hear the publisher's name and consider you a "real author."

A self-published book is just as real. And you might make more money that way. But self-publishing, whether in print or electronically with an e-book, brings less credibility and status than a traditionally published book.

People know it's difficult to find a publisher and that publishers are highly selective, so having a book with a big publisher impresses them. People also know that anyone who can write a check can pay a printer to print their self-published book; therefore they are less impressed when they see your title is self-published.

Some people may argue with my conclusion. That's their opinion. Mine is based on 20 years of experience having people ask me who my publisher is and observing their reactions, and I think it is accurate.

A famous self-publishing guru gave a lecture on book publishing to professional speakers. I asked him, "Doesn't publishing with a traditional publishing house impress people more than self-publishing?"

No, he insisted. People don't know publishers, so the name of the publisher doesn't matter. But I disagree. Recently I sat with an executive from a large pharmaceutical company who was reviewing my list of published books. "John Wiley," he said, nodding his head as he went down the list, "It's really difficult to sell a book to them." Who was I to argue?

## Selling Your Book Idea to a Major Publishing House

You have a great idea for a nonfiction book. Your significant other thinks it's a great idea. Your parents think it's a great idea. Even your neighbor who hates to read thinks it's a great idea.

But will a publisher think it's a great idea—enough to pay you an advance, commission you to write it, and publish and sell it?

That will depend largely on your book proposal. Here's where you demonstrate persuasively that your idea has merit. Of course, even a solid idea and a great book proposal can't guarantee success, but they surely can tip the odds in your favor. But if either the idea or the proposal is weak, your chances of a sale are slim to none.

It's no secret what book editors look for when reviewing book ideas and proposals. You'll improve your chances of winning a publisher's contract by testing your book proposal against the five key questions that editors ask. Let's look at those questions—and the best ways to answer them.

**Is there a large enough audience interested in this topic to justify publishing a book about it?**

The major New York publishing houses aren't interested in highly specialized books written for small, narrow-interest audiences. If you want to write the definitive work on LAN/WAN internet-working, for example, seek out a publisher of technical books.

Big publishers are primarily interested in "bookstore books"—that is, books that appeal to a general audience or at least to a large segment of the general population. Examples of such audiences include parents, small-business owners, corporate executives, fitness enthusiasts, movie buffs, users of personal computers, teenagers, and other large affinity groups.

A book aimed at a major publisher must appeal to an audience of hundreds of thousands of people, if not millions. To sell your idea to the editor, you must demonstrate that such an audience exists. In our proposal for *How to Promote Your Own Business* (accepted and published by New American Library), Gary Blake and I cited statistics showing there are more than 10 million small businesses in the United States and 250,000 new businesses started each year.

One excellent source of market data is *Standard Rate and Data Service (SRDS),* a book listing U.S. magazines that accept advertising and their circulations. *SRDS* is available at your local library or from the publisher (call 847-375-5000 for information). If you're proposing a book on freelance writing, for example, you could look up writers' magazines and find that the two largest publications in the field have a combined circulation of more than 300,000; this is the potential market for your book.

But only a small percentage of the intended audience will actually buy your book. And a major publisher hopes to sell at least 5,000 copies of your book. So if you're writing a book that appeals only to the 44,171 branch managers working at banks nationwide (say, *How to Manage Your Branch More Efficiently*), and 2 percent can be persuaded to buy the book, you've sold only 883 copies—not nearly enough to make the project worthwhile for either you or a publisher.

### Is this a book or an article?

At the onset of the 1991 recession, I came up with an idea for a book I thought would be a strong seller: *Recession-Proof Business Strategies: Winning Methods to Sell Any Product or Service in a Down Economy.* It was timely. It had strong media appeal. And it contained vital information readers desperately needed.

But, as my agent pointed out, there were two problems with the book. First, its timely nature. From conception to bookstore, it can take 18 months to 2 years to write and publish a book. If the recession was over by the time *Recession-Proof Business Strategies* came out, the book would bomb.

Second, my agent was concerned that there wasn't enough material to fill a book. And he was right.

The average nonfiction book is about 200 pages in typeset, published form, with approximately 400 words a page. That's 80,000 words; about 320 double-spaced, typewritten manuscript pages. Your book might be longer or shorter, ranging from 35,000 words (a slim, 100-page volume) to 200,000 words or more.

The trouble was, when I finished writing everything I knew about recession-proof business strategies, I had 5,000 words—too short for a book, too long for an article. The solution? I self-published *Recession-Proof Business Strategies* as a $7 booklet and sold several thousand copies. So a booklet, not a book, was the right vehicle for this material.

Many book ideas seem strong initially, but wilt under close examination. For example, a (to me) wonderful book title popped into my head a while back: *How to Survive a Midlife Crisis at Any Age.* My co-author loved it and wanted to do the book. But when we sat down, we couldn't think of anything to put in it! We soon abandoned the idea.

How do you know whether your idea is a book, article, or booklet? And how do you convince a publisher that your concept is a big one? Here are some guidelines:

First, see if there are other books on the topic. The existence of a few similar titles indicates that this idea is big enough to deserve a book, since other publishers bought and published book-length manuscripts on the topic.

Second, go to the library and see what else is written on the topic. If you feel overwhelmed by all the magazine articles, newspaper stories, booklets, pamphlets, surveys, reports, and statistics on your topic, that's a good indication the topic is "meaty" enough to justify a full-length book.

For example, I heard a public service announcement describing a toll-free number you could call to get safety information about any car that you were thinking of buying. I thought, "There seem to be a lot of these free consumer hotlines; why not organize them into a reference book?"

I researched the subject and discovered there were indeed hundreds of such hotlines. New American Library bought the book and published it as *Information Hotline USA*. If I'd uncovered only a few such hotlines, New American Library would have rejected my proposal.

The third step to convincing a publisher that your topic is broad enough to warrant a book is to organize your information into chapters. Think about how you would logically explain your topic or present your information, and organize it into major categories. These will become chapter headings.

A full-length nonfiction book typically has 8 to 15 chapters. If your outline has fewer, the publisher may think there is not enough information to fill a book on your topic. Shoot for an outline with at least nine chapters.

On index cards, organize all your research material by chapter. Then add the most important or interesting items as bullet points in your chapter outline to create a complete table of contents for your proposed book. Here's how my co-author and I described Chapter 15 in our proposal for *How to Promote Your Own Business:*

Chapter 15: On with the Show: Trade Shows and Displays

■ Why do people attend trade shows?

■ How to select the shows at which you will exhibit

- Creating effective trade-show displays
- Five things you can do to attract more prospects to your exhibit: demonstrations, product, samples, free gifts, contests, and entertainment
- Other uses for your display materials: retail point-of-purchase, malls, lobby displays

This type of detailed table of contents proves to the publisher that your topic is appropriate for a book, not just a magazine article.

**How is your book different or better than other books on the market on this topic?**

The first page or two of your book proposal must contain an overview of your idea. This describes what the book is about, who it's written for, and what's in it.

Your overview must also tell the editor why and how your book is unique, different, or better than other books already published on this topic. And you must do this within the first two paragraphs (if you don't, the editor probably won't read further).

The hook—the angle that makes your book different—can take many forms: It might be a slant toward a different audience, a better way of organizing the material, or inclusion of topics not covered in other books. The key to make your book seem both different and better.

For instance, if the other books aren't illustrated, say that your books will be—and explain why that's important. If the other books are lengthy, promise to write a more concise book. If the other books are incomplete, describe the topics they omit and tell how you'll cover them in your book.

When planning *How to Promote Your Own Business,* my co-author and I hoped to write a book on advertising that would appeal to small-business owners rather than advertising agencies,

PR firms and other advertising professionals. We used this as our hook; our proposal began:

> *How to Promote Your Own Business* is not a book for the professional publicist, promoter or advertising professional. Rather, it is a practical working promotion guide for the 10.8 million Americans who own their own businesses, and the 250,000 entrepreneurs who start new businesses each year.

We wrote a previous book, *Technical Writing: Structure, Standards and Style,* because we believed the existing technical writing books were too lengthy and dull to be suitable as references for working technical writers. We wanted to create a handbook for technical writers that emulated the concise, to-the-point style and format of *The Elements of Style,* William Strunk and E. B. White's popular style guide for general writers.

Our proposal called our book "the Strunk and White of technical writing," which instantly communicated the key appeal of the concept. Our agent sold the book, within three weeks, to the first publisher who looked at it. Interestingly, McGraw-Hill also used the phrase "the Strunk and White of technical writing" in publicity and promotional materials describing the book.

Another section of your proposal that positions your book in relation to others on the same subject is the "Competition" section. Here you list and describe competing books; each listing should emphasize how your book is both different and better. Here is an example from our *How to Promote Your Own Business* proposal:

> *How to Advertise and Promote Your Small Business,* by Connie McClung Siegel, John Wiley & Sons, 1978, 128 pages, $4.95 trade paperback. This book is part of John Wiley's Small Business Series. The author neglects several vital areas of small business promotion, including mail order sales literature, trade shows, and displays, contests and newsletters. There are very few examples of actual promotions, and the author gives no indication of the costs involved or the results achieved. The book does not provide step-by-step instructions for selecting and implementing promotions.

Include in the "Competition" section those books that cover the same or very similar topics as your book; are published by a major publishing house; and that are no more than five years old.

How many books you list in this section will be important. The presence of two to six competitive books shows there's a market for this type of book, while still room for one more. On the other hand, if there are seven or more books a publisher may think the field is overcrowded, and you'll probably have a difficult time making the sale.

### Will people pay $22.95 for this book?

The average hardcover nonfiction book sells for $22.95 or more; the average trade paperback for $12.95. Your book must be interesting or valuable enough to make readers part not only with their money—remember, they can always read your book for free at the library—but with their time as well. (Many people would rather watch TV, go to the movies, or nap than read a book.)

When it comes to nonfiction, readers typically buy books to learn something for reference or to be entertained.

A how-to or reference book proposal should stress the benefits readers will get when they buy the book. Will it help them save time and money? Make money? Look beautiful? Feel young? Live longer? If your book will make readers' lives better and easier. Say so. In our proposal for *How to Promote Your Own Business,* we said:

> *How to Promote Your Own Business* is unique because it goes right to the heart of the problem: How can the owner or manager of a small business—a person with little time, money and promotion expertise—promote his business as effectively as his bigger, wealthier competitors?

If your book is biography, journalism, history, or any other form of nonfiction written primarily to entertain, your proposal should highlight some of the more fascinating details of the book. Your aim is to make the editor want to read the whole story.

### Why should the publisher hire you to write this book instead of another author?

Your proposal must show why you are uniquely qualified to write the book. Such qualifications fall into two categories: writing credentials and expert credentials.

Writing credentials establish your expertise as an author. In an "About the Author" section of your book proposal, write a brief biographical sketch of yourself, being sure to include such information as:

- Titles, publishers, and dates of publication for any books you've written
- Total number of books and articles written (if the number is impressive)
- Names of major magazines and newspapers in which your work has appeared
- Excerpts from favorable reviews about your work
- Sales figures for your best-selling books (if they're impressive)

Expert credentials establish your position as an authority in the topic of your proposed book.

Actually, you don't have to be much of an expert. The trick is to make you seem like an expert to the publisher.

For instance, author Wilbur Perry wanted to write about mail order. To make himself more appealing as a potential author for a book on the subject, he started and operated a small part-time mail-order business from his home. This gave him the credentials he needed to convince John Wiley & Sons to publish two books by him on the topic.

In my experience, your expert credentials don't need to be in-depth. Editors understand you can research the topic, and they don't require you to know everything about it before buying your book. They just want to convince their editorial board that you know what you're talking about.

How do you present all of the above information to potential agents and publishers? At minimum, you write a book proposal. You can follow the model proposal reprinted in the appendix; it's the actual proposal that sold *Become a Recognized Authority in Your Field.*

Some publishers might buy your book on the strength of the proposal. Others may ask you for a couple of sample chapters before making a decision. For your sample chapters, do the strongest chapter plus Chapter 1. Why Chapter 1? Because the editor wants to see how you get into your topic.

## Agents and Publishers

Do you approach publishers directly? Or should you get an agent?

To sell your book to the major publishing houses, you need a literary agent to represent you; several are listed in Appendix B, "Recommended Vendors." A more complete listing may be found in my book *How to Get Your Book Published* (Roblin Press), also listed in Appendix A, "Bibliography."

You probably either know someone who has published a book, or else you know someone who knows someone who has published a book. Ask that person to refer you to his agent.

Or, go to the bookstore. Look at new books that have been published in your field. Does the author thank his agent by name in the acknowledgments? Call the agent, mention the book in which you found his name, and tell him you have something that appeals to the same audience.

Smaller publishers can be approached directly, without an agent. *Writer's Market* lists numerous small publishers and the types of books they publish. Write a letter describing your book and asking if they would like to see a book proposal.

If they respond positively, you of course need to send them the book proposal you promised. A book proposal, as the name implies, is a proposal to write the book you envision.

The book proposal presents an outline of the proposed book and describes the target audience. It answers the five questions we discussed earlier.

## Writing Your Book

The instant I get an idea for a book I might write, I create a file labeled with the title. I then clip and place into that file every item related to that topic I come across in my reading and Web surfing. This way, when I'm ready to write the book, a good chunk of the research is already done.

Part of putting together a winning book proposal is to write a detailed, chapter-by-chapter outline of the proposed book. Once you get a contract to write the book, you simply fill in the outline.

The first thing I do once I get the go-ahead from a publisher is to make a separate file on my computer for each chapter. It includes the chapter number and title, and numerous subheads relating to the subtopics described in my proposal. Once that's done, you just have to fill in each subhead with the material you've collected—through research and your own experience—about each subtopic.

I also print out the chapter number, heading, and subheads, and paste them on separate manila files for each chapter. Then I take the research I collected and sort it into chapter files. This further simplifies and organizes the task of writing the book.

## Self-Publishing

I cannot speak as authoritatively about self-publishing as I can about traditional publishing, simply because of my limited experience. I have self-published reports, manuals, videos, and audiocassettes, but I have never self-published a regular book.

The reason is that I write books to establish credibility, and as I mentioned earlier, I think publishing with a large publishing house is a big factor in building that credibility.

However, not everyone agrees, and many people tell me their self-published book has helped establish them as experts in their fields. Runner John Vonhof comments:

> I am the author of a self-published book, *Fixing Your Feet: Prevention and Treatment for Athletes.* As a marathoner, ultrarunner, and backpacker, I found a subject that was of interest to many athletes—foot care. I am often asked, "You wrote a book on *feet?*" This 300-page book has become the "bible" of foot care for distance runners, backpackers, and adventure racers. I have spoken to groups, given demonstrations on foot taping, and have become recognized as the expert on fixing your feet. I have become a guru on foot care! Many people would turn up their noses at being recognized as a foot expert, but I find it fun and rewarding.
>
> This whole project has led me into becoming a guru on creative self-publishing. I write and teach about using creative means to publish your work. So, not wanting to be a guru in only one area, I am developing myself as a guru in many different and diverse areas.

There are obviously pros and cons to self-publishing vs. traditional publishing. One of the great advantages of self-publishing is you are assured of becoming a published author. Anyone can write a book, take it to a printer, and have copies made. But if you go the traditional route, you may have difficulty getting a publisher interested in your book. It may take a long time or not happen at all. Thus, there is no assurance that you will become a published book author. If that's critical to your goal, you might consider self-publishing at least your first book.

Another advantage of self-publishing is that you keep more of the profits. In traditional publishing, when someone buys your $20 book, you (the author) may receive only $2 of that ... and many months after purchase. As the publisher, you receive the whole $20 (if you sell directly to the purchaser). If the book cost you $3 to print, your profit is $17.

As for the disadvantages of self-publishing, I've already discussed the major one: It doesn't carry the credibility you get with the brand-name of a major publisher on the title page. But there are several other disadvantages to self-publishing you should also be aware of.

First, cash flow. With traditional publishing, all the cash flow is in your direction. Upon signing the book contract, the publisher sends you an advance of $5,000 to $25,000 or more—instant cash in your pocket. You have no costs other than your time, research, and paying permission costs for any copyrighted materials from other works that you want to reprint in your book. Once the book starts selling and your advance is paid back,* you get an additional payment of $1 to $2 or more for each book sold.

Distribution for self-publishers is also problematic. A major publisher can afford to hire a sales force to visit all the bookstores and present the hundreds of books it publishes each season. As an individual with just a single book, you can't do that. So how will you get your book distributed in the trade? Often self-publishers can't.

Texts on self-publishing recommend alternative selling methods such as back-of-room sales and direct response. But for most authors, these simply won't work. Unless you are already a top speaker doing major association gigs, boot camps, or rallies, you don't reach a big enough audience with your presentations to generate significant back-of-the-room sales.

---

*The advance you get is just that—an advance against royalties, not a separate fee. Let's say your royalty is $1 per book and your advance is $10,000. If you sell 5,000 books, you have not earned your advance yet and get no royalty on those sales. If you sell 10,000 copies, you have earned back your advance. So on the next copy you sell, you get $1 in royalties. If sales reach 20,000 copies, you get a royalty check for $10,000.

As for direct response, costs for solo direct mail packages are so high today (60 to 75 cents apiece or more) and response rates so low (1 percent is typical), that it is nearly impossible to be profitable with a mailing selling a single book. The price point simply isn't high enough.

For instance, say you do a typical direct mail package selling your book—#10 outer envelope, 4-page sales letter, brochure, order form, business reply envelope. Your cost in the mail at small test quantities (5,000 to 10,000 pieces) is $700 per thousand.

You charge $25 per book. Out of that you have $3 cost for shipping and handling, and $2 cost per book for printing. That leaves you $20 profit per sale.

Just to break even and pay for the cost of the mailing, you have to sell 35 books (35 × $20 = $700) per 1,000 pieces mailed (remember your cost in the mail is $700 per thousand). That's a 3.5 percent response rate. Now, in direct mail, a 1 to 2 percent response rate is typical; a 3 percent response rate is great. Therefore, your chances of profitably marketing your book via direct mail are almost nonexistent.

Another disadvantage of self-publishing is lack of interest among the media. Many publications will not review a book if it is self-published. Many reporters and other people of influence do not take self-published books or self-published authors seriously.

## E-Books

"Published books give credibility and little cash," says Joe Vitale, who has written books for major publishers, self-published paperback books, and e-books. "E-books give cash but no credibility."

Joe Vitale is a guru in marketing and a prolific author who has published books in many different ways: through mainstream publishers, small presses, self-publishing, and now, quite lucrative for him, e-books.

An e-book is a book published in electronic form. The buyer purchases an electronic file, not a book made of paper, ink, and glue.

The file may be text, Word, html, pdf, or a proprietary format, such as Glassbook Reader or Rocket Books. It may require a specialized e-book reading device, or else the customer downloads it on a regular PC.

The e-book can be a profitable venture. Joe told me that from one e-book alone, he made $40,000 in revenues last year. And he has many more e-books in the works.

An e-book may be a good source of revenue for you. But on the book scale, it is at the bottom of the list as far as being a credibility builder. A regular book published by a traditional publisher is at the top. A self-published book doesn't have the prestige a publisher's brand name brings, but people are still impressed when they see a physical book with your name on the cover.

But with an e-book, there is no physical book, and with books, the physical presence of a printed, bound volume is what conveys a large portion of the credibility. People are not used to e-books and, even though they may enjoy reading them, don't put them in the same category as a "real book."

Therefore, if you pursue producing your own e-book, do it primarily for the revenue. It may contribute significantly to your bottom line, but only minimally—at least right now—to your guru reputation. That may not be fair, but it's the way things are today. ■

# Chapter 5

# Information Products

Gurus are focal points of information on a specific topic, and they enhance their reputations as experts by producing and marketing "information products" on these topics. In their book *The Witch Doctors* (Times Books), John Micklethwait and Adrian Wooldridge report:

> Like the Hollywood studios, the gurus have discovered how to sell their ideas through a range of outlets, including diaries, audio and videocassettes, and training camps. The Tom Peters Group produces videos, churns out a regular newsletter, and generally helps to stretch the brand. One of its more recent offerings is "The Tom Peters Business School in a Box," which comes complete with 42 "personal agenda cards," 14 "time cards," and two dice.

There are two major benefits to producing and selling information products. First, achieving and maintaining guru status depends on a steady flow of new thought on your subject. Creating and distributing information products contributes to this flow. Second, selling your information products can bring in significant incremental revenue.

The revenue from information product sales is "passive income," meaning the guru makes money independent of his personal labor. You can run an ad in a magazine selling your $99 audiocassette album, and you can receive 100 orders and checks for $9,900 on Saturday, even though you do nothing but sleep the whole morning. Information products, along with book royalties, are one of the keys to generating income beyond your own billable hours—an important element of achieving wealth.

This chapter shows what these products are and how to create and market them. It includes audiotapes, videos, CD-ROMs, software, directories, resource guides, special reports, market research, booklets, pamphlets, and more.

## What Are "Information Products"?

"Information products" are printed, recorded, or electronic files containing prewritten information sold at a per-unit price. Information products is a broad term referring to everything from pamphlets, special reports, books, audio cassettes, and videos, to CD-ROMs, software, computer-based training, newsletters, and fax advisory services.

Information products present in-depth data, information, or discussion of a topic related to the speaker's or seminar leader's area of expertise. One guru specializing in ISO compliance, for example, offers as an information product a "boilerplate" quality manual on a disk. The boilerplate can easily be customized to a client's operation, eliminating the time and effort of writing the quality manual entirely from scratch. Another information product produced by this ISO guru is a mini-directory of firms certified to perform ISO audits.

Traditionally, gurus have offered booklets (because they are inexpensive and easy to produce) and books (because of the prestige and credibility). But with the growth of the Internet, many prospects like to buy information in electronic form, whether as downloads from a Web site or on a CD-ROM or computer disk.

This actually works to your advantage as an information seller: You can package essentially the same information in multiple media, and sell it many times over. Not only will different people buy information in different formats, but some customers will actually pay for the same information several times over to get it in different formats!

ıru asked me, "What are the criteria for a
on product at a time when we are all suffer-
ı overload?" The answer: information prod-
: and detailed answers to questions and
problems in narrow-niche subjects not usually addressed by
newspapers, magazines, and general media. As Richard Saul
Wurman observes in his book *Information Anxiety* (Doubleday),
"The information explosion has backfired, leaving us inundated
with facts but starved for understanding." Information products
cut through the clutter, providing clients with the precise information they want in a minimum of words.

Another question I hear frequently is, "If I give away my
secrets in a free or inexpensive report or booklet, won't that eliminate the need for the client to hire me for my expensive training
program, coaching, consultation, or whatever?"

On the contrary, your potential clients don't want to do it
themselves. They want a professional to guide them. But they
also want to be convinced that, if they hire you, they are making
the right choice and you will not disappoint them. Information
products that demonstrate your knowledge of the field help give
them that comfort.

"People are silently begging to be led," observes marketing
guru Jay Abraham in *Stealth Marketing* (Abraham Publishing).
"They are crying out to know more about your product or service. When you educate your customers, you'll see your profits
soar. Educate your prospective buyers about everything (including a few of the bad or less positive aspects of your product or
service) and you'll sell to almost twice as many people as you do
now."

## Reasons Why Gurus Should Produce Information Products

The main reasons why speakers and seminar leaders should produce and offer information products, and why Howard Shenson said, "Publishing is every speaker, consultant, or seminar leader's second business," are as follows:

- Being published builds credibility. The highest-paid gurus are typically those who have written best-selling books in their fields.

- Information products let clients "sample" your information before they hire you. Once, the marketing director at a computer company said to me, "I am considering several consultants for teaching direct marketing to our staff; why should I choose you over them?" I sent him my book on direct marketing with a note that said, "If this doesn't convince you, hire someone else." I got the job and a large client with whom I've been working for years on numerous projects.

- Information products give you an advantage over the competition. If you have written a book or produced an audio album and your competitor hasn't, this gives you an edge in winning contracts.

- Information products allow you to profitably serve that segment of the market that can't or won't hire you for private consultation or speeches. Instead of turning away prospects who can't afford you, you can offer them a lower-priced alternative: an information product that delivers much of the same advice you would give in a private consultation. In this way, leads you've paid to generate that you'd otherwise have to turn down flat can become product buyers, generating additional income for you.

- Writing books, booklets, and articles sharpens your thinking, forces you to organize your information more logically, and builds your own expertise in your subject area. Creating information products helps you become more knowledgeable in your field.

Being the author of information products builds your reputation as an expert in your field. "The reverence people have for the printed word is amazing," writes Edward Uhlan in his book *The Rogue of Publishers Row* (Exposition Press). "Simply because a man appears in print, the public assumes he has something authoritative to say."

## Tips for Producing Specific Types of Information Products

Here is a quick overview of some of the more popular formats for information products, along with suggestions on producing each:

### Tip Sheets

Tip sheets are short, to-the-point fact sheets on a particular subject. They are usually printed on one or two sides of an $8^1/_2$ by 11 inch sheet of paper. Advice or information is typically (but not necessarily) presented as a series of short, numbered items or tips. You can write tip sheets as electronic files, then run them off one at a time on your laser printer as orders come in. You can also e-mail tip sheets to clients who prefer an electronic file. I typically charge $1 to $2 for a tip sheet.

### Booklets and Pamphlets

These are, in essence, expanded versions of tip sheets. They contain similar information except in more detail: In a booklet, there's space to flesh out each point more fully. Booklets are generally 4 by 9 inches, so they can be mailed in a standard #10 business envelope. A booklet is constructed by printing the pages and then saddle-stitching them together (saddle-stitching is binding by stapling through the spine). Booklets typically run anywhere from 8 to 16 pages, although they can be longer. I price booklets at $5 to $12 each.

### Special Reports

This format is typically longer than a booklet, and so can be even more detailed. Special reports, like tip sheets, are printed on $8^1/_2$ by 11 inch sheets of paper, but are multiple pages instead of one page. The larger page format allows for bigger illustrations, tables, and charts than you can put in a booklet. A special report can run anywhere from 5 pages to 100 or more, although typically they are 6 to 12 pages.

I desktop publish the master pages, then run off copies of the report on my office copier, collate, and staple them. The pages are reproduced on plain white copier paper; the cover, on a colored stock such as green or blue.

For a 10-page special report, I charge $6 to $7 for the print version. You can also produce special reports and post them on your Web site as pdf or html files. These can be available for free or for a fee. Typically, electronic versions are priced at half or less of the print version cost.

### Monographs

A monograph is an essay or article on a single subject. It is similar in look and feel to a special report, but often on the lengthy side (20 to 30 pages) and written in more formal, professional language. The medical products industry frequently uses monographs written by doctors to promote a drug, material, instrument, or piece of equipment. They give monographs away free, but you can charge $5 to $14 or more for a well-written monograph on a topic of interest to your prospects.

## Resource Guides

These are mini-directories of information resources in a particular field—for example, Web sites for quality control professionals. A resource guide of five or six pages might sell for $5 to $8.

## Manuals

Reference manuals are long, comprehensive special reports, usually placed in a binder or notebook and organized into sections. Manuals can range from 30 to 150 pages or more. Price can range from $10 to $30 or higher.

## Books

As discussed in Chapter 4, "Books," many gurus write books. Not only does the book promote your professional practice, but you can generate additional revenue from book sales. If you cannot find a publisher for a book, you can always self-publish it. A 200-page book will sell for $10 to $30 or higher. The more specialized the book, the higher the price. Costs for producing a self-published book are presented in the following table.

| Item | Cost |
| --- | --- |
| Proofreader | $12/hour |
| Copyeditor | $15/hour |
| Indexer | $2/page |
| Front cover design | $800 to $1,200 |
| Typesetting | $6 to $10/page |
| Printing of 5,000 copies of 224-page book | $1.20 to $1.30/copy |
| Printing of a 4-color cover, 5,000 copies | $1,200 to $2,800 |

*Source: "What Should Things Cost?" by Curt Matthews,* PMA Newsletter, *March 1997*

Although they complement one another rather than compete, learning through books in some ways has distinct advantages over the seminars and speeches we give. As writer Jerry Buchanan points out:

> A book that instructs in some profitable field is a priceless treasure. It stands patient and mute until you command it to teach. When it teaches, it teaches only as fast as you are capable of learning, and will repeat the difficult parts as often as is necessary to firmly entrench them in your brain. It will never rebuke you for tardiness to class, nor complain under a thousand interruptions. It never forgets even a minor principle of its conceptual message, yet it will not scold you if you forget even major ones. Such a book ranks with a faithful hound as one of man's best friends. If the bookseller offers it and you pass up the chance of ownership, who suffers the most: You? Or the bookseller, who will only sell it to the next one who browses?

## Audio Tapes

Audiocassettes are a popular medium for disseminating spoken-word business and how-to information. A single audiocassette is easy to produce. Just get a speaking engagement, and tape your talk. Then make duplicates, put a nice label on it, and sell the tapes. A single audio cassette retails for between $10 and $15. Duplication costs for small quantities are $1 to $2 each, depending on packaging. Appendix B, "Recommended Vendors," lists vendors who can tape and duplicate talks for you. Some organizations routinely tape speaker presentations and sell them to their members. You should make it a condition that you retain the rights to the tape and get a free master copy. This eliminates the cost of paying a professional or buying your own taping equipment.

## Audio Albums

Once you have done eight, six, or even four or two tapes on related topics, you can package them in a vinyl album and sell them as an audiocassette program. In the audiotape market, an "album" is a vinyl cover with plastic molded holders for multiple cassettes. A six-cassette album can sell for $49 to $79. Albums are a couple of dollars each and are available from any tape duplication service.

## Power Packs

A power pack is a multimedia information product. Typically, it's a combination of tapes, reports, perhaps a book or CD-ROM, all in a nice package. Power packs can sell for $50 to $150 or more.

## Video Tapes

You can video your presentation, duplicate it, and sell the videos. The video should be edited professionally in a video studio. Add graphics, special effects, charts, and other footage for a varied presentation that's more than just you talking behind a lectern. Have a nice label or package. A single video can sell for $29 to $59 or more.

The late seminar leader and consultant Howard Shenson told me that he often did a public seminar only once, and solely for the purpose of videotaping the performance and turning it into a video album he would then sell by mail. He said it was much more profitable to sell a program on tape than do it live again and again.

## Paid-Subscription Newsletter

As will be discussed in Chapter 6, "Newsletters and E-Zines," many gurus produce a quarterly promotional newsletter of four to eight pages they distribute free to prospects and clients. Make your newsletter meatier (more information; no self-promotion), longer (6 to 8 pages), and more frequent (monthly), and you can charge a subscription fee ranging from $29 to $249 a year or more.

### Software

If some of the processes you teach can be automated using software, consider working with a software developer to create custom software that you can sell to your clients and attendees. One consultant who gives workshops on how to write documentation for ISO compliance sold a disk containing boilerplate text and outlines for all the necessary documents she helped attendees create in her class.

## How to Design a Catalog Featuring Your Information Products

The greatest profit opportunity for selling information products is through your "bounce-back catalog." This is a mini-catalog of your entire information product line. It need not be elaborate; you can print it in black ink on white or colored paper (see Appendix C, "Sample Documents," for a model mini-catalog).

A bounce-back catalog should be included in every outgoing order you ship to your clients and customers. The beauty is that it promotes your entire product line at virtually no cost—there is no postage or envelope to pay for, since it is mailed with the product shipment. The only cost is the few pennies per catalog for printing.

For a small, home-based information business, including a bounce-back catalog in all product shipments can double your annual gross sales or better, with no added marketing cost.

You can promote your full line of information products in other ways, of course. For instance, you can periodically mail your mini-catalog or other special offers to your list of buyers. But the cheapest, easiest way to sell information products is by enclosing bounce-back catalogs with products being shipped. If you don't do this, you are missing out on a large share of the profits your information products business can generate for you.

Always insert your bounce-back catalog in every shipment, whether you are fulfilling a request for an inquiry or an order for a product.

## How to Sell Your Products Profitably to Clients and Prospects

You can get significant additional income with virtually no extra marketing cost by selling information products to clients and prospects.

Include your bounce-back catalog in the packets of information you send to potential clients. Many, even if they don't hire you, will place an order for information products. Those who do become further educated in your expertise—and are more likely to hire you.

Periodically re-mail catalogs to all leads who do not become clients. Many will place orders for your information products.

For those prospects whose business you actively seek, you can impress them by sending some of your information products, free, as an enticement to hire you and as a demonstration of your expertise. Books, booklets, article reprints, and monographs are more interesting than sales brochures alone and more likely to make the impression you want: that of the knowledgeable authority in your field.

I give away dozens of audiocassettes, article reprints, and full-length books each year to those prospects I want to close. It pays off handsomely. What's neat is that the information product has a high perceived value—that of the price listed on its cover and in your catalog. But it costs you only a fraction of that amount to produce and give away. And while a brochure might get lost in a file folder, a book sits on the client's shelf where he can always see it, and is therefore continually reminded of you and your expertise.

Consultant Dr. Jeffrey Lant says, "A book is a brochure that will never be thrown away."

## How to Use Direct Marketing to Boost Your Product Sales

Is the "information explosion" a good thing for information marketers? Actually, it's a mixed blessing:

- People have too much to read and not enough time to read it.

- More and more information is competing for their attention.

- There is a proliferation of low-cost/no-cost information sources eating into the market for your expensive information products.

Fortunately, you can still succeed in selling information by mail. It's tougher than it was in yesteryear, I think. So here are some rules and guidelines formulated specifically for information marketers competing in the Information Age.

### Narrow the Focus

Although the most profitable product may be one with wide appeal, such as Joe Karbo's *Lazy Man's Way to Riches* or Bob Kalian's *A Few Thousand of the Best Free Things in America,* "goldmine" concepts such as these are difficult to come by. Today we live in an age of specialization. People have narrow, specific areas of interest and eagerly seek the best information in these niche areas. Match your own interests and consulting expertise with the information needs of an identifiable market and you're on your way.

How big must this market be? Jerry Buchanan, publisher of Towers Club Newsletter, a how-to newsletter for information marketers and self-publishers, says that "any group large enough that some publisher has seen fit to publish a magazine about them or for them" is large enough for your purposes.

## Seize a Subject

The tendency of the typical magazine writer or book author is to wander from subject to subject to satisfy a never-ending curiosity about all things. But the speaker or seminar leader, an information marketer, must behave differently. He must latch onto a narrow niche or topic, make it his own, and produce a series of information products that meet the needs of information-seekers buying materials on this subject. Not only does this increase profits by giving you more products to offer your customers, it also helps establish you as a recognized expert and authority in your field.

## Plan the "Back End" Before You Start Marketing

Many entrepreneurial direct response advertisers dream of duplicating the one-shot success of Joe Karbo and of getting rich from a single mail order book. But it rarely happens. This "front end," or first sale, can be profitable, if cost-effective marketing techniques are used. But the real profits are in the back end—selling a related line of additional information products to repeat customers.

I advise you to come up with and plan this back end of related products before launching a direct response campaign. Otherwise, precious opportunities for repeat sales will be lost if you can only offer a single product to eager, information-hungry buyers.

## Test Your Concept with Classified Ads

Most information marketers want to immediately mail thousands of direct mail packages or place full-page ads.

That's fine if you can afford to risk $5,000 to $25,000 on an untested idea. However, I prefer to test with small classified ads first. By doing so, I can determine the product's sales appeal and potential for under $200.

Your ad should seek inquiries, not orders. All requests for information should be immediately fulfilled with a powerful direct mail sales letter, circular, order form and reply envelope.

What should all this cost? A successful classified ad will bring in inquiries at a cost of 25 cents to $1 per lead. A good sales package will convert 10 percent to 35 percent of these leads to sales. I have run classified ads that pulled up to 17 times their cost in product sales.

## The Importance of the "Bounce-Back" Catalog

As discussed, a bounce-back catalog is a circular containing descriptions and order information for your complete line of related information products. When a customer orders your lead product, you insert the bounce-back in the package and ship it with the order. Ideally, he sees the catalog, scans it, orders more items, and his order "bounces back" to you.

The bounce-back catalog doesn't have to be long or elaborate. For my mail order business, the catalog is printed on four 8$^{1}/_{2}$ by 11 inch pages in black ink on colored paper.

Additional sales generated by bounce-backs can range from 10 percent to 100 percent of the front-end sales generated by your original ad or mailing. The only cost is a few cents to print each catalog sheet. There is no postage cost, because the catalog gets a "free-ride" as an insert in your product shipment.

(Tip: When you fulfill a bounce-back order, send out another bounce-back catalog ... and another ... until the customer has bought every item in the catalog.)

## Create Low-, Medium-, and High-Priced Products

Different buyers have different perceptions of what your information is worth and what they will pay. You will get more sales by testing a variety of prices for your lead item and by offering a number of different products reflecting a broad range of prices.

My front-end product is a $12 book. The back-end consists of a series of $7 and $8 reports, a second book for $20, and a six-tape cassette album for $49.95. Dr. Jeffrey Lant, who sells business development products and services, has products ranging from a $4 report to a $4,800 consulting service.

Once I sent an inquiry to a well-known and successful marketer who specializes in selling information on how to make money as a speaker. I didn't buy because the only alternatives were a large cassette album or a one-year newsletter subscription, both of which are fairly expensive, and I wasn't ready to make that kind of commitment to the subject. Most buyers prefer to sample your information with a lower-priced product, such as a book, single cassette, or inexpensive manual in the $10 to $50 range.

## Let Your Buyers Tell You What Products They Want You to Create

Always put your name, address, and phone number in every information product you produce, and encourage feedback from readers. Many readers become advocates and fans, calling, writing, and establishing a dialogue with you.

Welcome this. Not only can you solve their problems and answer their inquiries by telling them which current products to buy, but their questions can suggest new products. Most of my back-end products were created to answer specific questions readers asked me repeatedly. Instead of having the same telephone conversation over and over again, I can simply sell them a report that contains the answers they seek. It saves time and generates revenue.

### Be the Quality Source

Your strongest advertisement is a good product. A clever or deceptive ad can certainly generate brisk sales, and returns may not be excessive even if your product is poor, but customers will feel cheated and will not favor you with repeat business.

A good product will have people actively seeking you out and will bring in a small but steady stream of phone calls, letters, inquiries, and orders generated by the product itself and not the advertising. You will be shocked at the enormous effort some people expend to locate the source of quality information products that are well spoken of by other buyers.

## Using Small Ads to Sell Information Products

The least expensive way to start in mail order is with small classified ads. Actually, these ads generate a greater return on investment than any other medium, including full-page ads. With a winning classified ad and strong inquiry fulfillment kit, you have the foundation for making your home-based information products business profitable.

You should not ask for an order directly from a classified ad. It won't work. There is not enough copy in a classified ad to make the complete sale.

Classified advertising is two-step direct marketing. In step one, you run a small classified ad to generate an inquiry, which is a request for more information about your product. In step two, you send sales literature describing your product along with a reply form the prospect can use to place an order.

The way to measure classified ad response for inquiry advertising is to count the inquiries, divide the cost of the ad by the number of inquiries, and thus determine the cost per inquiry. For instance, if you run a classified ad and it costs you $100, and you get 100 inquiries, your cost per inquiry is $1.

When people inquire, you send them an inquiry fulfillment kit, which is a sales package promoting your product. The inquiry fulfillment kit consists of an outer envelope, sales letter, circular or brochure, order form, and reply envelope.

Bernard Lyons, editor of KEY Newsletter, says that classified ads must follow the AIDA principle, meaning they must get Attention, generate Interest, create Desire for the product, and ask for Action. According to Lyons, sales appeals that work in classified mail order advertising include promises of obtaining love, money, health, popularity, leisure, security, entertainment, self-confidence, better appearance, prestige, pride of accomplishment, saving time, eliminating worry and fear, satisfying curiosity, success, avoiding work or risk, self-expression, pride of ownership, comfort, creativity, and self-improvement.

Lyons says the six most effective words and phrases to use in your classified ads are: free, new, amazing, now, how to, and easy. To this list I would add: discover, method, plan, reveals, show, simple, startling, advanced, improved, and you.

One of my most successful mail order ads ran continuously for many years in *Writer's Digest:*

> MAKE $85,000/YEAR writing ads, brochures, promotional materials for local/national client. Free details: CTC, 22 E. Quackenbush, Dept. WD, Dumont, NJ 07628.

Here are some other examples of how to write classified mail order ads:

EXTRA CASH. 12 ways to make money at home. Free details ....

MAIL ORDER MILLIONAIRE reveals money-making secrets. FREE 1-hour cassette ....

SELL NEW BOOK by mail! 400% profit! Free dealer information ....

GROW earthworms at home for profit ....

CARNIVOROUS AND WOODLAND terrarium plants. Send for FREE catalog ....

ANCESTOR HUNTING? Trace your family roots the easy way. Details free ....

The offer that will generate the most response is to ask for an inquiry, not an order. This is done by putting a phrase such as "free details," "free information," "free catalog," or a similar phrase, followed by a colon and your address (for example, free details: Box 54, Canuga, TN 44566).

Some mail order advertisers ask the prospect to pay for the information, either by sending a small amount of money (25 cents, 50 cents, $1, and $2 are typical), or by requiring the prospect to send a self-addressed stamped envelope.

The theory is that asking for postage or a nominal payment brings you a more qualified lead and therefore results in a higher percentage of leads converted to sales. My experience is that it doesn't pay to charge for your information kit, since doing so dramatically cuts down on the number of leads you will receive.

As a rule of thumb, whenever you offer information to generate an inquiry, make it free. The exception might be a very expensive and elaborate catalog, for which you charge $1 to cover your costs.

"Key code" all your promotions so you can track which ad or mailing each inquiry or order comes from. In your classified ads, put the key code in the address. For instance, in my ad

"MAKE $85,000/YEAR WRITING," the key code "WD" refers to *Writer's Digest* magazine. Since the ad runs every month, I don't bother adding a code number to track the month. If you wanted to do so, you could. For example, "Dept. WD-10" would mean *Writer's Digest* magazine, October issue (the tenth month of the year). Keep track of the key code on each inquiry and daily sales in a notebook or on a spreadsheet.

The measure of a successful inquiry classified ad is the cost per inquiry. Therefore, if you can get your message across in fewer words, you pay less for the ad, and as a result lower your cost per inquiry.

Make your classifieds as short and pithy as possible. Here are some tips for reducing your word count:

- Be concise. Use the minimum number of words needed to communicate your idea. For example, instead of "Earn $500 a Day in Your Own Home-Based Business," write "Work at Home—$500/Day!"

- Minimize your address. You pay the publication for every word in your classified, including your address. Therefore, instead of "22 E. Quackenbush Avenue," I write "22 E. Quackenbush." The mail still gets delivered, and I save one word. This can add up to significant savings for ads run frequently in multiple publications.

- Use phrases and sentence fragments rather than full sentences.

- Remember your objective. You are only asking for an inquiry, not an order. You don't need a lot of copy, since all you are asking the reader to do is send for free information.

- Use combination words, hyphenated words, and slash constructions. For instance, instead of "GROW EARTH WORMS," which is three words, write "GROW EARTH-WORMS," which counts as two words, saving you a word.

Place your classified ads in publications that run mail order classified ad sections. Send for free media kits, which include details on circulation, advertising rates, readership, and a sample issue of the publication. Ask for several issues, if the publisher will send them.

Look at the classified ad sections in the publications. Are there ads for products similar to yours? This is a good sign. See if these ads repeat from issue to issue. The advertisers would not repeat them unless they were working. If this publication is working for their offers, it can work for yours, too.

Classified ad sections are divided by various headings. Place your ad in the appropriate heading. If you don't see an appropriate heading, call the magazine and ask if they will create one for you.

If you sell information by mail, avoid putting your classified under the heading "Books and Booklets." This will reduce orders. Instead, put the ad under a heading related to the subject matter. For example, if you are selling a book on how to make money cleaning chimneys, place the ad under "business opportunities."

We have already discussed the two key measurements of two-step classified advertising, which are the cost per inquiry and the percentage of inquiries converted to orders.

The bottom line is whether the sales the ad generated exceed the cost of the ad space. If they did, it was profitable. If they didn't, the ad isn't working and a new ad should be tested. My goal is to generate sales at least twice what the ad space costs. Your objectives may be different.

You can test a classified by running it just one time in a publication. The problem is, most magazines and even weekly newspapers have long lead times—several weeks or more—for placing classified ads. If you place the ad to run one time only, and the ad pulls well, you then have to wait several weeks or months until you can get it in again.

In a weekly newspaper or magazine, I test a classified ad by running it for one month—four consecutive issues. For a monthly publication, I test it for three months—three consecutive issues. If the first insertion is profitable, I will probably extend the insertion order for several months, so the ad runs continuously with no interruption.

With a full-page ad, you usually get the greatest number of orders the first time the ad runs in the magazine. Response declines with each additional insertion, and at the point where the ad is not going to be profitable in its next insertion, you pull it and try another ad.

The reason is that the first time the ad runs, it skims the cream of the prospects, getting orders from those most likely to buy. Obviously, those who buy from the first insertion of the ad will not buy when it runs again. Therefore, each time the ad runs, it reaches a smaller and smaller audience of potential new buyers.

With a classified ad, however, the total response is much less for each insertion. Therefore, it doesn't materially affect the number of potential first-time customers the ad appeals to. In fact, some people who responded once, got your sales literature, and didn't buy, may respond several times—and get your literature several times—before they eventually break down and buy. Also, each issue reaches a number of new subscribers via subscriptions and newsstand circulation, so the total audience for a classified remains fairly constant.

While response to full-page mail order ads declines with each insertion, the response to a classified ad can remain steady for many insertions. Indeed, some information marketers (and I am one of them) have run the same classified monthly in the same magazine for years at a time, with no decline in response. In fact, response sometimes tends to increase during the first 12 months the ad is run, as people see the ad over and over again, and eventually become curious enough to respond.

A classified ad will generate a greater return compared to its insertion cost than any other size ad. However, the total sales are naturally modest. If you want to make more sales faster, use full-page display ads. ■

*Chapter 6*

# Newsletters and E-Zines

A powerful technique for building your reputation with a defined audience over a period of time is to regularly send them a newsletter, which can either be free or paid subscription.

Unlike newspapers, which are aimed at general audiences, newsletters are written on specialized topics for readers in specific niche markets. For instance, *Metalworking Marketer* covers marketing and is aimed at advertising managers in the metals industry.

Newsletters are written to offer these niche readers practical, useful strategies and tips vs. the more general feature or news articles published in trade journals. The following table summarizes the unique characteristics of newsletters vs. magazines and newspapers.

## Differences Between Newsletters and Other Media

| Newspapers and Magazines | Newsletters |
|---|---|
| Editorial driven | Market driven |
| Product driven | Customer driven |
| Information focus | Reader/solution focus |
| What happened | What it means |
| Interesting | Actionable |
| Journalism | Service |

*Source: Stephen Meyer, Progressive Business Publications*

This chapter tells how to produce and distribute traditional print promotional newsletters as well as electronic newsletters delivered via the Internet (e-zines).

## The Company Newsletter

A "company newsletter," which also used to be called a "house organ," is a promotional newsletter distributed free by a corporation or small business to its customers and prospects.

Thousands of company newsletters are published in the United States. The publishers range from the biggest corporations like Westinghouse, IBM, and Raytheon, to small service firms and independent professionals including lawyers, doctors, dentists, and chiropractors.

These newsletters, magazines, tabloids, or other regular publications are published primarily as promotional tools. They range from simple sheets published in-house to elaborate, four-color company magazines with photography and professional writing rivaling the quality of newsstand magazines.

The main purpose of such a newsletter is to establish your image and build your credibility with a select audience (the people who receive the newsletter) over an extended period of time.

Instinctively, most marketers recognize that they should be in touch with their customers and prospects more often than they actually are. You know, for instance, that there are many people in your life—business and social—whom you don't think about, see, or talk to for long periods of time simply because you are busy and not thinking of them.

Well, your customers and prospects are busy, too. And while you may be agonizing over why Joe hasn't placed an order from you recently or called your firm to handle a project, Joe isn't even thinking about you ... because he has so much else on his mind.

You know you should be doing something to keep your name in front of Joe and remind him of your existence. But how? You may want to call or send a letter, but you think this is too pushy ... and besides, there's no real *reason* to call, and you don't want it to seem that you are begging for business.

The newsletter solves this problem. It regularly places your name and activities in front of your customers and prospects, reminding them of your existence, products, and services on a regular basis. And you need no "excuse" to make this contact, because the prospect *expects* to receive a newsletter on a regular basis. The newsletter increases the frequency of message repetition and supplements other forms of communication such as catalogs, print ads, and sales letters.

## Size and Frequency

How long should your newsletter be? How often should it be published?

In my opinion, two to eight pages is the ideal length for a promotional newsletter. More than that is too much reading. Less is okay, especially if your newsletter is electronically distributed on the Internet. Even paper newsletters can be brief; several consultants have newsletters printed in postcard format.

As for frequency, four times a year—once every three months—is ideal. Publish fewer issues, and people aren't aware you are sending them a newsletter per se; they perceive that they're just getting a piece of mail from time to time. Four times per year is enough to establish credibility and awareness. Publishing six times or more per year is unnecessary, because some months you may prefer to make contact with your prospects using other media, such as the telephone or direct mail or catalogs.

What's more, my experience indicates that most companies don't have enough news to fill six or more issues each year. If your schedule is too frequent, you may find yourself putting unnecessary fluff and filler in the newsletter just to get something in the mail. Your readers will be turned off by the lack of quality and poor content, so this would hurt you rather than help.

## Building Your Subscriber List

Who should get your newsletter? Basically, it should go to anyone with whom you want to establish a regular relationship. These people can include the following:

- Current customers
- Past customers
- Current prospects
- Past prospects
- Expired accounts (past subscribers, "expires," and so on)
- Employees
- Vendors
- Colleagues
- Consultants, gurus, and other prominent members of your industry
- Referral sources (influential people who can refer business to you)
- Trade publication editors, business columnists, and other members of the press who might possibly use material in your newsletter in their own writings

"All your current clients should receive your client newsletter," says Steve Klinghoffer, president of WPI Communications, a company that produces newsletters for stockbrokers, financial planners, accountants, and other professionals.

The newsletter is an important vehicle for keeping in touch on a regular and predictable basis. It confers automatic high visibility and does so in the best possible way: by reflecting you as a professional, knowledgeable and competent. This not only builds your image, but also helps to insure that current clients will remain responsive to your recommendations.

Adds Klinghoffer:

Do not neglect to send the newsletter to clients who use your services or products in a very limited manner, or whom you have not visited with recently. You may not think of them as current clients, but of course, they are. What's more, rather than drifting away from you, the newsletter offers the kind of visibility that prompts many "limited clients" to expand their use of your products and services.

Here is how you build the subscriber list:

1. Put all current and past prospects and customers on the list. But don't use names that are too old. For past prospects and customers, for example, you might go back two or three years—but no more than that.

2. Get your salespeople to give you all the names of the people they call on regularly. Salespeople have their own favorite prospects, and these people may not be in the advertising inquiry files. So get them to give you names of people who should get the newsletter. You essentially want to convert the dozens of individual Rolodex files kept by various salespeople and sales reps into a single, integrated subscriber list for your newsletter.

3. Go to your PR department or agency and add its media list. Get the names of all editors who should receive the newsletter.

4. Make sure all new inquiries and new customers are added automatically to the subscription list. This includes every response, every sales lead generated by your targeted public relations campaigns.

5. For trade shows, create a subscription application form and offer a free one-year subscription to anyone who stops by your booth and completes the form.

6. Make sure the subscriber lists contain the names of your immediate supervisors, your product and brand managers, your sales and marketing managers, your CEO, and any other key personnel whose support you need to run an effective advertising department. Company managers enjoy getting the newsletter and often will offer ideas for articles and stories you can use. You might also approach your most important colleague and ask him or her to contribute a regular column.

## Promoting the Newsletter

In addition to compiling the list in this manner, you can do a number of things to promote the newsletter (and to use the newsletter as a promotion):

1. You can offer the newsletter as an extra incentive to people who respond to your direct mail. This can be as simple as adding a line to your reply cards with a box that says, "❑ Check here if you would like a free one-year subscription to our quarterly newsletter, [title of newsletter]." You could also stress the newsletter offer in the PS of your sales letter.

2. You can offer the newsletter as an extra incentive for responding to your space ads. Again, add an option to the response coupon that says "❑ Check here for a free one-year subscription to our newsletter, [title of newsletter]."

3. At speeches, seminars, and presentations, your company representatives can use the newsletter offer to get listeners involved in conversations with them. At the end of the talk, the presenter says, "Our quarterly newsletter, [title of

newsletter], will give you more information on this topic. Just give me your business card and I'll see to it you get a free one-year subscription." This way, the presenter will collect many more business cards for follow-up than he or she would get if there was no newsletter offer.

4. You could rent a list of names and send them the newsletter for free two or three times. The third or fourth time, you send it with a cover letter that says, "We hope you find [title of newsletter] informative and helpful, and we would be happy to continue sending it at no cost. To continue your free subscription, just complete and mail the reply card enclosed." Then you continue sending the newsletter only to those who return the reply card, which eliminates the cost of continually renting names.

5. Send out a press release offering a free sample copy of the newsletter to people in your industry.

6. Run small space ads with a picture of the newsletter. Offer a free sample copy to anyone who responds.

7. Post back issues on your Web site so that people who did not get them can read them.

8. Offer a free subscription as an incentive to get people to register on the guest page of your Web site (see Chapter 10, "The Internet").

## Designing Your Company Newsletter

Newsletters do not have to be elaborate, but the design should be consistent from issue to issue to build recognition and awareness. After a time, many recipients will come to welcome your newsletter, even seek it out from among the pile of mail in their in-basket. But this can happen only if the newsletter has a distinctive, recognizable, and consistent design.

Although many paid subscription newsletters are typewritten, you may want a design that is a little slicker, so as to enhance your image. Text is generally typeset or desktop-published in two or three columns. Paper stock may be white or colored, and the newsletter is usually printed in one or two colors of ink. The key to the design is a distinctive masthead highlighting the name of the publication.

The look, content, and "feel" of the newsletter are usually arrived at after a couple of issues. By the third issue, you know the approximate length of copy, the type of visuals needed, the technical depth of the content, and the types of articles to be featured.

For instance, you might decide that each issue will contain two feature articles, one biographical profile, a regular question-and-answer column on technical issues, one product-related story, three or four short news tidbits, and a box with short previews of the next issue. Your newsletter may be different, of course, but the point is, you'll eventually find a formula that works and stick with it from issue to issue.

Readers like this consistency of format because they know what to look for in each issue. For instance, some people opening the Sunday paper turn to sports first; some go to the comics; others read "Dear Abby" first. In the same way, some readers might check your "technical tips" column first, while others will read the profile. Make these features look and read the same in each issue (even position them in the same spot) so readers gain a comfortable familiarity with your publication.

I like simplicity in a promotional newsletter. I also have no graphic design skills, but want to be able to produce a camera-ready newsletter without hiring a designer. Therefore, I use Word to produce my original file. I type the body copy in Times Roman. The masthead is created by using another typeface in bold in a border at the top of page one.

A sample issue of my newsletter is reprinted in Appendix C, "Sample Documents." You can find back issues posted on my Web site, www.bly.com.

## Charging a Fee for Your Newsletter

One common question is, "Since so many newsletters charge hefty subscription fees, what about charging a fee for my newsletter?" Don't do it. A promotional newsletter is not the same as a paid subscription newsletter.

The paid subscription newsletter must deliver unique and valuable editorial material to the readers. Otherwise, they will not continue to pay a hefty price for it month after month. This material must be useful, informative, new, and special. In short, it must be material the reader cannot easily get elsewhere. The newsletter's purpose is to be the reader's source of critical information in the area covered by the publication.

The promotional newsletter is quite different. Although it should contain helpful and interesting information, readers expect less from a promotional newsletter than from one they pay to receive. As a result, they will accept a blend of how-to and technical information mixed with production information, company news, and sales talk. And this is the mix you want to give them. Remember, the ultimate goal of the newsletter is not to educate readers (you are not in the business of educating people for free) but to get them to do business with your firm and buy your products.

Because your newsletter is free, you're entitled to make some subtle (and not-so-subtle) sales pitches. But if you were charging, readers would not accept this. Another reason not to charge is that paid newsletters typically capture only a small percentage of any market as subscribers. If you want to reach a broader base of prospects, you must offer your newsletter free.

## Writing Your Newsletter

Putting your newsletter together is not terribly difficult. The first step is to make a list of possible story ideas. (Later in this chapter I provide a checklist of 29 such ideas.)

The material in your promotional newsletter does not have to be original, nor must it be created solely for the newsletter. In fact, a company newsletter is an ideal medium for recycling other promotional and publicity material created by your company speeches, articles, press releases, annual reports, presentations, and so on.

This fact helps you get maximum use out of material you've already created while minimizing the time and expense of writing and producing the newsletter.

The second step is to review your story ideas and select the ones to be featured in the next issue. If you are unsure as to how much room you have, it's better to select one or two extra ideas than one or two too few. You can always use the extra material in a future edition.

The third step is to create a file folder for each article and collect the information that will serve as background material for the person who writes the story. This background material typically includes sales brochures (for product stories), press releases (which are edited into short news stories), and reprints of published trade journal articles on a particular topic (which are often combined and compiled into a new article on a similar topic).

The fourth step is to write each story based on this material. Many businesses hire freelance writers to write and edit their company newsletters. A few hire their ad agency to do it. Using freelancers is usually more cost-effective. Besides, while most freelancers relish such assignments, most ad agencies don't like doing company newsletters, because they find them unprofitable.

Some articles may require more information than is contained in the background material. In this case, supply the writer with the names and phone numbers of people within your company whom he or she can interview to gather the additional information. Notify these people ahead of time that a freelance writer will be calling them to interview them for the newsletter. If they object, find substitutes.

Once you get the copy, the fifth step is to edit it, review it, and make any final changes. The sixth step is to give the final copy to your graphic artist or printer, who will create a mechanical. This should be carefully proofread and reviewed before it is printed. Many companies nowadays use desktop publishing systems in-house or hire outside desktop publishing services for newsletter layout and creation.

Once the mechanical is completed and approved, you print the newsletter. If subscribers perceive it as valuable, you can periodically offer back issues as a bait piece in your ads and mailings.

If your subscriber list is small—say, only a few hundred names—you can have your computer generate gummed mailing labels and affix them in-house. Once you have a thousand or more subscribers, you might want to use a letter shop, fulfillment house, or similar mailing service to handle the mailing and distribution on a regular basis. This will not be terribly expensive.

Here is a list of 29 sources of story ideas for company newsletters:

1. **Product stories:** New products; improvements to existing products; new models; new accessories; new options; and new applications.

2. **News:** Joint ventures; mergers and acquisitions; new divisions formed; new departments; other company news. Also, industry news and analyses of events and trends.

3. **Tips:** Tips on product selection, installation, maintenance, repair, and troubleshooting.

4. **How-to articles:** Similar to tips, but with more detailed instructions. Examples: How to use the product; how to design a system; how to select the right type or model.

5. **Previews and reports:** Write-ups of special events such as trade shows, conferences, sales meetings, seminars, presentations, and press conferences.

6. **Case histories:** Either in-depth or brief, reporting product applications, customer success stories, or examples of outstanding service or support.

7. **People:** Company promotions, new hires, transfers, awards, anniversaries, employee profiles, human interest stories (unusual jobs, hobbies, and so on).

8. **Milestones:** "1,000th unit shipped," "sales reach $1 million mark," "division celebrates 10th anniversary," and so on.

9. **Sales news:** New customers; bids accepted; contracts renewed; satisfied customer reports.

10. **Research and development:** New products; new technologies; new patents; technology awards; inventions; innovations; and breakthroughs.

11. **Publications:** New brochures available; new ad campaigns; technical papers presented; reprints available; new or updated manuals; announcements of other recently published literature or audiovisual materials.

12. **Explanatory articles:** How a product works; industry overviews; background information on applications and technologies.

13. **Customer stories:** Interviews with customers; photos; customer news and profiles; guest articles by customers about their industries, applications, and positive experiences with the vendor's product or service.

14. **Financial news:** Quarterly and annual report highlights; presentations to financial analysts; earnings and dividend news; reported sales and profits; etc.

15. **Photos with captions:** People; facilities; products; events.

16. **Columns:** President's letter; letters to the editor; guest columns; regular features such as "Q&A" or "Tech Talk."

17. **Excerpts, reprints, or condensed versions of:** Press releases; executive speeches; journal articles; technical papers; company seminars.

18. **Quality control stories:** Quality circles; employee suggestion programs; new quality assurance methods; success rates; case histories.

19. **Productivity stories:** New programs; methods and systems to cut waste and boost efficiency.

20. **Manufacturing stories:** SPC/SQC (statistical process control/statistical quality control) stories; CIM (computer integrated manufacturing) stories; new techniques; new equipment; raw materials; production line successes; detailed explanations of manufacturing processes.

21. **Community affairs:** Fund-raisers; special events; support for the arts; scholarship programs; social responsibility programs; environmental programs; employee and corporate participation in local/regional/national events.

22. **Data processing stories:** New computer hardware and software systems; improved data processing and its benefits to customers; new data procession applications; explanations of how systems serve customers.

23. **Overseas activities:** Reports on the company's international activities; profiles of facilities, subsidiaries, branches, people, markets.

24. **Service:** Background on company service facilities; case histories of outstanding service activities; new services for customers; customer support hotlines; online help desks.

25. **History:** Articles of company, industry, product, community history.

26. **Human resources:** Company benefit programs; announcement of new benefits and training and how they improve service to customers; explanations of company policies.

27. **Interviews:** With key company employees, engineers, service personnel; with customers; with suppliers (to illustrate the quality of materials going into your company's products).

28. **Forums:** Top managers answer customer complaints and concerns; service managers discuss customer needs; customers share their favorable experiences with company products and services.

29. **Gimmicks:** Contents; quizzes; trivia; puzzles; games; cartoons; recipes; computer programs; and the like.

"Make sure your newsletters contain timely, provocative information and advice that will be of specific interest to your targeted audience," recommends Klinghoffer. "The writing in your newsletters can make or break your newsletter marketing program. So make sure your newsletters feature solid information and advice framed in easy-to-read, action-oriented copy."

## What Will It Cost?

The cost for producing and distributing a promotional newsletter can vary tremendously. Factors that determine cost include:

- Length (number of pages, amount of text)
- Paper stock and color (one color versus two color)
- Number to be printed and mailed

With desktop publishing, you could, if you choose, write, design, and produce camera-ready pages for your newsletter on your desktop PC or Macintosh. The only cost, aside from printing and postage, is your time and labor.

What will it cost to have an outside firm produce your newsletter? A local graphic arts firm quoted me the following fee for producing 28,000 copies of an eight-page, two-color newsletter:

- One-time fee to design newsletter masthead and format (for first issue only): $850
- Production of eight-page newsletter (design, layout, mechanicals, type): $1,675
- Printing of 28,000 eight page, two-color newsletters: $6,500

These are prices for northern New Jersey, but at least they give you a feel for what's involved.

As for writing the newsletter, freelance writers will probably charge by the page (newsletter page, not manuscript page). The fee varies, and the range seems to be $350 to $750 per page.

Newsletters can be mailed in envelopes or without. If you mail in an envelope, consider using a 9 by 12 inch one so the newsletter can be mailed flat. A regular #10 envelope forces you to fold it, and it doesn't look as good. If you mail with no envelope, you must leave a blank space on the outer back cover for the mailing label, and your mailing indicia must also appear. You could affix postage, but that is unnecessary and labor intensive.

Mailing costs depend on quantity and weight. Klinghoffer advises companies to consult their local post office for details on third-class bulk rate mail if they plan to mail at least 200 newsletters at a time. Bulk rates can save almost $100 per thousand newsletters mailed.

If your newsletter contains valuable information, you might provide those who get it with a three-ring notebook or binder for storing issues. Store any extra issues left over from each printing, so you can fulfill requests for back issues if you get them or have extras to hand out at trade shows, speaking engagements, or seminars.

## Paid Subscription Newsletters

In addition to freebie newsletters published by companies as promotions, there are thousands of paid-subscription newsletters in the United States.

A company newsletter is a promotion *for* a business; a paid-subscription newsletter *is* a business—or at least a profit center for your business in its own right.

Anyone can produce and give away a company newsletter, but launching a paid-subscription newsletter business is a bit trickier. The process is more complex than I can adequately cover in this book. In fact, several books have been written on the topic of starting your own paid-subscription newsletters as a business; and some of these are listed in Appendix A, "Bibliography."

Appendix A also lists contact information for the Newsletter and Electronic Publishers Association (NEPA), which is the premiere trade association for the newsletter industry. They publish helpful guides and hold conferences on how to profitably start your own newsletter business.

Some would-be gurus successfully start their own paid-subscription newsletters. Another option is to become the editor of a subscription newsletter published by someone else.

For three years, I was the editor for "Bits & Pieces for Salespeople," a monthly newsletter published by Economics Press in Fairfield, New Jersey. I received a modest monthly per-issue editing fee plus a bonus based on any increase in subscriptions during my editorial tenure. I also got broad exposure to a core audience of thousands of sales and marketing executives.

NEPA publishes an annual membership directory listing publishers and their newsletters. A publisher probably already has an editor for an existing publication, but if you can suggest an idea for a newsletter that fits within their product line, you have a good shot of being appointed editor if they decide to launch the newsletter.

The fee you want to get paid is probably more than they want to pay. As part of your negotiation, ask for a number of free subscriptions that you may give away to whomever you choose in lieu of a higher fee.

You can then put your best clients and prospects on the subscriber list at no cost. They'll appreciate your generous gift, and you'll be getting your name in front of them on a monthly basis.

If you do not want to commit to the substantial work involved in being a newsletter editor, or if an editor's position is not offered to you, consider contributing articles to newsletters your target audience reads. Like trade journals, most newsletters do not pay for contributions, figuring you are writing the article in exchange for the exposure.

Newsletters typically have smaller circulations than trade journals, but the readers who pay a price (often hefty) for the newsletter vs. getting controlled circulation magazines for free are often highly responsive. So although the total readership of a newsletter may be only a fraction of the circulation of the leading magazine in the same field, you may find yourself getting more inquiries from your newsletter articles.

If a prestigious newsletter in your industry asks you to write a series of articles or a regular column, strongly consider accepting their offer. Such opportunities do not present themselves often.

You don't have to make a long-term commitment. Write your column for a few months. If you see results, continue. On the other hand, if no one seems to be reading or responding, you can drop it if the column is taking too much of your time.

But at the beginning of your quest for guruship, stick with the column for a while even if you are not getting a lot of response. Write at least half a dozen columns or more for a monthly newsletter; that means sticking with it at least half a year.

When you are finished, put a nice cover on the columns and reprint them in booklet form. Offer this free booklet to qualified prospects who are interested in your consulting, speaking, or professional services.

## E-Zines

An e-zine, or "electronic magazine," is a company newsletter in electronic form distributed on the Internet, usually via e-mail.

Doing an e-zine offers several advantages over producing a printed promotional newsletter:

- Graphics are simpler. Many e-zines are simple ASCII (text) e-mails with no graphics. To add graphics, you can produce your e-zine in html format.

- Printing costs are zero. The newsletter exists as an electronic file only.

- Postage costs are zero. The e-zine is distributed to your customer and prospect list electronically via e-mail broadcast.

- Delivery is instantaneous. The readers get their e-zine seconds after you send it.

- Since the cost is minimal, you can afford to distribute your newsletter with greater frequency. Most e-zines are monthly or weekly; a few are daily. The average print company newsletter, by comparison, is quarterly.

- It is easier for readers to respond to e-zines. All they have to do is click on hyperlinks in the text of the articles. The links can bring them to your Web site for more information or to fill out a form to request further action. With a print newsletter, they have to write you a letter or pick up the phone and call. Colleagues have told me that e-zines generate much higher responses to offers than the same offer being promoted in a print newsletter.

- One of the biggest problems in Internet marketing is how to get people who visit your site to give you their name and contact information by filling out an online form on your guest page or registration page (see Chapter 11, "Profiting from Your Guru Status"). Offering a free subscription to a valuable, informative e-zine on a topic that interests them can provide the necessary incentive and get many more people to register.

There are also several disadvantages of e-zines vs. printed newsletters:

- Not reading the e-zine is incredibly easy. The prospect just hits the Delete button and it's gone.

- There is already a glut of e-zines being produced and distributed. This, too, decreases the chances of yours being opened and read. At the same time, as e-zine publishing expands, printed promotional newsletters seem on the decline. Therefore, in this Internet age, a paper newsletter that the prospect can touch, feel, and hold in his hands may actually stand out from the crowd.

■ Corporate workers already get much more e-mail than regular mail. Their inboxes are overcrowded, and they have little patience for any e-mail that isn't personal and from someone they know.

There are many different formats for e-zines. Some html e-zines look like Web versions of color magazines. But most consist of half a dozen or so short articles on various topics of interest to the audience.

Some of these articles are one or two paragraph abstracts. Others may be a list of tips or tricks. Typically each article ends with an embedded URL or hyperlink that the reader can click on for more detail. These links can go to your site or to sites you recommend.

Take a look at the sample of my print newsletter, "Direct Response Letter," in Appendix C, "Sample Documents." This is the classic format for an e-zine: half a dozen short sections, each with a headline and a paragraph or two, with the sections separated by a line or border. I could easily publish this as an e-zine and may do so in the future.

There are a variety of methods for distributing your e-zine to your list of customers and prospects. You can buy software and do it yourself. Or you can hire a service bureau to do the e-mail transmission for you.

One company that specializes in e-mail and e-zine distribution is isellercentral.com. I recommend them because I have gotten to know them well. When I moved to a bigger office across the hall in my building a year ago, Peter DeCaro, owner of isellercentral.com, took my old office space. So we see each other every day! Their Web site is www.isellercentral.com. ■

*Chapter 7*

# Speaking

Giving keynote speeches at meetings and conventions quickly establishes your reputation as an expert. This chapter shows how to get these invitations and deliver a memorable talk that positions you as an expert in your topic.

## Why Gurus Give Speeches

Why is public speaking so effective as a promotional tool? When you speak, you are perceived as the expert. If your talk is good, you immediately establish your credibility with the audience so that members want you and your company to work with them and solve their problems.

Unlike an article, which is somewhat impersonal, a speech or talk puts you within hand-shaking distance of your audience. And, since in today's fast-paced world more and more activities are taking place remotely via fax, computer modem, and video-conferencing, meeting prospects face-to-face firmly implants an image of you in their minds. If that meeting takes place in an environment where you are singled out as an expert, as is the case when you speak, the impression is that much more effective and powerful.

Speaking is not ideal for every product or marketing situation. If you are trying to mass market a new brand of floppy disk on a nationwide basis to all computer users, television and print advertising is likely to be more effective than speaking, which limits the number of people you reach per contact. On the other hand, a wedding consultant whose market is Manhattan would probably profit immensely from a talk on wedding preparation given to engaged couples at a local church.

In his book *Effective Communication of Ideas* (Van Nostrand Reinhold), George Vardaman says speaking should generally be used when:

1. Confidential matters are to be discussed.
2. Warmth and personal qualities are called for.
3. An atmosphere of openness is desired.
4. Strengthening of feelings, attitudes, and beliefs is needed.
5. Exactitude and precision are *not* required.
6. Decisions must be communicated quickly or important deadlines must be met rapidly.
7. Crucial situations dictate maximum understanding.
8. Added impact is needed to sustain the audience's attention and interest or get them to focus on a topic or issue.
9. Personal authentication of a claim or concept is needed.
10. Social or gregarious needs must be met.

Speaking is also the promotional tool of choice when targeting a highly specific, narrow vertical market in which many of your best prospects are members of one or more of the major associations or societies in that market. For example, in the widget industry, if you wanted to reach widget buyers, you might run ads or write articles for the large-circulation magazines going to all widget people. But if your company specialized in widget polishing, you might be better off getting involved in a variety of ways, including speaking engagements or presentation of papers, at meetings of the Society for Widget Polishers and the National Association for Widget Cleaning and Polishing, if two such organizations existed.

# Finding Speaking Opportunities

Unless you are sponsoring your own seminar, as is discussed in Chapter 8, "Seminars," you will need to find appropriate forums at which you can be invited to speak. How do you go about it?

First, check your mail and the trade publications you read for announcements of industry meetings and conventions. For instance, if you design furnaces for steel mills and want to promote a new process, you might want to give a paper on your technique at the annual Iron and Steel Exposition.

Trade journals generally run preview articles and announcements of major shows, expos, and meetings months before the events. Many trade publications also have columns that announce such meetings on both a national and a local level. Make sure you scan these columns in publications aimed at your target market industries.

You should also receive preview announcements in the mail. Associations will send members direct-mail packages inviting them to attend their shows. That's fine, but you have another purpose: to find out whether papers, talks, or seminars are being given at the show, and, if so, to get on the panels or signed up as a speaker. If the show mailing promotion doesn't discuss papers or seminars, call up and ask.

If you are not on the mailing list to receive advance notification of meetings and conventions of your industry associations, write to request that they place you on such a list. Their names and addresses are listed in *The Encyclopedia of Associations,* published by Gale Research and available in your local library.

Propose some topics with you as the speaker. Most conference managers welcome such proposals, because they need speakers. The conference manager or another association executive in charge of the "technical sessions" (the usual name for the presentation of papers or talks) will request an abstract or short 100 to

200 word outline of your talk. If others in your company will be giving the talks, work with them to come up with an outline that is enticing so as to generate maximum attendance but also reflects accurately what the speaker wants to talk about.

Because many experts will be pitching speakers and presentations at the conference manager, the earlier you do it, the better. Generally, annual meetings and conventions of major associations begin planning 8 to 12 months in advance; local groups or local chapters of national organizations generally book speakers three to four months in advance. The earlier you approach them, the more receptive they'll be to your proposal.

You can "recycle" your talks and give them to different groups in the same year or different years, tailoring them slightly to fit current market conditions, the theme of the meeting, or the group's special interests. When you create a description, outline, or proposal for a talk, keep it on computer disk. Then, when other speaking opportunities come your way, you can quickly edit the file and print out a customized proposal or abstract you can fax or mail to the person in charge of that meeting.

Since your goal is to position yourself as a leader in your field, you want to pick a topic that relates to your specialty but is also of great interest to the group's audience. Importantly, the presentation does not sell you directly, but sells you by positioning you as the expert source of information in your specialized area. As such, it must be objective and present how-to advice or useful information; it cannot be a sales pitch for your services.

For example, if you sell computer-automated telemarketing systems, your talk cannot be a sales pitch for your system. Instead, you could do something such as "How to Choose the Right Computer-Automated Telemarketing Software" or "Computer-Automated vs. Traditional Telemarketing Systems: Which Is Right for Your Business?" Although you want people to choose your system, your talk should be (mostly) objective and not too obviously slanted in favor of your product; otherwise, you will offend and turn off your audience.

I once spoke at a marketing meeting where one of the other presenters, a manufacturer of such computerized telemarketing systems, was giving a talk. Although he was supposed to talk about how to improve telemarketing results with software, he proceeded to haul in his system and give a demonstration. The comments from attendees were openly hostile and negative. I'm sure he didn't get any business, and this did not enhance his reputation, either.

## Be Selective When Accepting Speaking Invitations

On occasion, meeting planners and conference executives may call you up and ask you to speak at their event, rather than you having to seek them out and ask them.

This is flattering. But beware. Not every opportunity to speak is really worthwhile. Meeting planners and committee executives are primarily concerned with getting someone to stand at the podium, and do not care whether your speaker or your firm will benefit in any way from the exposure. So before you say yes to an opportunity to speak, ask the meeting planner the following questions:

- What is the nature of the group?
- Who are the members? What are their job titles and responsibilities? What companies do they work for?
- What is the average attendance of such meetings? How many people does the meeting planner expect will attend your session?
- Do they pay an honorarium or at least cover expenses?

■ What other speakers have they had recently and what firms do these speakers represent?

■ Do they pay those other speakers? If so, why not you, too?

If the answers indicate that the meeting is not right or worthwhile for your company, or if the meeting planner seems unable or unwilling to provide answers, thank him or her politely and decline the invitation.

## Negotiating Your "Promotional Deal"

Often these speaking engagements pay a small honorarium or no fee at all. Yet there are things you can ask the sponsor for in lieu of payment that can be even more valuable in terms of self-promotion:

■ Tell the meeting chairperson you would be happy to speak at no charge, provided you receive a list of the members. You can use this list to promote your company via direct mail before as well as after your presentation.

■ At larger conferences and conventions, the conference manager provides attendees with show kits including a variety of materials such as a seminar schedule, passes to luncheons and dinners, maps, tourist sights of interest to out-of-town visitors, and the like. These kits are either mailed in advance or distributed at the show.

You can tell the conference manager, "I will give the presentation at no charge, but in exchange, I'd like to have you include my brochure in the conference kits mailed to attendees. Is that possible? I will supply as many copies of our literature as you need, of course." If he or she agrees, then you get your promo pieces mailed to hundreds, even thousands, of potential clients *at zero mailing cost.*

- Another is to get one or more PR placements in the organization's newsletter or magazine. For instance, propose to the meeting planner that you supply a series of articles to run in the organization's newsletter before the talk; this makes you known to the audience, which is good PR for your firm but also helps build interest in attending your program.

- After your talk, give the editor of the organization's newsletter the notes or text of your speech, and encourage him or her to run all or part of it (or a summary) as a post-talk article, so those who could not attend can benefit from the information. Additional articles can run as follow-ups after the talk to reinforce your message and provide additional detail to those who want to learn more, or to answer questions or cover issues you didn't have time to cover.

- If the editor will not run a bio with your phone number with the articles, talk to the meeting planner about getting some free ads for your product or service. For a national organization that actually charges for ads in its magazine, the value of your free ad space should be approximately twice what your fee would be if you were charging for your talk.

- The organization will do a program or mailing (or both) with a nice write-up of you and your talk. Usually it prints more than it ends up using, and throws out the extras. Mention that you would be glad to take those extra copies off its hands. Inserting those fliers is a nice touch in press kits and inquiry fulfillment packages.

- A professionally done audio recording or video of you giving a seminar can be a great promotional tool and an attention-getting supplement to printed brochures, direct mail, and other sales literature. But recording such presentations in a studio can be expensive.

One way to get an audio recording or video produced at low cost is to have someone else foot the bill for the taping. If an organization wants you to speak but cannot pay you, and especially if its audience is not a prime market for you, say, "I'll tell you what. Normally I charge $X for such a program. I will do it for you at no charge, provided you can arrange to have it professionally videotaped (or audio recorded, or both) and give me the master."

If the organization objects, say, "In exchange, you can copy and distribute the video or audio of my speech to your members, or even sell it to those who attend the meeting or belong to your group or both and I won't ask for a percentage of the profits. All I want is the tape master when you are through with it."

At many major meetings, it is standard practice for sponsoring organizations to audiotape all presentations and offer them for sale at the conference and for one year thereafter in promotional mailings. If you are being taped, tell the sponsor you normally do not allow it but will as long as you get the master. (Also make clear that, while you will allow the sponsor to sell it and will waive any percentage of the profits, the copyright is to be in your name. You can also ask for a 10 percent royalty on any sales of your tapes.)

■ If the group is a local chapter of a national organization, ask the meeting chairperson for a list of the other state or local chapters, along with addresses, phone numbers, and the names of the meeting organizers for each of those chapters. Then contact these chapters and offer to give the talk to their members.

## Planning an Effective Presentation

Of course, your objective is to sell yourself. But be careful. People attending a luncheon or dinner meeting aren't there to be sold. They want to be entertained. Informed. Educated. Made to laugh or smile. Selling your product, service, or company may be your goal, but in public speaking, it has to be secondary to giving a good presentation, and a "soft-sell" approach works best.

Terry C. Smith, author of *Making Successful Presentations* (John Wiley & Sons), lists the following as possible objectives for business presentations:

- Inform or instruct
- Persuade or sell
- Make recommendations and gain acceptance
- Arouse interest
- Inspire or initiate action
- Evaluate, interpret, clarify
- Set the stage for further action
- Gather ideas and explore them
- Entertain

I'd add "establish credibility" to this list; a good talk can go a long way toward building the image of the speaker and his or her firm as authorities in the field.

"Perhaps you are aiming for a combination of these," says Smith. "For example, there is nothing wrong with being both informative *and* entertaining; the two are not mutually exclusive. In fact, the two may complement one another."

Let's say your talk is primarily informational. You could organize it along the following lines: first, an introduction that presents an overview of the topic; next, the body of the talk, which presents the facts in detail; finally, a conclusion that sums up for the audience what they have heard.

This repetition is beneficial because, in a spoken presentation, unlike an article, listeners cannot flip back to a preceding page or paragraph to refresh their memory or study your material in more detail. For this reason, you must repeat your main point at least three times to make sure it is understood and remembered.

And what if your talk is primarily persuasive or sales oriented? In their book *How to Make Speeches for All Occasions* (Doubleday), Harold and Marjorie Zelko present the following outline for a persuasive talk:

1. Draw attention to the subject.

2. Indicate the problem, need, or situation.

3. Analyze the problem's origin, history, causes, manifestations.

4. Lead toward possible solutions, or mention them.

5. Lead toward the most desired solution or action.

6. Offer proof and values of the solution proposed.

7. Prove it is better than other solutions. Prove it will eliminate causes of problems, will work, and has value.

8. Lead toward the desired response from the audience.

9. Show how the desired response can be realized.

10. Conclude by summary and appeal as appropriate.

Janet Stone and Jane Bachner present a similar outline for persuasive organization in their book *Speaking Up* (McGraw-Hill):

1. Secure the attention of the audience.

2. State the problem.

3. Prove the existence of the problem.

4. Describe the unfortunate consequences of the problem.

5. State your solution.

6. Show how your solution will benefit the audience.

7. Anticipate and answer objections you know are coming.

8. Invite action.

Many other organizational schemes are available to speakers. For instance, if you're describing a *process,* your talk can be organized along the natural flow of the process or the sequence of steps involved in completing it. This would be ideal for a talk titled "How to Start Your Own Collection Agency" or "How to Design Mixers for Viscous Fluids."

If you're talking about expanding a communications network worldwide, you might start with the United States, then move on to Asia, then cover Europe. If your topic is vitamins, covering them in alphabetical order from vitamin A to zinc seems a sensible approach.

I allow at least one full day for preparation and rehearsal of any new short (20- to 30-minute) talk. Terry Smith says that for every brand new presentation, his ratio is one hour of preparation for every minute he plans to speak. "This is the preparation level at which I feel comfortable that I'm giving my very best," says Smith.

The trick to reducing preparation time is to have two or three "canned" (standard) talks that you can offer to various audiences. Even with a canned presentation, you'll need at least several hours to analyze the audience, do some customizing of your talk to better address that particular group, and rehearse once or twice.

## The Three Parts of a Speech

A talk has three parts: beginning, middle, and end. All are important. But the beginning and ending are more important than the body. Most people can manage to discuss a topic for 15 minutes, give a list of facts, or read from a prepared statement. And that's what it takes to deliver the middle part.

The beginning and ending are more difficult. In the beginning, you must immediately engage the audience's attention *and* establish rapport. Not only must members be made to feel that your topic will be interesting, but they must be drawn to you, or at least not find fault with your personality.

To test this theory, a well-known speaker put aside his usual opening and instead spoke for five minutes about himself, how successful he was, how much money he made, how in demand he was as a speaker, why he was the right choice to address the group. After his talk, he casually asked a member, "What were you thinking when I said that?" The man politely replied, "I was thinking what a blowhard you are."

How do you begin a talk? One easy and proven technique is to get the audience involved by asking questions. For example, if addressing telecommunications engineers, ask: "How many of you manage a T1 network? How many of you are using 56K DDS but are thinking about T1? And how many of you use fractional T1?"

If you are speaking on a health topic, you might ask, "How many of you exercised today before coming here? How many of you plan to exercise after the meeting tonight? How many of you exercise three or more times a week?"

Asking questions like these has two benefits. First, it provides a quick survey of audience concerns, interests, and levels of involvement, allowing you to tailor your talk to their needs on the spot. Second, it forces the audience to become immediately involved.

After all, when you are in the audience, and the speaker asks a question, you do one of two things: You either raise your hand or don't raise it, don't you? Either way you are responding, thinking, and getting involved.

## Ending Your Talk

While the beginning is important, don't neglect a strong closing, especially if you are there not just for the pleasure of speaking but to help promote your company or its products. As Dorothy Leeds observes in her book *PowerSpeak* (Prentice-Hall):

> Speakers, as you now know, are also in the selling business, and the conclusion is the time to ask for the order. Nothing will happen if you don't ask. And you ask by telling the audience what you want it to do with the information you've presented and *how* they can take that action. An effective speaker presenting a central idea ends by pointing out to those in his audience exactly what is needed from them to put that idea to work. For example … if you've been persuading them to give blood, tell them where. And make it sound easy to get there.

Action doesn't always have to be literal. If you simply want the people in your audience to mull over your ideas, tell them this is what you want them to do.

Although you want a great opening that builds rapport and gets people to listen, and an ending that helps "close the sale," don't neglect the body or middle of your talk. It's the "meat"; it's what your audience came to hear.

If your talk is primarily informational, be sure to give inside information on the latest trends, techniques, and product developments. If it's motivational, be enthusiastic and convince your listeners that they *can* lose weight, make money investing in real estate, or stop smoking.

If your talk is a how-to presentation, make sure you've written it so your audience walks away with lots of practical ideas and suggestions. As actor and Toastmaster George Jessel observes, "Above all, the successful speaker is sincerely interested in telling his audience something they want to know."

When speaking to technical audiences, tailor the content to listeners' expertise. Being too complex can bore a lot of people. But being too simplistic or basic can be even more offensive to an audience of knowledgeable industry experts.

## Length and Timing

Talks can vary from a ten-minute workplace presentation to a two-day intensive seminar. How long should yours be? The event and meeting planner often dictate length. Luncheon and after-dinner talks to local groups and local chapters of professional societies and business clubs usually last 20 to 30 minutes, with an additional 5 to 10 minutes allotted for questions and answers.

For technical sessions at major conferences and national expositions, speakers generally get 45 to 75 minutes. For a 1-hour talk, prepare a 45-minute talk. You'll probably start 5 minutes late to allow for late arrivals, and the last 10 minutes can be a more informal question-and-answer session.

The luckiest speakers are those who get invited to participate in panels. If you are on a panel consisting of three or four experts plus a moderator, it's likely that you'll simply be asked to respond to questions from the moderator or the audience, eliminating the need to prepare a talk.

Richard Armstrong, a freelance corporate speechwriter, says most of the speeches he writes are twenty minutes in length. James Welch, author of *The Speech Writing Guide* (John Wiley & Sons), says that a typed, double-spaced page of manuscript should take the speaker $2^1/_2$ minutes to deliver. This means an 8-page, double-spaced manuscript, which is about 2,000 words, will take 20 minutes to deliver as a speech.

That's about 100 words a minute. Some speakers are faster, talking at 120 to 150 words a minute or more. So the 20-minute talk can really be anywhere from 8 to 10 typed pages.

The most important thing is to not exceed the allotted time. If you are given twenty minutes with an additional ten minutes for questions and answers, stop after 20 minutes. People won't mind if you finish a bit early, but they will become fidgety and start looking at their watches if your time limit is up and you don't seem even near finished.

Since most of us cannot concentrate on two things at once—giving a talk and watching a clock—I ask someone in the audience to be the timekeeper, to keep me on track. For example, if giving a 45-minute talk, I ask him to shout out "Time!" every 15 minutes. The first two interruptions tell me where I am and how closely I'm on track; the last tells me to stop and shut up.

Incidentally, rather than finding this shouting of the word time annoying, audiences like it. I make it fun, telling the time-keeper, "You must shout out 'time' in a loud, obnoxious voice!" Then when he or she does, and the audience laughs, I ask them to rate, in a tongue-in-cheek way, whether the timekeeper was indeed loud and obnoxious enough. It gets a laugh every time.

## Handouts

Always have a handout when you give a talk. This ensures that attendees leave holding a piece of paper with your contact information. If you have your sales brochures on a table, few will take one. If you have a handout summarizing or expanding on your talk, almost everyone will take one.

The handout can take one of several formats: hard copy of the slides or overheads, article reprints, or reprints of the narration (with visuals incorporated, if possible).

It can be the full text of your talk, an outline, just the visuals, or a report or article on a topic that is either related to the presentation topic or that expands on one of the subtopics you touched on briefly in the talk.

Every handout should contain your company name, address, phone, and e-mail—and if possible a box with a brief summary of who you are and what you do, as should *every* marketing document you produce.

If the handout is the full text of your talk or a set of fairly comprehensive notes, tell the audience before you start: "There's no need to take notes. We have hard copies of this presentation for you to take home." This relieves listeners of the burden of note taking, freeing them to concentrate on your talk.

Handouts such as transcripts of a speech, articles, reports, or other materials with lots of copy should be handed out *after* the talk, not before. If you hand them out before you step up to the podium, the audience will read the printed materials and ignore you. You can hand out reproductions of visuals or pages with just a few bullet points in advance, so attendees can write notes directly on them.

Why do you need handouts? They enhance learning. But the main reason to give handouts is to ensure that every attendee (most of whom are potential customers, or you wouldn't be addressing the group) walks away with a piece of paper containing information on what you offer and how to contact you.

That way, when the person goes to work the next morning and thinks, "That was an interesting talk; maybe I should contact them to talk about how they can help us," he or she has your phone number in hand. Without it, response to your talk will be zero or near zero; most people are too busy, lazy, or indifferent to start tracking you down if they don't have immediate access to your contact information.

## Getting People to Take Your Handout Home with Them

It is most important to give a useful, interesting, information-packed talk that convinces prospects you know what you are talking about and makes them want to talk with you about doing work for them. But without the contact information immediately in hand, the prospect's interest and curiosity will quickly evaporate.

Since you cannot tell in advance who in the audience will want to follow up with you and who will not, your goal is to get everybody or as many people as possible to pick up and take home your handout material.

There are several ways to distribute handouts at your talk. The most common is to leave the materials on a table, either in the back of the room or at the registration table where people sign in for the meeting or your session.

But this is not effective. Most people will walk right by the table without picking up the material. Many won't even notice the table or stack of handouts. Even if you point out the table and say that reprints are available, many won't take one. And you might feel embarrassed at the silence that follows your announcement; it makes you seem less authoritative, more of a promoter.

Another technique is to put a copy of your handout on each seat in the room about a half-hour before the start of your presentation. Most people will pick it up, look at it; about one-quarter to one-half will take it with them when they leave and half or more will leave it on the chair. Disadvantages? People may read the handout and not pay attention to your presentation.

Also, some people resent this approach, seeing it as being too pushy and too salesy.

The most effective method of distributing handouts is the "green sheet" method. It maximizes the number of attendees who take handouts, increases their desire to have the material, and importantly, eliminates any hint of self-promotion or salesmanship.

Here's how it works. Prepare a handout that expands on one of the points in your talk, covering it in more detail than you can in a short presentation. Or make the handout a supplement, covering additional points not discussed but related to the topic.

Another option is to do a handout that's a resource guide; for example, a bibliography of reference books on your topic, tables of technical data, a glossary of key terms, a series of equations or examples of calculations, and the like. The important point is that the handout relates to *but does not merely repeat* information covered in your talk; instead, it *expands* on it.

When you get to that topic in your talk, which should be about halfway or three-quarters through the talk, discuss the point, then say something similar to the following (adapting it to your topic and handout, of course): "I can't cover, in this short talk, all of the techniques related to X. So, I've prepared a checklist of 25 points to consider when planning this type of project, and reprinted it on this green sheet." Pause, hold up the sheet for everyone to see, then continue: "I have plenty of copies, so if you want one, come up to me after the talk and I'll give you a copy."

After your talk, a large crowd of people will surround you at the podium with their hands out to get the free green sheet. Try it—it works. Oh, and why a "green sheet" rather than copying it on plain white paper? Doing it on colored paper and calling it a green sheet just seems to make it more special; also, instead of having to remember what's actually in the sheet (many people would not and therefore would hesitate to ask for it), people can just come up and say, "May I have a green sheet please?"

Handouts can also help you build a database of your speech attendees. Let's say the conference organizer will not release a list of attendees or those who go to your specific session, but you want to capture as many of those names as possible for marketing follow-up. In that case, offer your handout as a bait piece rather than giving it out at the session.

At the conclusion of your talk, discuss your handout and what it covers, and say, "So if you would like a free copy of our telecom security checklist, just write 'TSC' on the back of your business card and hand it to me. I'll mail a free copy of the checklist to you as soon as I get back to the office." The more enticing and relevant your bait piece, the more business cards you will collect. A really strong bait-piece offer can get you the business cards of 25 to 75 percent of attendees or more.

## The PowerPoint Question

It's an insidious trend: conference sponsors and meeting planners insisting that speakers create their presentations using a specific software product, namely PowerPoint.

Why is mandating use of PowerPoint by speakers bad? For six reasons:

1. Dictating format and software takes the focus away from where it should be—the content, message, and audience—and puts it on the technology. It's like telling a writer, "I don't care how good the piece is as long as it's in Word 7."

2. It encourages a conformity that can rob speakers and presentations of their individuality. Haven't you thought more than once that all PowerPoint presentations look alike after a while?

3. It's boring. So many bad presentations have been prepared with PowerPoint, I believe the very use of the medium itself can be a signal to some audience members that says, "Prepared to be bored."

4. It renders many speakers ineffective or at least less effective. When the speaker is focusing on his clicker, keyboard, or computer screen, he is not focusing on—or interacting with—his audience, a key requisite for a successful talk.

5. It locks the speaker in to the prepared slides, reducing spontaneity, ad libbing, and the valuable ability to adjust the presentation in response to audience reaction and interest—another requisite for a successful talk.

6. It can literally put the audience to sleep. What's the first step in preparing an audience to view a PowerPoint presentation? To dim the lights—an action proven to induce drowsiness in humans.

What should be done? Here are my suggestions:

1. **Don't feel you have to use PowerPoint.** If you want to use PowerPoint, fine. If you don't, also fine. Never force yourself to use any speaking aid you don't like or are uncomfortable with. It will compromise your performance and effectiveness significantly.

2. **Don't require visuals at all.** Does this surprise you? The fact is, many subjects—telephone skills, for instance—do not lend themselves to charts, graphics, tables, and other PowerPoint-type visuals. If you force visuals into every talk—even those whose subjects don't require it—you'll get that dreaded beast: a PowerPoint presentation created just because someone said the presenter had to have one. You know the type: full of word slides and lists of bullets that contribute nothing to clarity.

3. **Avoid the uniformity trap.** PowerPoint presentations suffer from sameness, which is the first cousin of dullness. Audiences crave freshness and difference.

4. **Avoid the handout trap.** A key advantage of PowerPoint is the ability to easily turn slides into hard-copy handouts. The trouble is, most of these slide printouts, removed from the speech itself, are cryptic when viewed in isolation if not totally meaningless. If the world could communicate effectively with just diagrams and bullets, sentences would never have been invented. Use instead the handout formats I suggested earlier.

Okay. Let's say you are putting together a presentation and PowerPoint is required. What can you do to make it more effective? I have four ideas for you.

1. Don't have the projector on all the time. Use PowerPoint selectively, not throughout the entire presentation.

   When there's a valuable picture to show, show it. When you're through with it, turn off the projector and turn the lights back on. The brightness rouses the audience out of their darkness-induced stupor. In a darkened room, it's too easy to close your eyes and nod off a bit.

2. Use visuals only when they communicate more effectively than words. If you are talking about quality, having the word "Quality" on screen adds little to your point. On the other hand, if you want to explain what an aardvark looks like, there are no words that can do it as effectively as simply showing a picture.

3. Consider adding other media as supplements or even alternatives to PowerPoint. When I taught telephone selling, the sound of a ringing telephone and a prop—a toy telephone—engaged the trainees in a way computer slides could not.

4. Design your presentation so that, if there is a problem with the computer equipment, you can go on without it. There's nothing more embarrassing than to see a speaker fall apart because he can't find the right slide. Use visuals as an enhancement, not a crutch.

Am I a dinosaur or a curmudgeon, to rail against PowerPoint in this manner? Perhaps. I don't own a laptop computer, wireless phone, pager, or PDA.

But one thing I have learned in 20 years of teaching and giving presentations: The best presenters have conversations with their audiences. If you believe you need to have a computer running to have an effective conversation, maybe that's a premise you want to rethink. ■

# Chapter 8

# Seminars

Virtually every guru gives seminars, both to reach new prospects and to solidify his or her position as a leading expert. Speeches are short talks, typically an hour long. Seminars, in comparison, are more comprehensive presentations ranging from a half-day to three days. This chapter outlines the various types of seminars you can give, the pros and cons of each, and how to use them effectively to promote yourself as a guru in your field.

Once thought of as strictly a means of training, educating, or informing an audience, seminars have become effective marketing tools for both business and consumer marketers. Almost every individual and organization that wants to be considered an expert in its specialty gives seminars to its target prospects or existing customers.

On the high-tech end, mainframe software vendors hold half-day product demonstrations/education sessions to educate IT (information technology) directors and systems analysts on how the software can fit into the corporate data center. On the consumer side, a producer of baby toys and products recently invited me and my expectant wife to a seminar on child care. The seminar is free, and we also get a free baby toy worth $35.

"Seminars can be effective marketing promotions," writes Herman Holtz in his book *Expanding Your Consulting Practice with Seminars* (John Wiley & Sons). "The Evelyn Wood speed reading school advertised weekly free seminars for a number of years, offering a demonstration lesson along with a sales presentation. Albert Lowry, the butcher turned real estate tycoon, has used many free seminars to promote his $500 weekend seminar on how to make money in real estate."

Why are seminars so effective? Because they fit in nicely with the transition sellers and consumers have undergone over the past two decades.

Twenty years ago, consumers were more open to traditional advertising messages. Salespeople were perceived as peddlers whose job it was to "move merchandise" regardless of whether that merchandise was right for the customer. "Pressure selling" was the predominant technique. We tended to feel an adversarial relationship with salespeople while believing much of what was force-fed us through TV commercials and magazine ads.

Today's consumers are more educated, more savvy, and more skeptical of advertising in all its forms. Consumers know what they want and are not afraid to question authority. That's why so many companies are putting more effort in their public relations, and why you, as a budding guru, should, too. When your message is carried by the media as editorial material, readers will not react with skepticism or scrutinize it as carefully as they would a paid ad.

I recently read an article that offers proof of the power of publicity and other "editorial" forums (I'd include seminars) versus paid advertising (I'd include sales presentations).

According to the article, an airline pilot and his wife noticed that many people holding garage sales were inadvertently selling, at low prices, items that had much greater value. They realized people did not know how to go through a garage or attic and separate the junk from the "hidden treasures": antiques, collectibles, and other items that could fetch a high price if sold to dealers or collectors.

The couple wrote and self-published a book called *I'll Buy That!* on how to find a profit from such hidden treasures and sent a press release to a number of magazines. *Family Circle* picked up the release and ran a half-page article, giving information on how to order the book, which cost $12.95 or so. The article generated 180,000 orders and more than $2 million in revenue!

The couple thought a natural follow-up would be to have the article repeated. Since the editor would not run it twice, they bought a half-page ad and reprinted the article in that space; the only difference was that it had the word ADVERTISEMENT above it. Want to guess the results? That second run of the article as an ad generated fewer than 20 orders—testimony to the power of "neutral" or editorial forums versus paid ads.

As the consumerism movement grows, consumers shift from being passive buyers to informed buyers. And to be informed buyers, they need information: information on products, information on trends, information on the very problems and applications the products address. Informed buyers prefer to buy from experts (gurus) who know what they are talking about and can explain it in plain English. This is where seminars come in.

## Why Every Guru and Would-Be Guru Should Consider Giving Seminars

Publicizing and marketing yourself, your product, or your company by giving a seminar offers a number of advantages:

1. Seminars are, by nature, educational, so they fill the consumer's need and desire to be better educated.

2. Presenting a seminar, or being a seminar sponsor, positions you and your company as expert sources of information. It in essence lets you make your "sales pitch" in a forum where you won't be perceived as a salesperson.

3. Getting a group of good prospects in a room for a seminar gives you a "captive" audience for making a sales pitch or giving some "commercials" before and after the seminar, as well as during the breaks.

4. Your product, if you sell one, can be demonstrated at the seminar, and demonstrations are a proven, powerful sales tool.

5. Seminars enable you to reach many prospects who skip over your ads, throw away your direct mail, and don't attend trade shows at which you exhibit.

6. Done right, the seminar gives attendees useful information. You will have done a service for your prospects, and their appreciation can translate into greater receptiveness to any follow-up selling you do, either in person or by mail or phone.

7. Seminars hold the prospects' attention and get them listening longer than they would listen to something that was pure sales presentation.

8. In fields where giving seminars is not a common PR tool, a seminar makes you stand out from the crowd and is more memorable than traditional ads, brochures, direct mail, and the like.

9. Because seminars, by definition, are local events, local media outlets are inclined to print publicity releases announcing your seminar.

There are six types of seminars to choose from. If you decide to try a seminar to promote your product, you have six options available to you:

1. Giving a free "tutorial" seminar

2. Giving a promotional or "product" seminar

3. Giving a self-sponsored fee-paid public seminar

4. Giving a seminar for a seminar company

5. Giving a short presentation at an association meeting or industry event

6. Teaching a college or adult education course

Let's explore each of these options.

## Option One: Free Tutorial Seminar

The free tutorial is a short morning, afternoon, or evening seminar presenting useful advice, suggestions, recommendations, or tips on a particular topic. The topic is one that would be of interest to potential clients of the seminar sponsor and relates to services offered by the sponsor. Length is usually one or two hours.

For example, a local financial planning firm offers a free seminar on retirement and estate planning. It attracts people, usually 40 and older, who want to build a "nest egg" for a comfortable retirement and leave a large estate for their dependents should they pass away. Subjects discussed include retirement investments, life insurance, pension plans, and wills.

Why give this seminar for free instead of charging a fee? The goal is not to make money on the seminar, but to attract the maximum number of prospects. Logic dictates that anyone attending a basic seminar on retirement planning and estate planning is interested in the topic, needs to do this planning, but probably is not an expert and needs the kind of help the financial planning firm, the sponsor of the program, can provide.

At such a seminar, the emphasis is on giving the audience useful, objective information—or at least information that the audience will perceive as helpful and objective. Actually, the content may be "slanted," subtly, leading attendees to become more interested in certain types of investments than in others ... investments that the sponsor just happens to specialize in selling.

Free tutorials are used most commonly by professionals, consultants, and service firms, but they can be successful for other types of businesses, too. For example, the drinking of vegetable and fruit juice as an aid to health is a hot trend. A big department store or small health food store could hold a free seminar on the health benefits of juice, which juices to drink, recipes, how to make juice in a juicer, and so on. Do you think the store could sell a lot of juicers to attendees after such a free seminar? Of course.

### Option Two: Promotional or "Product" Seminar

A promotional or "product" seminar—one designed ultimately to sell a product or service rather than be a profit center in itself—helps move consumers one step closer to a purchase decision. It does so by providing the knowledge consumers feel they need to make an intelligent buying decision.

Unlike a tutorial, which is more of a "pure" informational seminar, with the "pitch" for the service limited to the beginning, the end, and the coffee breaks, a product seminar usually combines advice on how to do something (such as how to stay fit and trim) with a lengthy demonstration of a specific product (how to use Brand X rowing machine).

The length of the program is typically two or three hours. For groups of business prospects, breakfast is usually provided at morning seminars; lunch at afternoon programs. Evening sessions can be followed by an open bar and light snacks.

Seminars help promote products and services in three ways: by establishing the seminar giver as the authority, demonstrating the product, and "setting the specs" for a product purchase.

Even if your seminar does not promote your product directly, just the mere fact that you and not your competitor is giving the seminar establishes you as the authority in your field, putting you in a superior position to make the sale to your attendee/prospect.

Those who write books, publish articles, make speeches, or give seminars are perceived as experts, as authorities, as leaders in their field. And whom do you want to buy from? An expert, of course. The seminar giver is perceived as more knowledgeable and better able to solve problems, and therefore is more likely to get the order.

For many products, the best way to sell the product is to demonstrate it. (Two examples that come immediately to mind are computer software and exercise equipment.) The seminar gives you a captive audience of prospects who will sit still for a lengthier demonstration than they might agree to in a store, at home, or in their office. And the more you show, the more you sell.

A common technique in a seminar is "setting the specs." In plain English, this means using the seminar to educate prospects on what they should be looking for in your type of product, the specifications to include in their request for proposal (RFP), the features they should want, the questions they should ask. Of course, you set these specs in such a way that your product satisfies them best. Your seminar tells prospects, "This is how you should shop for [name of product or service]." Of course, when they follow your shopping guidelines, your product or service clearly emerges as the logical choice.

Like the tutorial, the product seminar is free. The reason is simple: You are going to demonstrate and sell a product; attendees know it; and you can't ask someone to *pay* to hear your sales pitch.

Since the seminar is free and openly billed as a seminar on a specific product, attendees expect some selling and won't resent it.

## Option Three: Self-Sponsored Fee-Paid Public Seminar

If you work in a corporation, you probably get many invitations to public seminars on topics ranging from stress management and self-esteem building, to newsletter design and desktop publishing. These seminars are typically one or two days, with the fee ranging from $95 to $395 for a full-day program, $495 to $895 for a two-day program.

Although most of these seminars are done as a profit-making venture in themselves, some people do them primarily to promote their product or service, with revenue from the seminar being a secondary goal or by-product. The theory is that if people are interested enough to attend a full-length seminar on a topic that addresses a problem or need your product or service solves, then they are ideal prospects for buying that product or service.

A self-sponsored fee-paid seminar has several advantages over the product seminar or tutorial. First, it is the most impressive, offering intense education with no hint of sales hype.

Second, you can include mention of your products or services in the seminar mailing, or at least a description of what your company does (in an "about the sponsor" section) in the seminar brochure. Let's say you mail 5,000 brochures and get 75 people to attend. By putting a description about your company's capabilities in the brochure, you have promoted yourself to the 4,925 who did not respond as well as the 75 who do come.

Disadvantages of a public seminar are twofold. First, because people are paying, it is inappropriate to do promotion or self-selling. You have to let the seminar "sell itself"; that is, you and your firm gain credibility and generate interest simply by virtue of being the seminar sponsor and leader.

Second, fee-paid public seminars are a business in themselves, and you may not want to get into this business. It's time-consuming and a logistics challenge to coordinate and put on such events. Also, unless you are an expert in direct-mail seminar promotion, you could easily spend thousands of dollars putting together and mailing a brochure, and then get virtually no response. So it's risky.

## Option Four: Seminar Sponsored by a Seminar Company

You can be a seminar leader without sponsoring your own seminar. This eliminates the time, expense, and risk of promoting your own self-sponsored seminar, while providing the same forum for positioning yourself and your company as the experts in a particular field or topic.

There are many public seminar companies whose only business is to sponsor and promote, for a profit, public seminars on a variety of topics; see Appendix B, "Recommended Vendors," for a listing. You can write a letter to these companies explaining who you are, your qualifications, and the subjects you are interested in teaching. These subjects should either be topics they are already offering or related ones that would appeal to the same audience. Don't suggest a seminar on interpersonal skills to a public seminar company whose other programs are titled "LAN/WAN Internetworking" and "Troubleshooting T1 Networks."

The advantage of teaching a public seminar sponsored by a seminar company is that the company does all the marketing and arranging. All you have to do is show up and deliver the program. And if the seminar mailing doesn't generate registrations, it's the seminar company's money that has been spent, not yours.

You and your firm are promoted because the seminar company gives you the opportunity to lead the seminar and to provide your biography to thousands of people on the direct-mail invitation.

The disadvantage is that you are more restricted in your ability to sell your product, mention what your company does, and even in the information you present in the program. Some sponsors might encourage you to let the audience know about your products and services, while others have strict rules limiting such self-promotion. Some let you mix your information with theirs; others insist you present a program of their design as-is.

The other disadvantage is that there is a limited number of public seminar companies, and an even smaller number giving seminars on a topic that would be beneficial for you to present. If no company is interested in having you present a seminar, you'll have to pursue one of the other five options discussed in this chapter.

### Option Five: Speech or Presentation at an Association Meeting or Industry Event

Another way to find a "sponsor" for your program is to present it as a talk or speech, rather than a longer seminar, at an association meeting or an industry convention or trade show. This option is discussed in detail in Chapter 7, "Speaking."

### Option Six: Teaching a College or Adult Education Course

The sixth option is to give your seminar or lecture as a college course. Business people who teach do so primarily at adult education programs sponsored by local universities, colleges, and high schools.

Although prestigious, this would be my last choice because of its many disadvantages:

1. **Significant time commitment.** A typical course might be held in the evening from 6 P.M. to 8 P.M. every week for 10 or 12 consecutive weeks. That's a three-month commitment and more than twenty hours of your time.

2. **Low return.** During those 20 hours you'll only be addressing a single group: your students. And class sizes are usually small: 10 to 20 students.

3. **Wrong audience.** I taught adult education programs in topics related to my consulting practice (advertising and technical writing) for seven years at New York University's School of Continuing Education. While every class had several good prospects in it, most of the students (all working adults, by the way) did not hold positions that would make them potential clients.

4. **Not a selling forum.** I think it is inappropriate to take as a customer or client any student in your adult education class until the class is over. Reason: You must assign a grade to each student, and other students could claim you were favoring a student who was also a customer with a better grade.

The main advantage of teaching adult education at a local college or university is prestige. Especially when you want to build your guru credentials, it helps to add "Professor of Accounting at Andover College" to your resumé.

Another small advantage is that teaching adult education pays; however, the pay is usually low: $20 to $40 or so per hour of class time. A 10-week, 20-hour class might pay $600 to $1,000 but not much more.

## Will Seminars Work for *You?*

Whether a seminar is a useful way for you to promote yourself, your product, or your service depends on your marketing situation. Product seminars work well when introducing new products or technologies. They are also ideal for products that require an in-person demonstration, such as software or computer systems.

Seminars are also effective for introducing new concepts, new approaches to business, and professional and consulting services. For service firms, the seminar is the first opportunity to allow prospects to "sample" the service before they make a commitment to buy a larger chunk of it.

Also, if your product or service solves or addresses a major business problem or issue (such as plant safety, computer security, employee benefits planning, or life insurance), a seminar is a good place to educate your prospects on the subject.

Price is another factor. In most cases, seminars are appropriate only for expensive items, since it doesn't pay to rent a hotel room, mail invitations, and spend staff time presenting a seminar to people in the hopes of selling them a single product that only costs $10.

There are a few notable exceptions. "Tupperware" parties, in a sense, are mini-seminars on how to store food in the home. Also popular these days in the suburbs are crafts and decorating parties selling items such as candles or baskets. The average sale at such events is relatively modest.

At this point, you might ask, "Aren't most product seminars thinly disguised sales pitches for a specific product and not really seminars?"

Yes, and that's why they fail. Obviously, your purpose in presenting the seminar is to convince people to buy your product. But if the seminar is a blatant promotional pitch, people become annoyed, even disgusted.

On the other hand, if you present information of genuine value, attendees will think well of your firm and become more inclined to do business with you.

Attendees know they will be sold but want to learn something, too. They realize they cannot master a complex subject in a two- or three-hour seminar, but if you can present them with one or two new ideas, or a few practical how-to tips or techniques, you'll dazzle them. They'll walk away delighted with the seminar and will become "fans" of your firm—a desirable result.

## Setting the Seminar Fee

One early consideration is whether you charge for your seminars or give them for free. As a rule, seminars designed primarily to sell a product or service should be free. Every activity in business—promotional or otherwise—should have one primary goal and be wholly directed toward achieving that goal. Therefore, if your goal is to establish yourself as a guru or sell your advisory services, the seminar should be free. This allows you to maximize attendance to get the largest number of prospects in the room to hear your message and feel free to do at least some product selling.

Attendees at free seminars expect to get *some* sell and find it acceptable if not overdone. But if people have paid $295 to attend a one-day "Relational Databases" session, they want to learn how to manage, choose, or design relational databases. They don't want to hear what amounts to a reading of your sales brochure, and if they do get that they will feel cheated.

Some companies break this rule successfully, charging large fees for their seminars and still managing to generate both sales and immediate revenue at the same time. But they are the exception. If your goal is to sell, give free seminars and treat them as promotions, not profit centers.

Some companies seek a happy compromise by charging a nominal fee—say, $10 or $25. The idea is to qualify attendees. The reasoning is: "Someone who pays $10 or $25 must really be interested, and someone not willing to pay it is not a good prospect."

This sounds sensible, but I don't agree with the strategy. I feel free offers should be free. I don't think you impress prospects or make the seminar seem more valuable by charging a nominal fee.

What's more, if you charge the same fee as *regular* paid seminars ($50 to $125 for the general public and $100 to $300 per day for business seminars), then it would be inappropriate to do *any* selling, and the presentation would have to be 100 percent educational, which isn't your goal. If your purpose is to sell a product, make the seminar free.

## Fees and Scheduling

Most companies invite attendees to free seminars using direct mail. Response rates for free seminars in fields where the free seminar offer is common (software, computers, telecommunications) are generally not much higher than for paid seminars. Your response rate will probably be anywhere from ¼ to 2 percent. If you assume a 1 percent response rate, and want 25 people in your seminar, you will need to mail 2,500 invitations and probably should mail 5,000 to be safe.

Free seminars on a topic not usually presented in such forums often get a higher response. Gary Blake, a management consultant specializing in writing seminars, recently gave a free three-hour seminar titled "Effective Business Writing" and got a 10 percent response.

Most free seminars last half a day, typically two or three hours, either in the morning or the afternoon.

What day is best? Howard Shenson, author of *How to Create and Market a Successful Seminar or Workshop* (The Consultant's Library), says that for seminars aimed at business, Wednesday or Thursday are the best days, followed by Tuesday, Friday, and Saturday. Monday and Sunday are the worst days.

For seminars aimed at consumers and the general public, Thursday and Saturday are best, followed by Wednesday, Sunday, Tuesday, and Friday. Again, Monday is not a good day.

Are some months better than others? My own experience is that the best seminar seasons are March through May and September through mid-November. Summer interferes with vacations. Winter brings the danger of cancellation due to bad weather in most regions of the United States. And from mid-November to January 1, people are concentrating on the holidays.

## Choosing a Seminar Title

Does it matter whether you call the event a "product demonstration," "seminar," or "workshop"? Yes. The title is very important, as it connotes value.

"Product demonstration" is least desirable and should only be used when the event is indeed a pure and straightforward demonstration of a system. "Seminar" implies that the attendee will gain useful knowledge. "Workshop" implies hands-on participation and should not be used for most free seminars.

Copywriter David Yale suggests calling the seminar a "forum" and has gotten good results doing so. I also like "briefing" for a session aimed at executives and managerial types. Programs aimed at consumers can also be "luncheons" if a light meal is served around noon, or "parties" if given in a leisure atmosphere.

## Obtaining the Mailing List

You will get the best results by mailing your seminar invitations to your house list or database of current and past customers, clients, and prospects. People who know you, have had dealings with you in the past, or have in the past asked for information about your product or service are much more likely to attend than people who don't know you. A seminar is an ideal forum for reawakening interest in prospects who have not taken action as well as for reactivating inactive accounts.

When renting mailing lists, select people who are the most likely prospects for the product being featured in the seminar, and be sure they live within a 100-mile radius of the seminar site, ideally within 50 miles. Appendix B lists several mailing list firms from whom you can rent lists.

Mail your seminar invitations third-class about eight to nine weeks in advance of the seminar date if targeting a business audience. Based on a study of the seminar mailings that cross my desk, I would say that most arrive in my mailbox four to eight weeks in advance of the date.

You can probably mail on shorter notice for consumer seminars. Print ads can be placed a week or two, or even a few days, before the event to attract last-minute attendees.

Because the attendees do not pay, you don't collect money, but you still want them to register. Copy in ads and mail should read: "There is no fee to attend this seminar, but you must register in advance because attendance is limited. To reserve your seat, call [phone number] today."

And what about the mailing piece itself? There are a wide variety of formats. Some companies use self-mailers; others send personalized letters of invitation that include a circular or flier outlining the key points or benefits of attendance.

The copy doesn't have to be as long, complete, persuasive, and hard-hitting as it is in direct-response mailings selling costly paid seminars, but you probably have to sell it 75 percent to 80 percent as hard. The copy should tell prospects what they will learn at the session and the benefits of attending.

If you offer a free gift, stress this in your letter and on the cover of your brochure or self-mailer. Free gifts have tremendous pulling power. If the gift has a retail value, say "FREE GIFT guaranteed to be worth $35." Many people will come just to get the free gift. And if it's a sample of your product or related to your product line, that's fine.

The design of your mailing should be consistent with the event and audience. If you are inviting executives to a briefing on competing with the Japanese, the piece should be serious, somber, even urgent. If you are holding a party for expectant mothers to sell them on your diaper service, the mailing should be colorfully illustrated with pictures of babies, families, cribs, nurseries, and the like.

In your mailing, make it clear that the seminar is free—but don't make this fact your central theme or trumpet it in your headline. Write copy that makes the reader say, "This sounds wonderful. I would really love to go. How much does it cost?" Then tell him or her it's free.

Do not think that, just because the seminar is free, people will want to attend. "Despite being free, [free seminars] must be sold, just as anything else is sold," warns Herman Holtz. "The word free is one strong inducement to attend, of course, but few, if any, would attend if they were not promised a benefit they find attractive enough to merit the expenditure of their time."

## Controlling Costs

As discussed, free seminars are not a terribly expensive promotion, at least as far as incurring outside costs. The main expense is in the mailing. Sending out 5,000 invitations will run approximately $3,500 to $4,000, depending on the format. Self-mailers generally cost much less than packages with outer envelopes, personalized letters, insert brochures, reply forms, and reply envelopes. If you use a full-scale package, you should split test a self-mailer (a mailer with no outer envelope); often you get the same response at far less cost.

You can hold the seminar at your company facilities (but not your home, if you work from a home office), although a nice room in a good hotel is more pleasant and easier for attendees to find. In the suburbs, a seminar room can be rented for $100 to $300 a day; in a major city, it might run $300 to $500. The smaller your audience, the smaller the room and the lower the cost.

Food is the big expense. Coffee and tea run $1 to $2 per person per serving; soft drinks run $2 to $2.50 per can or bottle. Meals involve significantly greater expense but may be necessary if attendees expect to be fed.

Other expenses include development and reproduction of overheads, slides, handouts, and invitations. These costs can be amortized over the lifetime of the seminar. Because of the time, expense, and effort required to create an effective seminar, one-shot events do not pay off as well as repeats. So to maximize the benefit of the seminar, plan on giving it at least three or four times during the year in several different locations.

To develop a product seminar and give it once, a budget of $5,000 should be sufficient, assuming you do the work yourself and do not hire outside consultants.

## Self-Promotion at the Seminar

The key to making your seminar an effective promotional event is to give a good seminar—one that lives up to the promise of its brochure or mailing and delivers an interesting, useful, helpful, informative presentation prospects will appreciate. If they walk away happy and pleased, you've achieved your primary goal: to make them "fans" of your company.

To further enhance selling effectiveness, you can sell your product before, during, and after the seminar. This is acceptable (because your seminar is free, and they expect it), but only if done in a gentle, reasonable, pressure-free way. Don't push your product on people or mention it every minute. When people ask questions, don't answer every one by saying "Buying our product solves it!" Instead, give them an answer that helps them regardless of whether or not they become customers.

Following is a checklist of things you can do to maximize the promotional benefits of the seminars you give:

In advance of the seminar ...

■ Mail a questionnaire asking prospects what topics they want addressed during the seminar. Ask them to return the questionnaire. Answer those topics at the seminar.

■ Put them on your mailing list so they get at least one promotional mailing from your company before the seminar.

■ Put them on the subscription list to receive your free company promotional newsletter.

■ Send a confirmation letter acknowledging registration. Include easy-to-follow directions to the seminar site both by mass transit and car.

■ Call them to confirm that they are coming.

Before the seminar starts ...

- Serve coffee and tea.

- Meet and shake hands with attendees. Welcome them to the seminar. Engage them in conversation to learn more about them.

- Leave product literature on a table at the back of the room and put one copy of your catalog or brochure on each chair in the room.

- Distribute an article reprint or other interesting piece for people to read before the seminar starts. Some people come early; others come late; and you want to give the early people something to do.

- Have an unannounced door prize to create additional interest and excitement. Hold the drawing at the first break. A good door prize is a copy of a book you have written on the seminar topic. (Having a door prize prevents people from walking out.)

- Give them a simple survey or questionnaire to complete while they wait for the session to start. This will be a useful tool in planning your sales approach to these people. If possible, address some of the concerns expressed on the questionnaires during your talk. (Don't identify the people asking the question unless they volunteer their identities.)

- Use name tags so attendees feel comfortable mingling. The session will be more meaningful and enjoyable if attendees can network with their peers.

During the seminar ...

- Work your product or service into your presentation and mention it briefly two or three times each hour. But only for a sentence or two. And don't overdo it. Let common sense be your guide.

■ At the end of the presentation say, "You've been a great audience. Thanks for your attention." Then name the company salespeople in the room and ask them to identify themselves by standing or raising their hands. Then say, "Rick, Sue, and I [or whoever the salespeople are] will stay around a while to talk to you if you have more questions about [topic of seminar] or want more information on [name of product]. We welcome your questions and comments."

■ Let people come to you. Don't have salespeople descend like hawks to "capture" prospects or put on the hard sell. If people want to leave, let them. But be sure they have your catalog or brochure and business card before they go.

After the seminar ...

■ Send a follow-up note thanking them for coming, along with a form they can use to place an order or request more information.

■ Follow up on any specific inquiries or concerns expressed to salespeople or on questionnaires.

■ Place all prospects on your in-house database list to receive future mailings.

■ Do not forget to deliver any free gifts you promised to distribute if they were not handed out at the seminar.

■ When giving out a free product or sample or literature, include price-off coupons the attendees can use to purchase your products at a discount at retail outlets.

■ Did the mailing piece generate the desired attendance? If not, why not? Are you using the wrong lists, or is the piece itself ineffective? Maybe your topic does not appeal to your intended audience.

- Did the right people attend for the right reasons? Did you get a room full of eager prospects who showed interest and enthusiasm in your proposition? Or were you talking to the wrong people, or prospects who just wanted the free doughnuts and couldn't care less about your widgets?

- Did the seminar itself generate the desired sales results? That is, did prospects show interest, become involved, approach salespeople, and take the next step in the buying process?

- What percentage of attendees were genuine prospects? What percentage demonstrated real interest in your product? What percentage eventually became customers or clients?

- If the results were not satisfactory, is there anything you can do to improve attendance or the quality of the presentation? Or is it possible that free seminars simply don't work for your type of offer?

Why should every would-be guru give seminars? To sum it all up:

- We are trained from early childhood to listen and defer to teachers. Seminar leaders are teachers for adults.

- Seminars demonstrate your grasp of your subject matter and your ability to communicate this knowledge in an organized fashion—exactly what people look for in a guru.

- Seminars give you prolonged, close, personal exposure to your audience in a way the Internet and other remote communications do not. ■

*Chapter 9*

# Public Relations

Why pay for advertising when the media can help you establish your guru image for free? In this chapter, we look at how to get the print and broadcast media—newspapers, magazines, radio, TV—to interview you and feature you in stories related to your area of expertise.

## How PR Works

While public relations (PR) is a big and sometimes complex business, here is the simple fact you need to know: Most of what you read, see, and hear in the media got there with the help of a PR firm.

Why would legitimate journalists use PR materials? Because they're busy, lacking the resources and time to fill programs and publications with worthy material of interest to their readers, viewers, and listeners. As David Yale explains in his book *The Publicity Handbook* (McGraw-Hill):

> Publicity … involves supplying information that is factual, interesting, and newsworthy to media not controlled by you, such as radio, television, magazines, newspapers, trade journals, newsletters, e-zines, and Web sites. Your goal is to earn coverage because journalists think that your material will be of interest to their audiences. Your material, if it is used, may stand on its own as a separate story, or it may become part of a larger story that draws on information from several sources.

As a rule, the narrower your niche, the easier it is to get publicity for yourself, your organization, and your ideas. Large media reaching general audiences are bombarded by materials from publicists because of their large circulation and the broad variety of stories they run. Media targeting specialized audiences or industries have fewer publicists trying to get them to run materials, since their audiences are smaller and their editorial scope narrower.

If you are a guru in a highly specialized niche, I recommend you target about 80 percent of your PR efforts to the few industry publications reaching your market. Regular exposure in these publications, unknown to the general public but read avidly by most people in the industry, can dramatically raise your profile with this audience.

At the same time, take a shot now and then at getting into large national media, such as *The Wall Street Journal* or CNBC. Coverage in these media is prestigious. It will impress clients and prospects as well as other editors and producers to whom you are trying to sell your story.

## Develop a Hook

Obtaining publicity is somewhat a function of supply and demand. On the one hand, the media has a huge appetite for story ideas—they desperately need material to fill pages and airtime. On the other hand, they are bombarded by PR agencies, all pitching ideas that look fairly similar.

To stand out and get noticed, you need a hook—an unusual angle. The media and their readers/viewers are jaded and easily bored by the "same old thing." If you can promote your service or idea with a fresh angle, you increase your chances of getting press coverage for your story.

Fran Capo, a guru in publicity and humor, tells how she came up with the PR hook that skyrocketed her fame:

> I'm a stand-up comic by profession. After the *Daily News* interviewed me a few years ago, the reporter asked, "What are you planning to do next?"
>
> Well, at the time there was nothing I was planning on doing next. But here was a woman from the *Daily News* telling me she was interested in following my career. So I thought I'd better tell her something. What came out was, "I'm thinking about breaking the *Guinness Book of World Records* for the Fastest Talking Female."
>
> The newspaper article came out the next day. That evening, at 5 P.M., I got a call from CNN asking me to go on *Larry King Live*. They wanted me to try to break the record. They told me they would send a limo to pick me up at 8 P.M. That was only in three hours. They insisted because they wanted me to do it that same night. Talk about pressure!
>
> I had a gig that night in New Jersey, but it didn't take a rocket scientist to figure out which of the two engagements I should do. I started calling every comic I knew, and by the grace of God, I found a replacement for my 7 P.M. stand-up show.
>
> Next I called Guinness to find out what the rules were to break a fast-talking record. They said I would have to recite something from either Shakespeare or the Bible.
>
> Suddenly I started saying the ninety-first Psalm, a prayer for protection that my mom had taught me. Shakespeare and I had never really gotten along, so I figured the Bible was my only hope. I began practicing and practicing, over and over again, timing myself with a stop watch to see how fast I could do it.
>
> At 8 P.M., the limousine picked me up. I practiced all the way there, and by the time I reached the studio, I felt as if my tongue would break off. "What if I don't break the record?" I asked the producer. She replied, "Larry doesn't care whether you break it or not. He just cares that you try it on his show first."
>
> So I asked myself, "What's the worst thing that could happen? I'll look like a fool on national television." A minor thing, I told myself. I could live through that. Then I asked myself, "And what if I break the record?" Now that would be great.

So I decided just to give it my best shot, and I did. I broke the record, becoming the World's Fastest Talking Female by speaking 585 words in one minute in front of a national television audience. I broke it again 2 years later, with 603 words. My career took off.

People often ask me how I did that. Or how I've managed to do many of the things I've done, like lecturing for the first time, or going on stage, or bungee jumping. I tell them I live my life by this simple philosophy: I always say yes first, then I ask, "Now what do I have to do to accomplish that?"

Then I ask myself, "What is the worst thing that can happen if I don't succeed?" The answer is simply: I don't succeed. And what's the best thing that can happen? I succeed.

What more can life ask of you? Be yourself, and have a good time!

By the way, when Fran was in the audience at one of my seminars, I introduced her. On the spot, she gave the world's fastest recitation of "The Three Little Pigs." It brought the house down!

Now, getting into the *Guinness Book of World Records* may not have wide applicability for most of us. But there are a number of PR "hooks" that other gurus have used, and which you might adapt successfully to your business.

Gary Blake, director of The Communication Workshop (Port Washington, New York), is a guru in business writing. His firm presents business writing seminars to major corporations worldwide. Each year, he sponsors an award for the worst business writing, which gets a lot of publicity.

A safety consultant could sponsor a "safest plant in the USA" contest. A dentist could have a brightest smile contest for local schoolchildren. Or a "best brusher" contest. You get the idea.

Predictions are another hook that people in many fields can use. If you are a market timer, you can gain attention by predicting the Dow will hit 500 or 5,000 or 15,000 within a year.

Ken McGill, a reporter with *iMarketing News,* warns: "Predictions are a prime opportunity to look like an ass." But I don't think it turns out that way. If you are right, you publicize the accuracy of your forecast. If you were wrong, you pontificate on the new market factors that changed the market in ways no one could have foreseen.

Prediction is a bit of a racket, but it can work. Psychics do it all the time. They make a whole bunch of predictions. The few that come true make headlines; the ones that didn't come to pass die quietly.

## Letters to the Editors

Entrepreneurs frequently complain that big corporations get all the press, because they spend the big advertising dollars. How can you, the independent guru, compete? By writing a "letter to the editor" of the publications that your prospects read—and in which you'd like to be featured.

Marketers and publicists almost universally ignore the fact that the "letters to the editor" column is usually the best-read part of any publication—getting much higher readership than the average article.

"Regular news stories never really reveal how involved people get in what goes on around them," says Winifred Bramley. "For that, you need letters to the editor. There's enmity, empathy, love, loss, anger, angst, fear, feistiness, facetiousness, felicity, griping, grit, congratulations, cunning, consideration, confession (well, rarely that), bragging, bravado, and gentility. In short, everything needed for a good story."

Here's a formula for writing an effective letter to the editor to promote the solutions you sell. Let's say, for instance, that there's a new regulation or requirement being imposed on your prospects—by government, regulatory agencies, or customers—and you sell a system that automates compliance.

Your letter says, in essence, "Your readers need to know about and comply with this new rule, or they will suffer [name the penalties]. They should set up their computer systems with software capable of automating this paperwork to make sure every document is in compliance, and should ask their computer vendor for assistance in this area."

Of course, the reader assumes his current computer vendor doesn't know anything about this, or he would have brought it up and offered to fix it. Who does he turn to for help? You, the knowledgeable solutions provider who wrote the letter that told him about it.

## Press Releases

The press release is a one- or two-page typed document of news or information about a company and its activities. It is the standard vehicle through which publicists and businesses communicate their news and information to the press in the hopes the media will run a story on them.

We talked in Chapter 5, "Information Products," about producing information products to promote yourself as a guru. A very effective PR tactic is to send out press releases about your information products. This is my "secret weapon" in PR and the single most effective type of release I know of.

It works as follows: You write a free booklet, report, or other giveaway item along the lines described in Chapter 5. You then send out a release that ...

1. Announces the publication of your new booklet or report.

2. Describes some of the useful information it contains.

3. Offers it free to readers of the publication or to the audience of the radio or TV show.

All three elements are critical. Editors are primarily interested in what's new, so if you are offering a new booklet on a topic, your headline should always begin NEW FREE BOOKLET ... followed by a description of the topic, contents, or issue the information addresses.

Next, your press release should repeat (either word-for-word or edited) some of the key points highlighted in the booklet or report. This is done so the editor can run your release as a "mini-feature article" on the topic.

Just saying you have a booklet available might get you a small mention. But if you allow editors to reprint some of its contents, by putting such material in the release you send, they'll run longer, more in-depth pieces featuring all the useful information you've provided.

"But if all of the information in my booklet is revealed in the article, then people will have no reason to send for my booklet!" you might protest. That sounds like a logical objection. But experience proves the opposite is true: The more the article describes the contents of your booklet, the more people will read the article and send for the booklet.

Experience has shown that even if the entire text of a booklet is reprinted in an article (or an ad), people still want to get that text in booklet form. Why? Perhaps people don't like to tear out an ad or article, and find booklets and reports are a more permanent medium.

Remember, *put excerpts from your booklet into your release.* Do not assume that the editor will read your booklet and pull out pertinent material for an article. The press release should be a self-contained mini-article ready to use "as is," without the editor having to refer to any enclosures or other materials.

Finally, your free booklet release must call for action. In the last paragraph you say "For a free copy of [title of booklet], call or write [your company name, address, phone]."

Many editors will include that contact information and a call to action when running your releases, and you will get many requests. Some editors will not print such contact information. But you have no control over that. However, if you do not put in contact information and a call to action, *no* editors will tell their readers how or where they can request your booklet, and without such information, no one will contact you. So, always close with the call to action.

Finally, should you include a copy of your free booklet with the press releases you mail? Including a sample of the booklet may be desirable, but it is not necessary. I have had great success mailing press releases that did not include a sample copy of the booklet or report being offered.

The main benefit of leaving out the sample booklet is cost savings: Including a sample booklet can add another 10 to 70 cents or more per release being mailed, depending on the cost to print the booklet and the weight of the booklet (which increases postage). For example, a tip sheet or slim pamphlet will add less cost than a bulky special report, book, or manual.

If the extra 10 to 70 cents per piece is significant to you, omit the sample booklet and pocket the savings. Be sure to put a line after the close of your release that says:

EDITOR: REVIEW COPY OF "[TITLE OF BOOKLET]" AVAILABLE UPON REQUEST. CALL JOE JONES AT XXX-XXX-XXXX.

Some editors may insist on seeing a copy before they'll promote it in their publication, so you should offer to send a copy free to any editor who requests it.

If your free booklet is slim and inexpensive, or if cost is not a factor, include a sample copy with each release you mail. It certainly can't hurt. And some editors may pay extra attention when they open the envelope and see your report or pamphlet.

One of my more successful new booklet releases was for my booklet, "Recession-Proof Business Strategies." I think it's a good model for anyone offering free information via press release: The format is easily adapted to any information offer and has worked for everyone who has tried it.

This press release was mailed to 300 business magazines, 50 advertising and marketing magazines, 80 syndicated newspaper columnists who write on business topics, business editors at the nation's 500 largest daily newspapers, and a few other publications. Because I included a sample booklet with the release, total cost for mailing approximately 950 releases was a bit under $1,000.

The release generated dozens of pickups, ranging from brief mentions to magazines that reprinted almost the entire text word for word. I do not know the specific number of pickups since I did not use a clipping service to keep track of all the placements.

Virtually every pickup included information on how the reader could order the booklet. From this press release alone, I sold well over 3,500 booklets at $7 each, for a gross of over $24,000. The follow-up sales included several consulting assignments, half a dozen paid speaking engagements, and additional sales of other booklets and reports.

The release worked for two reasons. First, because the topic was timely. The release was issued during the worst of the recession of the early 1990s, so it was a "hot" topic with inherent media appeal. Second, it precisely follows the three-part formula of (a) announcing the availability of a new booklet, (b) excerpting highlights so editors could run a mini-feature article on the subject, and providing contact information and a call to action.

The only way in which it violates the formula for the free booklet release is that the reader must pay $7. I did this because my primary motivation at the time was to make money selling this booklet as well as a line of related booklets and reports I offer, and I felt the need for such a booklet was so great that charging $7 would not prevent a person from ordering.

For someone selling a consulting or advisory service, however, I would probably make the booklet free or ask for a nominal sum if the objective was to generate sales leads for the service. Here is the release as I mailed it:

FROM: Bob Bly, 174 Holland Avenue,
New Milford, NJ 07646
CONTACT: Bob Bly,
phone 201 385-1220

*For immediate release*

### NEW BOOKLET REVEALS 14 PROVEN STRATEGIES FOR KEEPING BUSINESSES BOOMING IN A BUST ECONOMY

New Milford, NJ. While some companies struggle to survive in today's sluggish business environment, many are doing better than ever—largely because they have mastered the proven but little-known strategies of "recession marketing."

That's the opinion of Bob Bly, an independent marketing consultant and author of the just-published booklet "Recession-Proof Business Strategies: 14 Winning Methods to Sell Any Product or Service in a Down Economy."

"Many business people fear a recession or soft economy, because when the economy is weak, their clients and customers cut back on spending," says Bly. "To survive in such a marketplace, you need to develop recession-marketing strategies that help you retain your current accounts and keep those customers buying. You also need to master marketing techniques that will win you *new* clients or customers to replace any business you may have lost because of the increased competition that is typical of a recession."

Among the recession-fighting business strategies Bly outlines in his new booklet:

- **Reactivate dormant accounts.** An easy way to get more business is to simply call past clients or customers—people you served at one time but are not actively working for now—to remind them of your existence. According to Bly, a properly scripted telephone call to a list of past buyers will generate approximately 1 order for every 10 calls.

- **Quote reasonable, affordable fees and prices in competitive bid situations.** While you need not reduce your rates or prices, in competitive bid situations you will win by bidding toward the low or middle end of your price range rather than at the high end. Bly says that during a recession, your bids should be 15 to 20 percent lower than you would normally charge in a healthy economy.

- **Give your existing clients and customers a superior level of service.** In a recession, Bly advises businesses to do everything they can to hold onto their existing clients or customers—their "bread-and-butter" accounts. "The best way to hold onto your clients or customers is to please them," says Bly, "and the best way to please them is through better customer service. Now is an ideal time to provide that little bit of extra service or courtesy that can mean the difference between dazzling the client or customer vs. merely satisfying them."

■ **Reactivate old leads.** Most businesses give up on sales leads too early, says Bly. He cites a study from Thomas Publishing which found that although 80 percent of sales to businesses are made on the fifth call, only one out of ten salespeople calls beyond three times. Concludes Bly: "You have probably not followed up on leads diligently enough, and the new business you need may already be right in your prospect." He says repeated follow-up should convert 10 percent of prospects to buyers.

■ **Repackage your product line or service to accommodate smaller clients or customers on reduced budgets.** Manufacturers and other product sellers can offer compact models, economy sizes, no-frills versions, easy payment plans, extended credit, special discounts, incentives, and smaller minimum orders to appeal to prospects with reduced spending power. Service providers can be more flexible by selling their services and time in smaller, less-costly increments.

■ **Keep busy with ancillary assignments.** Another recession survival strategy is to take an ancillary assignment to fill gaps in your schedule. For example, a carpenter who normally handled only large, lucrative home remodeling jobs took on lots of smaller jobs and "handyman" work to keep the money coming when his home renovation work fell off.

■ **Add value to your existing product or service.**
While prospects may seem reluctant to spend money
in a soft economy, their real concern, says Bly, is making sure they get the best value for their dollar. You
can retain existing accounts and win business by offering more value than your competition. For instance,
says Bly, a firm selling industrial com-ponents added
value by computerizing its inventory system so it
could give customers faster telephone quotations on
the availability and pricing of needed parts.

■ **Help existing clients or customers create new sales
for you.** Bly advises businesses to call their existing
accounts with new ideas that will benefit the client or
customer while requiring them to buy more of what
the vendor is selling. "It's a win-win situation," says
Bly. "They get your ideas, suggestions, and solutions
to their problems at no charge, while you sell more
of your product or service to help them implement
the idea you suggested."

To receive a copy of Bly's booklet, "Recession-Proof
Business Strategies," send $8 ($7 plus $1 shipping
and handling) to: Bob Bly, Dept. 109, 174 Holland
Avenue, New Milford, NJ 07646. Cash, money
orders, and checks (payable to "Bob Bly") accepted.
(Add $1 for Canadian orders.)

Bob Bly, an independent copywriter and consultant
based in New Milford, NJ, specializes in business-to-
business, hi-tech, and direct-response marketing. He
is the author of 18 books including HOW TO PRO-
MOTE YOUR OWN BUSINESS (New American
Library) and SELLING YOUR SERVICES (Henry

Holt). A frequent speaker and seminar leader, Mr.
Bly speaks nationwide on the topic of how to market
successfully in a recession or soft economy.

## Pitch Letters

A press release is effective when you have a particular story to sell
to the media. But another way to get the press to help publicize
you as a guru is to be interviewed by them when they are doing
their own stories and need comments from an expert in your
field.

The vehicle for getting the media to call you is a pitch letter. In a pitch letter, you introduce yourself as the expert. You say
what topics you are qualified to speak on, give your credentials,
and let the recipient know you are available and eager to do interviews.

Pitch letters can be used to position either an individual or
a company as an expert. Following is a pitch letter a publicist sent
to promote the Skin Cancer Foundation as a source of cancer
prevention information.

---

June 14, 2000

Editor
Publication
Address
City, State Zip

Dear:

A freckle. It may be small and just one of many that we see on our bodies
every day. But no matter how small—each of these freckles is significant
and has an impact on our lives—especially when we cease to acknowledge
its importance.

With the start of summer, the Skin Cancer Foundation and Cactus Juice want to increase awareness of the importance of checking your skin for freckles and melanoma and inform people of the dangers of sun exposure.

So those freaks in New York are walking around with fake freckles, so what else is new? ... What does that have to do with the price of tea in Tulsa, or Texas, or Tampa? Well perhaps that fake freckle is a symbol that New Yorkers have taken the time to educate and protect themselves from skin cancer. With the ozone problems and the country more active than ever, that stupid freckle might just have national significance.

To kick off the first day of summer and national tour "S.O.S.—Save Our Skin" ... the Skin Cancer Foundation and Cactus Juice and the City of New York Parks and Recreation invite you to learn how to protect your skin from the harmful effects of the sun.

- Learn how to examine your skin for melanoma and pre-cancerous beauty marks
- Learn how to protect your friends and family from sun damage
- New all-natural skin/sun care products
- Before and after sun-damage photos

If you would like to schedule an interview with an expert from the Skin Cancer Foundation or would like to conduct a live remote, please feel free to call me at 212-645-6900 at ext. 109.

Best regards,

Beth Scheffer

## Syndicated Columns

A really big coup for a guru is to get a syndicated column on his area of expertise. It is not exactly easy to achieve but is probably less difficult than most writers believe.

Most people are aware that such well-known columnists as Carl Rowan, James Kilpatrick, and William Buckley are nationally syndicated—selling their columns regularly to newspapers all over the country. Not so well known is that it is not only political columnists and "big names" whose columns are syndicated in this manner.

Writers of "service" columns are also widely syndicated. "Dear Abby" is one example. There's also Sylvia Porter, Rona Barrett, Eliot Janeway, and many others. They write on personal problems, household hints, finance and economics, investment, medical matters, career concerns, and other topics.

Even this is not the complete list of types of materials that may be syndicated. The crossword puzzles, comic strips, political cartoons, and many other such items in your morning newspaper are also syndicated (as are many radio and TV programs!).

In short, almost anything that would interest newspaper readers generally may be syndicated, including completely new ideas.

The market may be easy or difficult to crack, depending on many factors:

1. Opinion columns—"think pieces"—are extremely difficult to sell, almost impossible if you are not a recognized authority of some sort. Walter Lippman was able to do it, and probably Walter Cronkite and a few others of great reputation can do it, but it's an uphill, almost hopeless battle otherwise. (That is not the same thing as true analysis columns, such as those analyzing the stock market or the latest medical findings. But even then you must be able to demonstrate impressive credentials.)

2. Humor usually sells well. But it is much more difficult to write than most people believe. You will have tough acts—for example, Dave Barry and Erma Bombeck—to follow. You must be good—very good.

3. Something truly different and original will go—if readers like it.

And that—"if readers like it"—is what it always comes down to. The readers are the final judges.

The editor buys what he thinks readers will like. He or she may be right—or wrong. Of course, he or she will never know without trying the column. Still, they are hard to sell after all the years they spent as reporters, correspondents, and newspaper editors. They "have seen it all," or believe they have. (Maybe your "new" idea is not so new, after all, to an old hand in the business.)

Syndication is usually done through an established organization, such as the King Features Syndicate or United Features, two of many syndicates. They are the true professionals in syndication. They have a good idea of what is salable as a syndicated feature and what is not. They are also realists; they know that even a good idea takes time to sell to enough subscribers—newspapers—to make the proposition viable. That is why you must pay them as much as 60 percent of the selling price as their commission. And that is why it is not easy to get them to accept you as a client.

But it is not hopeless. There is another way: do it yourself. Be your own syndicate by selling your material directly to a number of newspapers on a syndicated basis.

Bear in mind that you are up against experts, some with large reputations, as competitors. Try to specialize as much as possible. It's much easier to be a true expert in a narrow specialty than in a broad one. Choose an area where you truly do have credentials as an expert and in which there are not an excessive number of competitors.

Obviously, for many of the areas, you must be a professional expert. But you could also be an "amateur expert" in many areas, such as wine, gardening, home-based second-income careers, and household hints.

Don't underestimate the value of research to supplement—even replace—your own expert knowledge. You don't have to know it all yourself. If you are in a position to get good information on a continuing basis, you can turn that to advantage. Many journalists, for example, are not experts in their subjects, but they are expert in finding information they can use—where/how, who to call/interview, what bulletins to read.

You can easily get yourself placed on distribution for news releases, for example. All you need do is make up a letterhead announcing that you are a columnist, news service, publisher, or other relevant entrepreneur and request that your name be placed on the mailing list.

The marketing departments of most manufacturers issue such releases, as well as full press kits, and will be happy to add your name. There are dozens of trade publications that are distributed free of charge to many people. Your local librarian will help you find lists of such periodicals.

You don't have to apply for many releases and periodicals; it is almost self-perpetuating, once you have started: Your name will find its way onto many mailing lists, and before long you will be getting many mailings from people and organizations you never heard of before.

You must decide about your audience. For the general public as an audience, you want to shoot for the daily newspapers. But if you are after a more specialized audience, such as professionals or business owners, you want to consider the trade papers. *DM News,* for example, is a tabloid for the direct-mail community, and *Target Marketing* is a smooth-paper magazine for the same audience. Both are "controlled circulation" periodicals, incidentally, which means free subscriptions for qualified applicants.

Talk to your friends and colleagues. Some of them may come up with a great idea or two. Ask them what they would like to see in their newspaper. Do lots of reading and researching. Read columns and features, form critical opinions, try to turn those reactions into new ideas.

Once you settle on an idea, be sure that you haven't over-specialized so that you would have trouble doing the column regularly or finding enough interested readers. But don't allow it to become too general, either, for it is not worthy of a column if it is not distinctive in some manner. That's the art: finding that right middle ground.

Once started, listen to feedback from readers. Let them guide you in what they want, and give that to them if you want to be successful.

Also listen to editors. Editors are commonly confronted with more copy than he or she has space for; it's the classic problem. Space is almost always at a premium.

Most of the time, therefore, an editor must cut stories to fit available space. But he or she usually winds up with leftover space—odd and assorted small bits of column inches—"holes" in the page makeup. (It's generally pretty easy to cut news stories to fit; columns and features are much more difficult to trim.) That's why you see those filler items, for example, "The blue whale is the largest mammal on earth."

You are well advised to make your column about 500 to 750 words, and certainly not more than 1,000 words. At least, not in the beginning. You may write 2,000 words in your first draft—you should, if that is what is necessary to get your complete story down—but then take the blue pencil to your copy and start cutting. Cut it to that optimal limit by chopping out everything that is not absolutely essential to the story. You will have far better copy—terse, tight, more vigorous, and more directly to the point—as a result.

Now you have selected your topic, gotten your flow of information started, and written your first column, right? You are ready to seek buyers, right?

No, not right. First of all, write several more columns. Whether you are trying for a monthly, weekly, or daily column (most newspaper columns today are daily or two to three times each week), you must have a number of columns prepared, probably at least a half dozen as a minimum. Editors will not buy your column without seeing a number of them first, for at least two reasons:

1. The editor wants to be sure that you can produce the columns steadily, with each one able to stand on its own merits.

2. The editor wants to be enough columns ahead to be independent of the vagaries of mail service, your continued good health, and other hazards to faithful appearance of each manuscript when it is due.

Having gotten six or more columns of A-1 quality written, you are organized and ready to turn out your columns regularly, and you are now ready to roll, to sign up your first subscribers. Now what?

You will probably have to give your first few columns away. You offer them gratis to a number of editors as a free trial to sample their readers' responses. You send copies of at least three columns to each editor, with a brief letter explaining that this is an introductory freebie. Don't explain what your column is about; if it does not explain itself—editors are usually quite intelligent—you are dead anyway.

Better yet, call the editors and try to get their agreement to see you and give you a few minutes, if possible. If you can arrange that, try to do this in your meetings:

1. Make a good appearance and try to impress the editor that you are a true professional, bright, dedicated, and capable.

2. Try to get their views on coverage, perhaps columns they would like to see, suggestions, and perhaps what it would take to sell them.

3. Editors you visit may not be able to use your column, but may be able to suggest other editors who can. Don't wait for the idea to occur to the other however; solicit such ideas, and if they are forthcoming, try to get notes of introduction to those other editors. Such notes help greatly.

Caution: Editors are invariably very busy people and not appreciative of having their time wasted. If an editor is gracious enough to see you, get to the point promptly and don't waste his or her time.

You will probably do well to try marketing your column to weekly newspapers at first, for several reasons: Editors of weekly newspapers are often easier to see and talk with, although they tend also to have rather limited budgets. If you can give your column local interest, it will be more attractive to a weekly also, since they are the journals of small towns, neighborhoods, and suburbia. The editor will probably be pleased to have a local writer doing a column and presumably available to discuss coverage of the column, perhaps even to accept special assignments. Certainly, the small weekly is easier to sell to than the big daily.

Another way to improve your chances for success is to pay attention to local businesses and organizations of all kinds. Mention them when it is compatible with your columns to do so. Their endorsement of you and what you write goes a long way to persuade editors that your column is catching on.

Encourage readers to write you with questions and comments; mail arriving from readers is another excellent persuader. Too, editors are well aware that any column that involves the readers directly is likely to become quite popular. And don't be bashful about working on your family and friends to read your column and write to the editor about it.

A mass mailing to editors who might be interested in running your column will help also, although it means a good bit of work and some expense. First, take the trouble to compile a list of editors. Don't send your copy to the newspaper's general address. It will wind up in the mailroom, and probably never get to an editor's desk, much less the right editor. Newspapers have many editors: financial or business editors, feature editors, sports editors, literary editors, state editors, editors for copy concerning adjacent states, society editors, style editors. Find out which editor ought to see your copy—even try to get the individual's name, if possible, but certainly the right title—and address your copy to that editor.

It's a "numbers game"—playing the percentages or probability statistics. If your column has worth and you send samples to enough editors, you will make a few sales, inevitably. It will take patience and endurance, but if you persist you will succeed. It is those first few sales that are hardest to make. Once you are started, it will gradually become easier.

Persistence and perseverance mean going back to that list for additional mailings. Many prospects who ignored the first mailing will pay more attention to the second one, and a few more will order. Each mailing will produce better results—more orders—than the previous one, to the point where the response begins to level off. That's the inherent nature of advertising; if the copy and the product are worthy, persistence produces sales eventually. Persistence is the magic ingredient; no obstacle can endure forever against it. Most successes depend on it.

You must be sure to mention that the subscriber will have your column exclusively in his or her distribution area. That is, you cannot sell your column to two newspapers that compete directly with each other—two in the same city or two weekly newspapers serving the same small town or neighborhood. That exclusivity is one of the inducements, especially where there is a directly competing newspaper. Once you have sold one, you cannot sell the other.

You can charge subscribers to your column in either of two ways: a flat fee per column or a sliding scale, based on the circulation of the paper. (The latter is not an uncommon practice.) The rates, however, vary enormously, so that you may be able to get only $5 from some weekly paper, where you might get several times that from a large daily—if you are fortunate enough to sell your column to that daily.

Use this as the most general of guidelines in setting a price for your column. Start low—you'll be giving the first ones away as a promotion, anyway—while you are trying to land a few subscribers. You can always raise your rates later, as you become established and accepted.

In fact, one way to handle this gracefully and leave the door wide open to adjust your prices later is to offer a low "introductory" bargain price, clearly signaling the customer that the price may go up later. In any event, that will serve also as an inducement to try your column, while it is available at such a bargain figure. (That is always a good marketing strategy.)

Once you have those first legitimate sales—a base of subscribers—and are actually being paid for your column, you are ready to begin the work of expanding it. And there are at least two ways to do this:

1. Go back to your original mailing list with another offer. This time, ask for a price and explain that such and such newspapers are now carrying your column regularly. Include any favorable comments you have had from readers or editors. Offer the "special introductory price" here.

2. Go to an established national syndicate (your librarian can help you find a reference source listing all major syndicates) and offer your column. You now have an excellent chance of being accepted, since you have shown that it is a salable product, even with your limited resources. You will probably earn far more by marketing your column through them.

If you decide that you prefer to do it yourself, use your mailing list over and over, adding to it when you discover some newspapers you did not know about before. Do a fresh mailing every 30 to 90 days, revising your sales letter to reflect your current success with the column frequently.

You don't have to limit yourself to newspapers. Consider other kinds of periodicals, including trade tabloids—many trade journals are published as "slicks"—smooth-paper magazines—but there are many published on newsprint as tabloids. Try also the Sunday supplements—many of those are syndicated, and those regional slicks also.

## Radio Talk Shows

There are hundreds of talk radio shows. You should mail your press releases to the producers of these shows. (Bacon's, listed in Appendix A, "Bibliography," has their names and addresses.) If they are interested in your topic, they might invite you to be a guest.

The good thing about talk radio is you don't have to go to their studio. They can interview you over the telephone, from the comfort of your home or office.

Dottie Walters, publisher of the newsletter *Sharing Ideas,* offers the following tips for being interviewed on radio:

- Prepare. Write out the 15 most likely questions you'll be asked. Develop your answers and practice answering them.

- Restate the question before giving your answer.

- Be brief. After twenty to thirty seconds, you're probably over-answering. If an answer goes beyond that, summarize it.

- Use humor. But don't tell jokes. Short anecdotes are effective.

- Demonstrate you're an authority. Use facts, enumerating your points. Use dramatic, startling statistics and findings.

- Elaborate beyond yes or no. Make specific points. Use examples to bring home each point. Give reasons.

- Speak personally, concretely, and colorfully. Look at the interviewer when you talk. Address people by name: the person interviewing you and the people calling into the show. Later in the show, refer by name to people who have called in.

- Be positive and show energy through enthusiasm and conviction. Don't repeat or paraphrase a caller's damaging question. It's okay to interrupt a question based on a false fact or premise. End each segment with an upbeat, summarizing benefit.

Put a sign on your door that says "I AM ON THE RADIO—Do Not Disturb" when you are doing a radio interview. You don't want your interview interrupted by a loud knock on the door or a visitor barging in and talking.

## TV Appearances

Al Parinello, in his book *On the Air: How to Get on Radio and TV Talk Shows and What to Do When You Get There* (Career Press), says that to get on a radio or TV talk show, you must begin by contacting the producer. It is the producer, not the host, who decides who will be the guests on the show.

Parinello recommends the following steps for contacting producers to get yourself as a guest on their radio or TV show:

1. Look up the producer in the media directory and call him or her.

2. Be brief. As in any sales call, you must immediately say who you are, why you are calling, and give reasons why the person should listen to you and have you as a guest on the show.

3. Do not pretend to be a publicist. If you are calling for yourself, say so. Do not try to overimpress or exaggerate, and don't lie. "Producers can tell a phony immediately," says Parinello.

4. If the producer is not interested, thank him for his time, get off the phone, and call the producer of the next show you want to get onto. Do not argue with a producer who turns you down, or try to prove that you indeed are a good potential guest; producers know what they are looking for in a guest. Do not ask producers who turn you down for a referral or recommendation to another show; they are not in business to be your publicist.

5. You are unlikely to get booked for the show over the phone. Producers who are interested will ask you to send a package of information about you and your topic.

6. What should the package include? Parinello says the media kit can include such items as press releases, a personal biography, testimonials or endorsements, reprints of articles written by or about you, a sample of your product, and a tip sheet. The latter is a list of 10 to 15 suggested questions the host might ask you about your topic. In addition, if you have made prior appearances on radio or TV, include a list of them (program names, stations, dates,

and topic). I'd also recommend including an audio- or videotape of a recent media appearance if available.

If you get invited to appear on a show, be there at least a half-hour earlier than they tell you. Study your topic well enough beforehand so you are comfortable. Remember that, as a guest, you are not given a script, cue cards, or other aides to help you talk.

Years ago, my wife and I co-authored a book on real estate. She was the professional real estate agent; I was the writer. But she does not like public speaking, so we decided I would do the media interviews.

Although I didn't know the subject nearly as well as she did, I kept our book in front of me while I did phone interviews for the talk radio shows. And with the book as my "cheat sheet," I got through a dozen interviews okay. Then I was asked to be a guest on CNBC.

When we were walking onto the set to get ready, the host saw me carrying my "cheat sheet" and said, "You can't have that on-camera, you know." Panic! How would I talk about real estate without my *Cliffs Notes?* Fortunately, doing all those radio shows etched the information temporarily into my brain, and I got through the TV interview without a hitch. But it was an experience I would not want to repeat! ■

*Chapter 10*

# The Internet

Another central component of establishing yourself as a guru is building a Web presence, the centerpiece of which is a Web site that is both an online resume and an information resource on a subject relating to your core expertise. This chapter shows how to create a guru Web site and covers other Web marketing techniques including e-zines (as discussed in Chapter 6, "Newsletters and E-Zines"), e-mail marketing, forums, chat rooms, content, and discussion groups.

## Do You Need a Web Site?

People seeking guru status frequently question whether they need a Web site. The answer is an unequivocal "yes."

In a few short years, the Internet has irreversibly become an integral element of business, communication, and information dissemination. As we have been discussing throughout this book, the key methodology of attaining guru status is to continually disseminate relevant information on your specialty to one or more niche markets or audiences.

The Internet was tailor-made for information dissemination. In fact, the entire culture of the Internet is based around freely sharing information. To achieve your quest of attaining guru status, you want to give away information; and the people on the Internet want to take all you're giving. It's a perfect match.

When people want information on a topic today, they do not turn first to the library, the bookstore, the newspaper, or the *Reader's Guide to Periodical Literature*. They surf the Web to find what they need. You need a Web site of your own to maximize exposure of you and your information on the Web.

Gurus are expected to keep up with the state of the art in technology and business, if not lead it. Without a Web site, you look old-fashioned and behind-the-times—not the image you want to convey.

## What's in a (Domain) Name?

Network Solutions (www.networksolutions.com), a company offering domain name registration services online, registered nearly one million unique domain names last year alone. And a domain name is a unique entity: If I own www.business.com, no one else can.

Corporations, small businesses, and individuals are buying up domain names at a frantic rate. So if you don't have one, pick a suitable domain and register it right away. The longer you wait, the greater the chances that someone else will snap it up.

Surveys from GreatDomains.com, a company that resells domain names on the secondary market, reveal few surprises about what makes for a desirable domain name. A short name is easier to remember and therefore better than a long name. A one-word domain name is better than a multiple-word domain name. Avoid domain names with hyphens or numbers.

Domain names with the word "and" are difficult to remember correctly. For instance, is Barnes & Noble online www.barnesandnoble.com or www.barnes&noble.com? (Actually it's neither.)

Also a problem are two-word domain names where the last letter of the first word is the same as the first letter of the second word. Would you think to look on www.bobbly.com or www.bobly.com to find me? (Fortunately I was able to get www.bly.com.)

Notice that the above names all end in .com. Right now, the major domain name suffixes—the letters after the last period—are .com, .org, and .edu. These suffixes are called top-level domains (TLDs).

At a recent meeting in Japan, the Internet Corporation for Assigned Names and Numbers (ICANN) said it will create new TLDs, making many more domain names possible. These new suffixes include .biz, .info, .aero, .pro, and .museum.

And you have yet another alternative: Country Code Top Level Domain Names (CCTLDs). These are extension you can get based on the name of the nation from which the domain originates. But you do not have to have a physical presence or even operate in that country to use their domain name extension. CCTLDs are plentiful and available for registration now.

There are 243 country-specific domain extensions (like .de for Germany, .fr for France, .jp for Japan, etc.). These domains have been in existence for many years, but they are becoming increasingly popular. Total registrations in country-specific domains have increased from just under 1 million in 1998 to nearly 4 million in early 2000, a jump which until last year had gone relatively unnoticed.

Although there are multiple suffixes available (.org, .tv, .md, .net, .aero, .edu), .com is still the most popular.

## Guru-Focused vs. Topic-Focused Web Sites

The basic decision you have to make is whether to build your Web site around you and your company—or around your topic. The name you choose should match that choice.

For instance, my domain name is www.bly.com—my last name. And my site is built around me as a service provider (freelance copywriter and consultant) in direct marketing. It is not about direct marketing *per se*. I call this type of site a *guru-centered Web site*.

Having the Web site focused on the guru, and not the topic, is a good choice if you are fairly well-established and already have a steady flow of leads.

In my office, Fern, my office manager, handles the sales leads. She saves an enormous amount of time (not to mention photocopying, envelopes, and postage) referring most of these leads to my Web site for further information on my copywriting services.

In fact, the entire site is designed for the purpose of inquiry fulfillment. This makes sense only if you already get a lot of inquiries and need a way to fulfill them efficiently and rapidly.

What items should be included in a guru-focused Web site? I recommend that your site have the following pages:

- A home page describing the guru—who he is, his experience and background, clients served, services offered, results achieved
- Biography of the guru and, if appropriate, key staff members
- Company profile
- A client list
- Client testimonials
- Products sold
- Services offered
- Seminars, speeches, and presentations
- Bookstore—featuring books by the guru as well as books he recommends

- Articles—downloadable library of free articles written by the guru
- Travel and speaking schedule (for speakers, trainers, and consultants who serve out-of-town clients onsite)
- Press release archive
- Newsletter archive (back issues of his newsletter)

The main purpose of a guru-centered Web site is to give potential customers enough information to enable them to make a decision about hiring the guru or buying his products.

The secondary purpose is to impress site visitors with the guru's credentials and breadth of experience, convincing them that he is indeed a leading expert in his specialty.

The second type of Web site used by gurus is the *topic-centered Web site*. Unlike the guru-centered site, which focuses on the guru, his company, and his credentials, the topic-centered Web site focuses on the specialty or niche in which the guru wishes to establish himself.

Topic-centered sites are packed with useful, free content relating to the topic. The idea is to draw people to the site, where they can get the free content. The objective is to establish the guru's expertise in the topic.

For example, Dan Seidman used the Web to establish himself as a sales guru. His award-winning Web site, www. SalesAutopsy.com, is in his words "a collection of the worst sales horror stories." Dan explains:

*Sales & Marketing Management* magazine has called me a "cult hit" among salespeople. I've created my own niche in sales and the entrepreneurial world and am leveraging it into speaking and coaching engagements, syndicated articles in trade publications, and a book. I give expert analysis or "postmortem" to add value to each story. This brands me as a sales training expert.

Gerald Kostecka says his books and Web site, www.dragon4kids. com, helped establish him as a guru in his field: "I have become a recognized authority in the field of children's and parenting issues and I did appear as a panelist on a recent *Sally Jessy Raphael* show on school shootings."

Topic-centered Web sites are recommended for business owners and independent professionals who want to establish themselves as gurus in a niche but are not quite in that position yet. They are packed with articles and other free content relating to their central topic.

The more pages you have with articles relating to the topic, the more often Web surfers using search engines will be brought to your site. Therefore packing the topic-centered site with content not only increases your credibility; it also generates more traffic on the site.

An established guru with a guru-centered Web site may not be all that interested in driving volumes of traffic to his site, which after all is primarily designed for use by serious clients and prospects, not the masses of Internet surfers munching on free content.

But for the expert looking to build his reputation in a topic, building the preeminent information resource on that topic on the Web can go a long way toward helping him achieve the recognition he seeks.

## Building Your E-List

Many small business owners, independent professionals, and other entrepreneurs would like to know who has visited their Web site and be able to contact them again.

But when you get a hit to your site (a user accessing any page on the site), the only information captured about that person automatically by the computer is his IP (Internet Protocol) address.

You can put a counter on your site to keep track of the total number of hits. But to track the individuals who visit your site and build a database of these folks, you need to capture their information using a *guest page.*

A guest page is an online form where users can register at your site. You can find sample guest pages you can add to your own site at www.scriptsearch.com.

The visitor fills in his personal information on the guest page including name, company, title, address, city, state, zip code, phone, fax, and e-mail address. When he clicks the "Submit" button, he is registered, and all this information goes to you via e-mail.

Most people won't fill out and submit a guest page unless you give them a compelling reason to do so. This can be any number of things: a free report or downloadable e-book, free software demo, a discount coupon to a conference at which you are speaking, a free consultation, or free access to a special portion of your Web site.

For instance, you can post exclusive reports, surveys, or other data in a password-protected portion of your Web site. To get the password, the visitor has to give you his personal data by filling out and submitting the guest page.

## E-Mail Promotion to Your Web Site Visitors

Why would you want to encourage people to submit a completed guest page to you while visiting your site?

As we discussed in Chapter 2, "How to Join the Guru Elite," you need to communicate with your target audience many times, not just once, to build awareness of yourself and your services in their minds.

By getting Web visitors to submit a completed guest page, you obtain their contact information—phone, address, and e-mail address—making it possible to communicate with them on a regular basis.

Obviously e-mail is the fastest, easiest, and lowest-cost option for repeat communication to a database of your Web site visitors. But laws concerning spamming do not allow you to send e-mails to someone without their permission.

Therefore, on your guest page, place a check box with the following text next to it: "I am willing to receive e-mails from time to time about information and special offers of interest to people visiting this Web site."

If the visitor checks the box, and then submits the form, he has in effect given you his permission to send future e-mails, and you can do so without fear of violating either the law or Internet etiquette. Lists of Web surfers who have agreed to receive promotional e-mails in this manner are known as "opt-in lists." If you ever do an e-mail marketing campaign to a rented e-list, opt-in lists are the only ones you should ever use.

Let's say you get people to opt-in using your guest page. What can you send them via e-mail that would interest them while building your guru reputation with them?

- Announcements of upcoming speaking engagements and seminars.

- Announcements of your latest books.

- Links to articles by and about you posted on the Web (your site or other sites).

- Actual copies of articles by or about you. (Send these as text pasted into the body of the e-mail. Most people will not open an attached file because of virus concerns.)

- Periodic commentary by you on issues relating to your industry or specialty. Some marketers call these "e-mail alerts."

- Special discounts—for instance, on close-out or remaindered merchandise you may be selling, or "customer-only" specials.

- Notification of pricing or policy changes.

## Publishing on Your Web Site: The E-Zine

In Chapter 6, we talked about publishing an electronic newsletter, or e-zine.

Many gurus who have their own Web sites offer e-zines, most sent either on a weekly or monthly basis.

On many of these sites, there is a separate box for subscribing to the e-zine. All you have to do is fill in your e-mail address (nothing else) and hit submit.

If your goal is to maximize guest page submissions, then don't let people subscribe to the e-zine with a separate box. Require them to complete the entire guest page to subscribe to the e-zine. If you're going to give away valuable information, you may as well get some valuable marketing data in return.

## Publishing on Your Web Site: Articles

As discussed in Chapter 3, "Articles," a core task in the guru action plan is to write and publish articles.

You can and should post a large selection of your published print articles on your Web site. When you're just starting out, you'll probably only have a few articles published, so you'll want them all available on your site.

Once you've been in business as long as I have, and can count your career in decades instead of years (and your published articles by the dozen instead of on the fingers of one hand), you'll reach the point where posting all your articles on your site would overwhelm the Web surfer.

When that happens, you have to be selective. But which articles should you post?

- **The most recent.** If you have five articles on the same topic, the most recent (all else being equal) should be selected, since the examples and references are the most up-to-date. If you post an old article you wrote ten years ago, edit it to remove dated references.

- **The best.** Some of your articles are better than others. If you have written several articles on the same subject, post the one that is the clearest and most interesting to read.

- **The shortest.** Web surfers like conciseness and brevity. A short article, perhaps containing 10 tips and taking no more than 1 or 2 pages, is preferable to a Ph.D. thesis.

- **The most specialized.** There are tons of general articles on your topic already posted on the Web. Favor articles you've written that cover niche markets or specialized situations. A specialized article may appeal to fewer readers, but those who are facing the situation the article describes will be duly impressed and motivated to find out more about your services.

I post my articles in two versions—Word and html—and let the reader choose. The html version is for reading on the screen. The Word version is for the visitor to download and print out, if he wishes.

Having a downloadable version of your articles available on your Web site makes it easier for other Web site owners to take and use your articles. That's bad if you are worried about copyright violation and want people to pay you for your articles, as many content owners do.

However, if you want to publicize yourself, having downloadable articles on your site will get them wider distribution on the Web. It's a form of viral marketing: the easier it is for people to take and use Web content, the more readily they do it.

## Publishing on Your Web Site: Reports and E-Books

Your Web site—your "home" on the Internet—is a good place to test online publishing ventures.

You can produce special reports, monographs, and even books as electronic files—text, Word, html, pdf—and post them on your Web site for reading and downloading. You can "test drive" them in electronic form, and refine the content based on feedback, before committing documents to the permanence of print.

Some gurus post chapters of books in progress on their Web sites. They allow visitors to download and read the chapters for free. In return, the authors ask for (but do not insist on) feedback and comments.

The interactive nature of the Internet makes it a uniquely valuable research tool. One example is the posting of documents-in-progress on the Web site for feedback from site visitors.

You can also ask visitors questions and solicit feedback on your home page or in an issue of your e-zine.

The nice thing about using the Internet as a research tool is it eliminates the need to transcribe interviews (necessary when you interview a prospect in person or over the phone and tape your conversation). When you ask questions of people online, they will reply via e-mail, which forces them to type out their answers.

There are two major benefits to doing interviews via e-mail. First, the prospect gives you a more articulate, well-thought-out response, because he has to write out his thoughts.

Second, you save time. You can just cut the reply out of the e-mail, paste it into your document, and edit for style. Many of the longer success stories quoted in this book were written by the experts quoted, and then e-mailed to me. I merely cut and pasted them into the chapters with minor editing. It has the added advantage of letting the subject speak in his or her own voice.

## Your Online Bookstore

When you write your first book, you may want to feature it heavily on your home page and elsewhere on your Web site. Once you have written a few books, as I have, you may want to put them in an online bookstore.

You can sell the books yourself directly to customers. To do so, you have to add e-commerce functionality to your site. That means having a shopping cart or online order form and the ability to accept credit cards online.

If you wish to sell your information products online as a profit center, setting up an online order form or shopping cart system makes sense. With online e-commerce, your customer can get everything you sell—videos, audiocassette albums, reports, directories, software, books, CDs, flash cards—from a single source: your online store.

If you do not want to bother taking orders for your information products, and your books are already available on Amazon.com, you can become an Amazon Affiliate and link your online bookstore to their Web site.

When a customer clicks on the title or image of your book on your Web page, he is automatically brought to a description of your book on Amazon.com. For each book sold through this link from your Web site to theirs, Amazon.com pays you a 15 percent commission.

Do not see the Amazon Affiliate Program as a way to make extra money. Most of us who participate find our periodic commission checks from Amazon.com to be modest at best. The best way to think of the Amazon Affiliate Program is as a value-added service for your Web site.

Except for my books, my information products are typically free to qualified prospects, and since I choose not to focus on product sales (my business focuses solely on my custom copywriting for corporate clients), I don't bother marketing these information products to nonprospects who might buy them. Therefore, I don't take orders for products on my Web site, and articles are given away free.

But I do want to offer my clients and prospects the convenience of getting my books from my site. Since they are not free and I do not take product orders on the site, the solution is to link to the Amazon Affiliate Program. That way, everything the prospect wants or needs from me is available from a single source: my Web site.

## You Ought to Be in Pictures (and Audios and Videos)

For a long time, because I don't think I'm an attractive person, I preferred that my picture not be printed on my book covers, with articles, or in seminar brochures.

But now I have changed my mind. I still don't think my photo is appealing per se, but I now believe people want to put a face with the guru's name.

On my site, I have a standard head shot photo on my bio page. There is also a candid shot of me at the podium on a page describing the seminars and workshops I give.

Also on my seminar page is a short video clip of me giving a workshop. I didn't actually put the streaming video on my site. A speaker's bureau put the video on their site, and I merely link to it from my site.

Having streaming video or real audio on your site takes advantage of the Web's interactivity in a way that posted documents do not. One company that can put audio on your Web site is Wild Blue Media, listed in Appendix B, "Recommended Vendors."

Think about how you can use the Web's interactivity to your advantage. One of my clients is a mailing list broker, and I wrote a lot of pages for their site to establish their credibility and demonstrate their expertise.

But we also added interactive features to the site that add value to the firm's customers and prospects. For instance, there is a search engine that can quickly tell you what lists are available to reach a given market and what the list counts (quantity of names on each list) are.

Another client is a leasing company specializing in financing for computer systems. Their site has lots of pages about leasing, but it also contains a calculator you can use to calculate the monthly payments on any lease based on the dollar amount and terms.

## Online Polls and Surveys

I mentioned a moment ago what a great tool the Internet is for research, and gave the ability to conduct interviews by e-mail as an example.

Another huge advantage the Internet gives you is the ability to do instant polls. If your Web site gets a large volume of traffic, you can get quick survey results by putting a poll on your home page.

Netscape's home page has a poll almost daily. It allows you to vote as well as see an up-to-the-minute tabulation of the results.

You can use a similar poll on your home page. Polling scripts are available at www.scriptsearch.com.

Since attention spans are short on the Web, limit your posted poll to single yes or no questions. You can run several polls over a period of a couple of months, then write an article reporting on and analyzing the results.

Alternatively, if you've built a database of opt-in e-mail addresses, you can send a short survey form via e-mail. Such a form can have half a dozen questions or more.

The recipient is asked to answer the questions and e-mail the completed form back to you. Response rates to an e-mail survey of your Web site visitors from an opt-in database are around 20 percent. If the subject of the survey is of personal interest to the people being surveyed, you can increase response by promising them a report on the survey results once it is completed.

Surveys are an extremely effective means of building your reputation as a leading expert in your field. Why is this so?

Earlier I mentioned that most gurus do not in fact create revolutionary new concepts, but basically repackage existing information. Surveys are the exception, because when you do a survey, you are automatically creating new information (the survey results) that did not exist before. It belongs to you and differentiates you from competing gurus who have not conducted their own survey.

For instance, Drake Beam Morin is an outplacement consulting firm whose marketing strategy is to position itself as a leader in career transition and job hunting. Each year they do a survey to determine the average number of months it takes an executive who has been fired to find a new job.

The release of the survey results gains broad distribution, since it is a topic of wide interest. People worry about what would happen to them if they lost their job, and are interested in how long it would take them to find a new one. When they read the number and see Drake Beam Morin as the source, they gain an impression of Drake Beam Morin as an expert authority in career issues.

## Building a Community of Interest on Your Site

Web marketers often speak of the "3 C's" of Web sites—commerce, community, and content.

*Commerce* is the ability to take orders over the Internet. *Community* means the site provides a forum, chat group, bulletin board, or other mechanism for visitors to share thoughts, opinions, and information about the subject of the site. *Content* is the information available to visitors on the site.

A "community of interest" on the Web is a group of like-minded people sharing information, experiences, and anecdotes on a topic of common interest. Why should you consider establishing such a community of interest on your site? Several reasons.

First, community increases Web site stickiness—how long people spend on your site and how frequently they return. If your Web site is not merely a place to buy products or read articles, but rather a place to gather, visitors will stay longer and come more often. To understand the importance of a gathering place in marketing, merely visit any Starbucks. People come for the coffee but stay for the environment.

Second, you can add community features at modest cost. It's a lot of added value for a small investment.

And third, as the "supervisor" or manager of your online community, you see and hear everything that goes on. This can tell you a lot about your visitors and what they want.

There are very few online communities that target every Internet user. Those few that do become portals.

Most online communities focus on a specific topic aimed at a specific audience. Example: Kibu.com aims at generating sales for its sponsors by becoming a community—they call it a "digital hangout"—for teenage girls. Experts in such areas as fashion, wellness, and relationships moderate chats on these topics in which the girls can participate.

CyberSite, Inc., oversees about 20 communities of interest. Their most popular is AncientSites, which is aimed at pre-Medieval history enthusiasts and has 90,000 registered members. "It (the community of interest) is a superior environment for selling merchandise," says CyberSites COO Keith Halper.

When I was putting together a new Web site on communications in the Internet age, www.espeakonline.com, Web programmers quoted me a high price to create custom software that would build the online community I wanted—for instance, a chat room, message forum, and online polling.

I wondered whether it was really necessary for these programmers to reinvent the wheel for each new client. Turns out, it's not. A lot of the online community functionality you want for your site is available as free CGI shareware scripts.

CGI stands for Common Gateway Interface, which is a standard for running external programs from a Web server. An interface-creation scripting program, CGI allows Web pages to be made on the fly based on information from buttons, checkboxes, and text input. For this reason, most interactive forms for building online communities are created using CGI.

To improve performance, Netscape devised NSAPI and Microsoft developed ISAPI. These standards allow CGI-like tasks to run as part of the main server process, thus avoiding the overhead of creating a new process to handle each CGI invocation.

Programmers have created large libraries of CGI scripts that you may use to create community-of-interest type functionality on your Web site. One such library, mentioned several times earlier in this chapter, is available at www.scriptsearch.com. There is usually no fee to use most of these scripts. Some allow free use in exchange for running their banners on your site.

The key to creating community on your Web site is having some kind of mechanism where visitors can exchange ideas, information, opinions, and resources on the topic of your site.

For instance, if you sell welding equipment, your community should deal with tips, techniques, and problems encountered in welding. *Welding*—not your particular product line—is the focus of the community. What promotes your product line is the fact that this community exists on your site. When participants need welding equipment or supplies, and their community is on your site, they are likely to look there first to fulfill their needs.

You have probably already seen or participated in many of the vehicles used to create online communities of interest:

- **Polls.** People love to give their opinion. You can use CGI scripts to do online surveys on your site. The scripts instantly tally the results and display them numerically and graphically, so you can learn how your opinions compare with other members of the online community.

- **Voting.** Voting is a variation of the online survey, the difference being the vote asks for an opinion on a single issue, while the survey has multiple questions. The voting results are tabulated and displayed for each voter after they vote.

- **Tests and quizzes.** In addition to giving opinions, site visitors also like to test their knowledge of your site's topic. Giving and scoring an online quiz adds an element of fun and challenge to the site. Be sure to change the quiz frequently so people come back for the new quizzes.

- **Message boards.** On a message board, forum, or "bulletin board," people can post and reply to messages on various topics. By reviewing the content of these discussions, which remain posted on the board, you can learn a lot about your visitors and their interests. You can also quote from these forums in articles and books you write. Just ask permission of the person who posted the material first.

■ **Chat rooms.** A chat room is a live discussion on a topic. Messages are not posted and left for consideration; they are typed and immediately responded to by people who are online at that moment.

■ **Guestbooks.** You can invite members of your online community to join as official members by filling out and submitting an online registration form or "guestbook." By doing so they qualify themselves by giving you a lot more information (address, company, phone number) than just their IP address.

To the online marketer, community may be the most important of the 3 C's. The greater the sense of community, the stronger the relationship between the users and the Web site.

Therefore, the users who have registered as members of your community and are on your e-list (and you can get almost all of them to opt-in by requiring them to register to use chat rooms, forums, and other favorite site features) have a great relationship with the site. This maximizes their receptiveness to e-marketing messages sent both by you and by other companies you allow to rent your e-list.

## Third-Party Endorsement Postings

Any company in business for any period of time will begin to get testimonials from satisfied customers. If you do not have testimonials, you can use the sample testimonial solicitation letter in Appendix C, "Sample Documents," to get customers to give them to you. My experience is that sending this letter to ten clients will get you three or four good testimonials.

If you already have testimonials, you should still get written permission from the client to use them in your promotions. Use the testimonial permission letter I have provided in Appendix C to secure it.

Start a separate page on your Web site where you post testimonials. Then—and this is the key—keep posting as many as you get. I know the Web usability experts say to keep Web pages short, but your testimonial page is the exception. Just keep piling on the testimonials.

As of this writing, my testimonial page is the equivalent of nine typed pages. An Internet consultant told me, "That's too long; no one will read it all."

She misses the point. It's not important whether the prospect reads all the testimonials. The sheer number impresses visitors as much or more than the specific content of the testimonials. The prospect sees the endless list and thinks, "If this guy has all these testimonials, he must be good."

Put the new ones in front as you get them; the old ones move to the rear. That way, the testimonial page appears fresh and new when visitors return to the site (most returning visitors will only glance at the top of the first page).

## Networking Online (and Offline, Too)

A lot of freelancers and self-employed professionals spend a lot of time networking online in various forums, chat rooms, and discussion groups.

I would caution you against spending any significant portion of your time doing such activities. Others, of course (and I am thinking in particular of Internet marketing gurus like Joe Vitale, Ilise Benun, and Marcia Yudkin) may disagree.

There are two reasons I feel this way. First, it is too easy to become addicted to this kind of online chatting. Minutes easily slide into hours. For small business owners and independent professionals, time is money, and productivity translates directly into revenue. Wasting time online means productivity and revenue suffer.

Time is a nonrenewable resource. Once it's gone, you can't get it back. Many gurus derive the bulk of their revenue by selling their time. If you spend all your time playing on your computer, you're not making money or getting your real work accomplished.

Second, aggressive networking presents an image you do not want to convey: that you are hungry and need the work. The late Howard Shenson, an authority on consulting, observed that clients want to work with vendors they perceive as busy and successful. He called this the "Busy Doctor Syndrome"—the doctor who has the fullest waiting room and the busiest schedule is the one who attracts the most patients. If people see you constantly putting out feelers in online forums, it shows you to be in a business-seeking mode—which, if you were a guru, you would never be.

The Busy Doctor Syndrome applies to offline networking as well as online. Entrepreneurs think of networking as "free advertising," but in reality, it's tremendously expensive.

Here's why: In offline networking, it's axiomatic that any networking opportunity eats up, at minimum, half a day of billable time. If you bill $2,000 a day, going to a networking event costs you at least $1,000 in lost billings. The tab for going to 10 such events can exceed $10,000.

Also, if you show up at every meeting, participate in every group, and are actively involved on half a dozen committees, people view you as having too much time on your hands—again, not the image a guru wants to convey.

Does this mean I oppose online and offline networking? I am certainly against the traditional approach to networking, which is to be a busy beaver, flitting from meeting to meeting.

If you are going to network—online or offline—I suggest you limit yourself to one activity each, online and offline. Online, that might be a particular forum or discussion group. Offline, pick one association or club.

If you overnetwork, you'll spread yourself too thin. Limiting your networking to one or two activities allows you to gain steady exposure to a group without excessive commitment of valuable time.

Make sure the venues where you have chosen to network are squarely focused on your niche market, not the world at large. If you sell database systems to directory publishers, attending meetings of the Directory Publishers Forum is more time-effective than, say, joining the Chamber of Commerce.

## Search Engines

When Web surfers are looking for goods and services like yours, you want your site to show up at the very top of a search engine's list, not on the tenth (or even the third) page. But the way search engines work is a mystery to most. So let's debunk a few myths and then put the search engines into perspective.

First of all, not all search engines are alike, and the difference boils down to the various ways that they acquire, store, categorize and search through data. Some send automated robots (called "spiders" or "crawlers") out to scour the Web, then take the data back to index it. Others wait for you to submit your site to them. And still others do a little bit of both.

So if you want to be included in the search engines you have to do two things:

1. Design your Web site so that it will be easily found by the search engines that scour the Web.

2. Submit your site to the major search engines and directories.

As soon as your site goes up, companies may e-mail you and say "Just pay us $99 and we'll get you top search engine rankings!" It would be nice if that was true, but if it was true then everyone would do it, and everyone can't get onto the first page of a popular search, right? So you're better off learning how to make sure your site is ready for search engines, and submitting your site yourself.

If you want the robots and spiders to find you, your Web site needs a relevant title for the home page. The title of a Web page appears in two very important places: at the top of the browser window when someone visits your site, and as the name of the bookmark when a visitor bookmarks your site. Search engines also often display your title when your Web site appears in their search results.

Sometimes the title is the only thing a person will see, and on which they'll base their decision to click or not to click, so make sure your title is a phrase or sentence that clearly describes your Web site. For example, if your site was about a sewing service, you might title it, "Sewing services, custom design, and production on curtains, pillows, slipcovers, and clothing alterations." That way you've not only said what your service is—but also included *key words* which people might search for.

A word that appears in your title is considered more important by most search engines than words that appear in the body of your page. So try to include specific words you think people looking for your products or services would search for.

Most search engines *don't* have a limit on how long a title can be. But only 70 or so characters will actually *appear* in the results. These are all the words related to your product or service that your customers will use to search for your site. Your keywords should be included in the html code of your Web site (these are known as meta tags). You should also include your keywords in an introduction to visitors on your home page.

For example, Everyday Gaiters is a small business run by Sarah Tyree and her husband. Their site, www.boothuggers.com, sells gaiters and boothuggers. Their meta tags include words that relate to their product, such as gaiters, boots, gloves, mittens, winter, snow, skiing, snowboard, snowmobiling, ice fishing, children, kids, sliding, clothing, hunting. So when someone performs a search using one of these keywords, www. boothuggers.com should appear in the results.

More and more, the number of links to and from a Web site is being used to rank a site. The idea is that the more links you have, the more popular your site must be, so it deserves a higher ranking. That's why, in addition to submitting your site to the search engines, it's essential to spend time trading links with sites of similar topics. And be sure to have a links page of your own with lots of links to sites of similar interests.

It's essential to submit your site to the search engines. Because there are so many search engines, there are search engine submission services, like www.selfpromotion.com and www. submitit.com available to help you—some free, others for a fee. Just make sure you submit your site yourself to the major search engines, to make sure it's done correctly.

The search engines you should register with include Yahoo!, AltaVista, Excite, Lycos, HotBot, Ask Jeeves, Google, and Go. Yahoo! is a special case. It's a directory, rather than a traditional search engine, and you are required to submit your site manually by filling out an application on the site. Then, they send a real person (not a robot) to visit your site, to evaluate it and place it in the hierarchy of the directory, which can take several months, so be patient.

For those in a hurry, Yahoo! offers a service where, for approximately $100, your site gets a priority viewing, but that *doesn't* guarantee that you get listed any faster. Although Yahoo! requires a lot of extra effort, it is one of the most popular directories on the Web, so listing your site here is well worth it.

There are also search engines, like Goto.com, where you can buy your way into the results. They offer an inexpensive pay-for-placement arrangement that can provide a fast jump start. You select the search terms or keywords that you think people will use to find a site like yours, then you decide how much you are willing to pay on a per-click basis for each of those search terms. The higher your "bid," the higher in the search results your site appears.

Creative Webmasters are using Web sites such as eBay.com as a search engine. An eBay listing costs as little as $2, and can generate lots of leads from people who are in the market for your product, so it's a fast, effective way to reach a targeted group. (This works best for people with products, rather than services.)

According to an article in *The Industry Standard,* the trend for the future is away from the currently popular general search engines and toward topic-specific search engines that specialize in particular industries, such as music or graphic design. Voila, a company based in France (www.voila.com), is one of the Web sites experimenting with this.

You don't have to sign up for every search engine on the planet—just the major ones, and ones that specialize in your particular field (if they exist). In some fields, there are no search engines, but there are popular sites that contain a lot of lists. If you find a site like this, contact the Webmaster to see if you can trade links.

Search engines are important when it comes to online marketing, but there's still no guarantee that if you follow these steps, your site will be listed in the top rankings. So don't make the mistake of depending on search engines to drive traffic to your Web site.

Be proactive, and use other forms of marketing to spread the word. First and foremost, put your Web address everywhere you can think of. Spend time networking—online and offline. Go to the Web sites where people are already researching and discussing your topic.

Participate in the discussion forums on those sites. Get a link to and from those sites. Do whatever you can to get your name out there in cyberspace, because it's the accumulation of references and links to your site that will turn surfers into visitors, and visitors into buyers. ■

# Chapter 11

# Profiting from Your Guru Status

Praise, recognition, and some degree of fame in your industry are wonderful, but for most people who take the time and effort to become gurus, the bottom line is making more money. In this chapter we look at how to capitalize on your guru status and use it to sell lots of your products and services at higher prices than you charged when you were less well known.

## Referrals

The easiest way for you, the guru, to get new clients is through referrals from existing clients, prospects, colleagues, fans, and even competitors. Yet asking for referrals is often neglected in favor of other marketing techniques such as cold calling, letter writing, and proposals.

"Without question, selling through referrals is the most powerful way to build your business, not to mention the most enjoyable," writes sales trainer Bill Cates in his book *Unlimited Referrals* (Wheaton, Maryland: Thunder Hill Press). "Your buyers would rather meet you through a referral. The endorsement and testimony of others makes them feel more comfortable opening their door to you and giving you their business."

How do you go about getting referrals? You do it by calling your best customers and asking them for referrals.

Although this can be a separate call, it's better if combined with a call for another purpose—to keep in touch, check on customer satisfaction, follow up on a job you submitted, or check on the status of a project. Here's how it might go:

**You:** Mike, can I ask you a question?

**Prospect:** Sure, go ahead.

**You:** You seem pretty satisfied with the work I have done for you … am I right?

**Prospect:** Yes, very.

**You:** Would you be comfortable recommending my speaking services to colleagues of yours who are not direct competitors with your firm?

**Prospect:** Of course.

**You:** Which of these people could I get in touch with to let them know about my program and how it can help him?

**Prospect:** Joe Doakes at Hummingbird Industries.

**You:** And do you have Joe's phone number?

**Prospect:** XXX-XXX-XXXXX.

**You:** Joe Doakes at Hummingbird. May I use your name when I call him?

**Prospect:** Certainly.

**You:** Great. I'll call Joe. Who else do you know who might be able to benefit from our services?

You then repeat the cycle, ending with "And who else?" until the prospect gives you all the referrals he or she is going to give you right now. By asking "And who else?" you will probably get two or three referrals instead of the one the prospect was going to give you. Three is probably the limit for one call—the prospect will run out of ready names and get tired of giving the referrals—but ask until they say "That's it."

I recommend you send a thank-you note to customers who give you referrals. A small, tasteful gift is optional. (I send a copy of one of my books.)

Keep the customer up to date if anything comes from the referral. If you get business out of it, send another thank-you and a slightly better gift (my choice is a gift basket of muffins from Wolferman's—1-800-999-1910) or one of your expensive video tape programs.

You can ask these same customers for more referrals later on. Just don't do it too frequently. Once every four or five months seems about right. If you do something particularly good for them, such as solve a problem or complete a successful project, by all means ask for a reference as you bask in the glow of their praise.

Don't neglect *internal* referrals: Getting someone you know in an organization to refer you to the training buyer. Executives are often more willing to see you if the referral is from someone in their own organization than from someone outside.

## Repeat Orders

Most speakers concentrate on new business. Here's how to win lucrative ongoing repeat business from existing clients. Repeat assignments are easier to get and take less time to prepare for, since you are already familiar with the audience and their needs.

Because many salespeople love the thrill of the chase, and because they often get bigger commissions for bringing in new customers, soliciting repeat sales and reorders from active accounts is often ignored at the expense of pursuing new business.

Not every salesperson makes this mistake. Stockbrokers, for example, know the value of working existing accounts. If you have an account with a brokerage, you get frequent calls from your broker offering new ideas for companies he wants you to invest in. But salespeople in some other industries are not as savvy. For example, the company that sold me my computer has never contacted me to offer any upgrades or new services, despite the fact that they sell many I would want—more memory, a better CD-ROM drive, higher resolution laser printer, or home page design. A mistake? I think so.

Have a plan for periodically contacting active customers to remind them of your existence and give them news of any special offers, discounts, new services, or new ideas for writing projects they might benefit from. Doing so will substantially increase reorders and repeat sales from your database of existing clients.

In particular, let existing customers know of new services or products you are offering. This cross-selling will get existing customers to give you orders they would have never thought to call you for before.

Experience shows that an active customer is 5 to 10 times more likely to buy something from you than a prospect you cold-call from a prospecting directory or telemarketing list. That means "working your database" can yield 5 to 10 times the response of a new business or customer acquisition effort aimed at a similar number of prospects.

How frequently should you keep in touch with existing customers? It's different for every business, but for gurus in the maintenance stage of their careers (see Chapter 2, "How to Join the Guru Elite"), a contact every quarter—a call or mailing once every three months, for a total of four in a given year—makes sense. It's frequent enough so the customer doesn't forget about you. But infrequent enough so that you're not pestering customers or spending an inordinate amount of time and money making these contacts.

If possible, make most of the contacts phone calls. You can increase frequency of contact by adding one, two, or three mailings a year ... or by substituting a mailing for one or two of the four annual phone calls … and by using e-mail. The mailing need not be elaborate. Remember, this is just to keep in touch and keep your name before the customer. A simple postcard or short sales letter is more than sufficient.

"Seek a reason to keep in touch with your existing clients so they don't fall into a dormant cycle," writes Loriann Oberlin in her book *Writing for Money* (Writer's Digest Books). "It takes much less effort to sell a previously satisfied client on a new job than a customer unfamiliar with your work. Send correspondence and clippings your clients might appreciate and schedule lunch meetings periodically to discuss your client's changing needs."

## Resales

Never create a product, system, program, or report that you only do once. If you customize a program for a client, create a generic version (eliminating anything proprietary you created for them, of course) and sell that to other firms with similar training needs.

Consider creating versions of your programs that corporations can license from you. For the client who wants to train thousands of their employees in your area of expertise, it might be better and more cost-effective for them to have their own in-house trainers give your course rather than bring you in so many times. You create workbooks and a teacher's guide for the trainer, including camera-ready handout masters they can reproduce with their photocopier or reprographics department.

You get a fee—maybe $1/10$ or $1/4$ of what your fee would be if you conducted the session personally—for each time the course is presented. They save on your travel expenses and the majority of your fee. You in turn earn passive income, getting paid whenever they give the course, even though you are not doing the presentation yourself.

When you have such a reproducible course in a binder and with workbooks so trainers other than you can give it, you can also franchise your program. Other trainers can buy the rights to give the presentation using your materials. You could charge a flat franchise fee, a per presentation fee, or some combination.

## Investing Your Guru Income

My father once told me, "Money is not important, as long as you're happy." But I disagree. Direct marketing guru Ted Nicholas, writing in his *Direct Marketing Success Letter* (April 23, 1997, page 2), says: "The happiest possible life ideally rests on a balance between four elements: health, career, personal relationships, and money." I share Ted's view.

We became gurus for a variety of reasons. Freedom to do work you enjoy is one factor that motivates us to leave the corporate world and become self-employed. Another is the opportunity to earn more money than we would working for someone else.

The old definition of rich was $100,000 a year in income or $1 million in net worth. People still use these benchmarks mentally to judge income or wealth, but inflation has made them less valid. Even with a modest annual salary of $50,000, a two-income couple earns $100,000 a year. And people now become millionaires weekly on TV game shows or playing the lottery.

## How to Calculate Your Earning Potential

To plan your financial life, you need some idea of what you will earn. For the independent professional selling his or her services, it's fairly easy to calculate income potential.

Most gurus charge by the day. If you charge $2,000 per day, and bill clients for 150 days a year, that's a gross income of

$300,000. Not all of your time is billable. You don't get paid for self-education and development. Nor do you get paid for marketing, following up, cultivating clients, or administrative tasks such as bookkeeping and billing.

The amount of billable time a guru has per week varies with the individual. Typically, half your time is spent on work for which you can bill the client. A quarter is spent on self-promotion, marketing, sales, and program design. The rest is spent on running your office and continuing education (reading books like this one, subscriptions to industry journals, taking seminars).

This does not take into account income from sources other than straight billable time, such as commissions, performance bonuses, royalties, and any additional compensation you have negotiated with clients. If you have these kinds of fee arrangements, your income can be more variable.

An income of $300,000 makes you a top wage earner, but far from wealthy. In his book *Money* (Scribner, 1997, p. 67), Andrew Hacker notes that 9 percent of American households have annual income of $100,000 a year or more. "This is far from being rich," Hacker says.

## Financial Planning for Self-Employed Professionals

The most important piece of advice I can give to any person as far as investing and money is concerned is: Start early. In fact start now. Don't wait. The longer you wait to start investing, the more difficult it will be to achieve your financial goals and retire in relative comfort and wealth.

Why is getting an early start so important? *Compound interest.* Investments earn annual returns ranging from 1 percent to 25 percent and sometimes much more. Naturally, the longer you hold an investment and it earns a return, the more its value increases.

But thanks to compound interest, the increase in value is not merely linear; it's almost exponential. Therefore, when you start early, your investments will grow in value much more spectacularly than someone who gets a late start. In his book *Money Doesn't Grow on Trees* (Cumberland House), investment counselor Mark Dutton says, "Compound interest is the eighth wonder of the world."

And with this comes a warning: If you don't start now, you'll lose out. The most important thing you can do to assure a healthy financial future is to start at 20 instead of 30, or if you're 30, start at 30 instead of waiting until 40.

If you start late, you lose 10 years of compound interest— a 10-year start on building your wealth. The total you end up with will decline enormously. And once you let those early years go, you can never reclaim them; the "magic" of the compound interest is lost forever.

For instance, Merrill Lynch says that a person who puts $2,000 a year in an IRA starting at age 18 will retire with more than double the savings of a person who starts only 10 years later, at age 28.

Wayne Kolb, CPA, had an even more dramatic example in his *Tax Planning* newsletter (June 1995). Let's say an 18-year-old invests $2,000 annually in an IRA through age 25, with an annual return average of 10 percent, and then stops. By age 65, his IRA will be worth more than $1 million! Not a bad return for a $16,000 investment.

By comparison, if a person waits until age 25 to start an IRA, as I did, he or she will need to invest $2,000 a year until retirement to have $1 million. Two thousand dollars a year for 40 years, from age 25 to 65, is $80,000—meaning the person who started his IRA 7 years later, at age 25 instead of 18, had to put in 5 times the investment of the person who started earlier.

But whatever your age when you read this, if you haven't started investing in earnest, the best advice I can give is: Do so now. Not in a week, but now. An example from Prudential Securities dramatizes this point: If you open an IRA at age 50, and contribute $2,000 a year earning 8 percent compounded monthly, at age 65 your IRA will be worth $54,300.

Had you opened the same IRA when you were 25, and put in the same amount of money annually earning the same rate of return, at age 65 your IRA would be worth more than half a million dollars—almost ten times as much.

It is never too late to start investing, but the earlier you start, the better off you will be in your later years.

## Be a Saver, Not a Spender

Be a saver. Invest. Americans are notoriously behind the rest of the world when it comes to accruing wealth. The average American family saves only 5 percent of their earnings each year, compared with nearly 10 percent in the UK and almost 13 percent in Sweden.

Before you spend your paycheck, invest at least 10 percent of it. My habit is to invest in increments of $10,000: Once I have an extra $10,000 in my bank account, beyond the balance I need to maintain to pay bills and living expenses, I invest it, whether in a mutual fund, bond, or stock. I advise you to do the same.

In the young Generation X, a spirit of entrepreneurship, combined with a rash of technology entrepreneurs who became multimillionaires, leads younger people to the erroneous conclusion that wealth can always be generated quickly and solely through one's ingenuity, ideas, and labor.

But in reality, the richest Americans are savers and investors. Among Americans who have an annual income of $1 million or more, the average makes only a third of that income from their job or business. The rest is generated from investments: money making more money. By comparison, the average American earning under $50,000 a year gets almost all of that income—85 percent—from employment; only 15 percent is passive income generated from investments.

Because Americans are not savers, the median total net worth of families with parents in the 35- to 45-year age group is only $35,000. Their share of the national debt, by comparison, is $78,000 per family.

More than half of all wage earners become dependent on their families, pensions, the community, or social security to live in their old age. Yet according to Prudential Securities, social security and employer-sponsored pension plans provide only 59 percent of aggregate retirement income. Only 5 percent of the population retires financially independent and in relative comfort.

The best financial advice I ever received was, "Live below your means." Do not build debt by acquiring so many possessions that decrease in value. Invest in assets that appreciate in value. Collect interest rather than pay it.

## Invest for Return

Do not be too conservative in your investments, especially when you are young and can afford to take risks. My father lived through the Great Depression, the aftermath of the Stock Market Crash of 1929, and therefore associated the stock market with poverty and loss. He owned little or no common stock, and only later in life would he invest, minimally, in mutual funds (once he even took a test and got licensed to sell them, but never pursued it).

The fact is, however, stocks produce a greater return than other investments over time. The 71-year inflation-adjusted rate of return of stocks is 9.83 percent. Government bonds returned only 2.16 percent and treasury notes only 0.62 percent over the same period.

A doctor whose office is a few blocks from mine once told me, "You will never get rich doing piecemeal work, no matter how much you charge. To become wealthy, you have to participate in the market." Make your money work for you. If you content yourself with the paltry returns of CDs and other below-market investments, you will have to work harder and longer, and inevitably wind up with less.

Many novice and less-sophisticated investors lean too heavily on mutual funds to give them the returns of stocks without the risk, volatility, or the need to thoroughly understand the industries and businesses they're buying.

But I would steer you away from putting all of your portfolio in mutual funds—and encourage you to put some of your money in individual stocks—for this reason: Eighty percent of mutual fund managers underperform the S&P 500.

Why is this so? The Investment Act of 1940 requires diversified mutual funds to have at least 75 percent of their total assets invested in securities, with no single holding exceeding 5 percent of the total.

As a result of this legally mandated "forced diversity," the average equity portfolio holds 131 stocks—a quantity, says *The Wall Street Journal,* that "presumably provides for each manager's best down to his rainy day flotsam and jetsam, and maybe even a few he wouldn't wish on his own worst enemy." But instead, why not simply buy the one or two best stocks these money managers own—by buying them directly—and avoid the flotsam and jetsam you're forced to own when you buy their fund?

*The Wall Street Journal* gives a powerful condemnation against the overdiversifying of today's fund managers: "By owning too many names, they are reducing the impact of the stock-picking ability that supposedly got them their jobs—like a home-run hitter squaring to bunt." In a small, tightly focused portfolio of best-of-the-best picks, *The Wall Street Journal* observes, "there is no room for warm-hearted hospitality toward a stock that has reached its value."

*Barron's* states the problem this way: "Many funds—and the industry itself—have gotten too large to deliver superior returns." In 1977, mutual funds controlled 8 percent of the stock market. Today, funds control 22 percent of a $9.5 trillion stock market.

Jack Bogle, former chairman of the Vanguard Group, says it's "virtually inconceivable" that mutual funds controlling one-fifth of the market could actively outpace the market. And the facts prove him right. During a $2^{1}/_{2}$-year period ending June 1997, the average mutual fund returned 76 percent vs. 104 percent for the S&P. On an investment of $100,000, the mutual fund investor ended up $28,000 behind the market!

A $20 billion mutual fund can hold a whopping 362 stocks, assuming no holding exceeds 2 percent of its total portfolio or 10 percent of any company's outstanding shares.

But the usual "rap" money managers and others give you about safety in diversity is vastly overstated. One major research study shows that by owning only 8 stocks, you get 92 percent of the safety from diversity you would owning dozens or even hundreds—as long as your 8 are in several different industries. So the idea of a mutual fund as safer than stocks is largely inaccurate.

With so many stocks in their portfolios, mutual funds are, in reality, collections of investments with wildly varying performance. By selecting the top performers and spurning the rest, you and I can generate superior profits.

If you are not certain of your ability as a stock picker, but don't want to leave it up to a money manager either, considering buying stock index funds or annuities. They produce a return that mirrors the S&P 500, which was 21 percent in 1999, 28.58 percent in 1998, 33.36 percent in 1997, 22.96 percent in 1996, and 37.58 percent in 1995. For the 5-year period, that's a cumulative return on your investment of 450 percent. A $100,000 investment made in 1995 and held for those 5 years would have climbed to $351,111 by 2000, more than tripling your money in half a decade.

## Be Frugal

In addition to investing more, spend less. Lower your expenses. Were I to start over, I would live in an area where the lifestyle is good and employment opportunities are plentiful, but the cost of living is reasonable. According to an article in *USA Today* (February 17, 1998, page 6B), the median price of a single-family home in San Francisco, CA is $304,600. That's almost five times the average home price of $64,200 in Waterloo, Iowa, the hometown of seminar leader and speaker Tom Winninger.

The difference in cost of living within the United States is staggering. As noted, in San Francisco, the median home price is a whopping $304,600. In San Antonio, Texas, you can get the equivalent home for just $88,600. In the New York City metro area, where we live, the price is $177,700. I only stayed in the New York metro area because I wanted my kids to be close to their grandparents and have a strong relationship with them. Had our parents retired to Florida, my wife and I would have probably moved to a less costly area of the country. In the expensive cities, such as San Francisco and New York City, you don't get a lot of house for your money.

You might argue, "Yes, but the salaries are proportionally higher in the more expensive cities." They're higher, but not in proportion to the greater cost of living. Note that the home price in San Francisco is almost $3^1/_2$ times higher than the home price in San Antonio. Yet the median household income in 1995 for California, $37,009, is only 16 percent more than the $32,039 a year median household income in Texas. Those of us who live in or near the expensive cities usually have an overall higher cost of living than those who live in less central areas.

Do not throw money away. Combine abundance with thrift. When my net worth reached a million dollars in my late 30s, I was driving an 11-year-old Chevrolet Chevette, for which I had paid $6,500 in 1984.

Andrew Tobias says, "There is no smell more dangerous or costly than the new car smell." My father taught this lesson to me early. He drove me through the poor sections of Paterson, the city where he had his office and in which I was born. "What do you see, Bob?" he asked me. What I saw was that the poorest people, living in near-slum conditions, all had shiny new Cadillacs parked in front of dilapidated apartment buildings.

Now this luxury-car-as-status-symbol syndrome has moved up a notch. Scores of middle-class families with ordinary levels of income buy or lease a Mercedes Benz, Lexus, Infiniti, BMW, or other luxury car. Yet the average man age 35 to 44 earns a modest $31,420. As Thomas J. Stanley and William D. Danko observe in their book, *The Millionaire Next Door,* "Most millionaires do not drive luxury cars. Most luxury car drivers are not millionaires." Stanley and Danko also found that ordinary people who built wealth:

- Live well below their means
- Allocate their time, energy, and money efficiently

- Choose businesses and professions with good income potential
- Believe that financial independence is more important than displaying high social status

I am not against enjoying material possessions—in moderation. But being financially secure, not enjoying luxuries, is clearly my priority. When my wife, Amy, makes these comparisons between us and others who seem to have more status symbols in their lives, my reply is, "Yes ... but how many of them are millionaires?"

A large part of what you pay for brand-name luxury products is for the prestige of the name. A $100,000 car is rarely five times better than a $20,000 car. A lot of the $80,000 is for the status of driving the luxury model, not better comfort or performance. Most millionaires live in modest homes and drive used cars.

## Time vs. Money

There is one way, however, that I am not frugal where others seemingly are, and I advise you to follow my lead in this regard. I don't waste money or buy unnecessary luxuries. But unlike many people, I won't trade time for money. Money is a precious resource, but it can always be replaced. Time is even more precious, as it is a nonrenewable resource: Once an hour is gone, it is gone forever.

"Time is the most precious currency of life, and how we spend it reflects what we truly value," writes Richard J. Leider in his book *The Power of Purpose*. "Once we have spent it, it is gone forever. It cannot be re-earned."

I almost never go to price clubs, discount outlets, and other bargain basement retailers ... because there is no service. There are bargains to be had, but finding them takes time and energy I'd rather spend elsewhere. Merchants who sell better quality goods usually offer premium service. For the extra price, you get a sofa or table that you like better and that lasts longer—so although the purchase price is higher, the cost of ownership over its lifetime is equal or better than the bargain item. Add the time-savings and elimination of frustration that good service offers, and excessive penny pinching and bargain hunting makes little sense.

For example, I don't clip coupons. Some people argue that by not clipping coupons, I am literally throwing money in the garbage when we recycle our old newspapers.

But they ignore the time factor. I know what my time is worth, and everyone should. I bill $250 an hour in my consulting practice. Therefore, in one measure, my time is worth $4.17 a minute.

Using coupons not only requires you to search through the paper, clip, and meticulously file the coupons; you also have to check your coupon file before shopping, pull the appropriate coupons, put them in your pocket, find products on the shelves covered by the coupons, and then remember to present the coupons at check-out.

The bottom line: Clipping and redeeming $4 worth of coupons might take me 15 minutes total time. That's a cost of $62.50 to save $4. I'd rather skip the coupons, not waste the time, spend the extra $4, and put in 15 more minutes of work (something much more pleasurable to me than coupon clipping) and make the $62.50.

It makes sense to seek a bargain when it's right in front of you, but many people spend more resources shopping for the bargain than they save by buying the bargain. I marvel at a friend who will drive 20 minutes out of her way, each way, to pick up paper towels at a lower price than the grocery store offers. What a waste of time, energy, and human life!

There have been several articles about penny pinchers who, through vast ingenuity, live well on near-poverty levels of income. One even started a newsletter on the subject, *Tightwad Gazette*. But the penny pinching seems three times as hard work—and much more frustrating and grinding—than living normally. If these folks put the same energies toward their careers, they'd have better and easier lives.

Of course, your expenditures should be less than your revenue. But how much is going out? Try this simple technique: get a receipt for *every single purchase,* no matter how small, for one month. Save all the receipts in a box. At the end of the month, add up all the receipts. The total gives you a good sense of what you spend monthly.

Here is the easiest rule I have learned for putting investment returns in perspective. Divide 72 by the annual return on investment, and the answer tells you how long it will take to double your money at that rate. If you are earning 8 percent after tax annual return on an investment of $10,000, divide 72 by 8, and you get 9. That means in 9 years you will double your money, and your original $10,000 will be worth $20,000.

Lord Kelvin said, "When you can measure something, and talk about it in numbers, you know something about it." Many of the important things in life—love, relationships, kindness, caring, behavior, and ethics—cannot be measured quantitatively. But your net worth can be calculated to the penny.

There's an old saying: "Money isn't everything in business; it isn't the sole factor defining success; but it is how people keep score." Throughout your life, you will often ask yourself, "Am I successful?" The search for a meaningful answer can be difficult and frustrating. Many of us spend our lives in search of that answer.

At least the money portion can be measured. Don't sacrifice your life for money. Don't put it so far ahead of the other elements of your life—family, friends, health, career, accomplishment, personal fulfillment—that these other elements go largely unfulfilled.

But do make the accumulation of wealth a priority in your life. When you have enough money that you can describe yourself as "comfortable," that's indeed how you feel: more secure, more content, less worried, proud of what you have accomplished, and more comfortable with who, what, and where you are in life. This I can attest to from personal experience.

## Retirement Plans and Other Retirement Investments for Self-Employed Professionals

Joseph E. Kehoe, a manager at Prudential Securities, says "recent Social Security Administration data suggests that, on average, social security and employer-sponsored pension plans provide only 59 percent of aggregate retirement income."

The best advice for retirement savings is to start early. According to Merrill Lynch, an individual who starts an IRA at 18 will retire with more than double the net wealth they would accrue by starting at age 28.

Start and contribute annually to a self-funded retirement plan, such as a 401(k) or IRA. I prefer the 401(k), since you can contribute more money than in an IRA.

## Tax Deductions

As a self-employed professional, one of your most miserable financial burdens will be paying for your own health insurance. Fortunately, the government may step in to help you by at least making these costly premiums tax-deductible.

According to an article in the Fall 1997 issue of *Perspective,* a Prudential Securities newsletter, the percentage of health insurance premiums for the self-employed and their families that may be deducted will increase to 50 percent in 2001, 60 percent in 2002, 80 percent in 2003, 2004, and 2005, 90 percent in 2006, and 100 percent starting in 2007.

As for medical expenses not covered by insurance, the itemized deduction for these costs is limited to the amounts exceeding 6.5 percent of adjusted gross income (source: *Tax Report,* September 1997, Dunich Kolb LLC).

The June 1995 issue of the *Tax Planning Letter* discusses a long-practiced but little-known tax deduction: hiring your children to work for your business. You can hire a child to do routine clerical or clean-up tasks. Your child's salary becomes a tax-deductible business expense, and at least $3,900 of each child's income from your consulting business is tax-free. Income in excess of $3,900 is taxed at your child's annual income level, which is much lower than yours. Even better, you can put up to $2,000 a year of the working child's compensation into an IRA for that child, which will enjoy years of tax-deferred growth.

The most popular and talked-about deduction for work-at-home professionals is the ability to deduct for home office expenses. Consult your accountant or other tax advisor before doing your taxes.

As a rule, you can deduct the cost of space in the home that is used solely for your business. So if you have a seven-room house and use a spare bedroom as the office for your consulting practice, you can deduct the cost of this space as a percentage of total home square footage. On the other hand, if you work at the kitchen table during the day, then sweep it clean and eat dinner there each night, you can't take the kitchen as a home office deduction.

When you are self-employed, it's critical to keep detailed, meticulous records of all business-related expenses. So many work-at-home professionals I know are sloppy about receipts, either not getting them or not filing them. As a result, they miss out on hundreds, even thousands of dollars of legitimate expense deductions they haven't kept track of, which in turn means a bigger tax bill. Financial advisor Bill Bresnan notes, "You will see rich people writing down every penny they spend in a notebook, because they take every deduction to which they are legally entitled."

According to the American Express booklet *Financial Facts for the Small Business Owner*, the most commonly overlooked business deductions include the following:

- Accounting fees for legal or tax work related to business
- Books for business purposes
- Business calls charged to a personal phone
- Business conventions, workshops, and meetings
- Business entertainment expenses
- Dues and fees for professional organizations
- Twenty-five percent of passport fees for business travel
- Subscriptions to business periodicals and newspapers
- Uniforms and the cost of their care
- Investment management and advice fees
- Appraisal fees to determine a casualty loss
- Certain employee education expenses
- Dividend reinvestment plan fees
- Safe-deposit box rental
- Business parking

Independent professionals are running small businesses, and their tax returns reflect that complexity. Even though a good tax accountant may charge $1,000 and up to prepare your personal and business returns, having such an advisor on your team is well worth the price.

## Health Insurance Is the Number-One Financial Problem of Self-Employment

The skyrocketing cost of medical care in the United States is a national issue, and health insurance is a major problem for thousands of self-employed people. When you work for a large corporation, you get medical insurance as a benefit; when you are self-employed, you have to provide your own coverage—and, it's expensive.

Even through groups, self-employed people can rarely match the coverage they received when they were under a corporate plan. Your health insurance premiums will likely run you thousands of dollars a year. In return, your coverage will be more limited than what you enjoyed under your corporate plan. For example, our policy does not reimburse us for medical care until the total bills for a single condition or illness exceed $500. So we end up paying for virtually all minor and routine doctor visits out of our own pocket.

With the rise in managed care, you now have the option of joining an HMO or other care plan. This is often the only way of getting coverage equivalent to what a corporate employee would have, at an affordable cost. The drawback may be an inability to continue seeing your current doctor, as most plans force you to use physicians of their own choosing.

Health insurance is often available to independent and free-lance professionals at reduced group rates through their associations. If you are not a member of the association in your trade or industry, consider joining it for the insurance benefits.

## Life Insurance—How Much Do You Need? What Type Is Best?

If you are single, you probably don't need life insurance. Married people whose spouse earns a good income also don't need life insurance. But if you have a family that depends on your income, life insurance is probably a good idea.

Life insurance is designed to provide you with an "instant estate," so that if you die, your family has enough money to live without hardship. For those of us who have already achieved significant net worth, life insurance isn't necessary; our own estate will leave our heirs the money they need. But if you have a more modest net worth, are just starting out, have many children, or are saving to put your kids through college, life insurance can provide your heirs with an estate beyond your current assets.

Many associations offer members life insurance. You can also contact a local insurance agent. Prices vary widely, so shop around.

*Term* life insurance has a low monthly or annual premium, and can pay a death benefit of $10,000 to $300,000 or more, depending on the policy you buy. You pay for it every year. It's the most affordable life insurance coverage. The premium can and does usually go up—and up—as you get older, so many people drop their term policies as they approach an age when they're more likely to die. And unfortunately, once you stop paying, you lose the benefit.

*Whole* or "universal" life insurance is a combination of insurance and investment. The policy pays a death benefit, but also has cash value; both increase as the years go by. The premium is fixed and cannot go up. Some insurance companies offer a "vanishing premium," meaning after a certain number of years, you don't have to pay anymore, but still own the policy and are entitled to the benefits.

The disadvantage of whole life, according to many experts, is the premiums are high—many times greater than premiums for term insurance of comparable coverage—and the return on the investment portion of the policy is frequently below-market. Take a look at both types of coverage and decide; perhaps you'll have both types of coverage.

## Disability Insurance

What happens if you become disabled and cannot work? Disability isn't only for blue-collar workers, tradespeople, and others doing physical work. Suppose you lost your ability to use a keyboard or talk on the phone. The consequences to your earnings potential could be devastating.

Disability insurance pays a predetermined sum weekly or monthly if you cannot work. Policy terms and conditions vary widely. Some policies start paying right away; others have a 90-day or longer period before the payments begin. Some policies pay off for as long as the disability lasts; others are more limited.

The best place to shop for disability insurance is through associations. They will offer a group rate that you, as an individual, cannot hope to match. For the self-employed seminar leader grossing $100,000 to $200,000 a year, a disability policy paying at least $50,000 annually should be sufficient coverage, unless you have exceptionally large expenses. ■

*Appendix A*

# Bibliography

## Books

Bly, Robert. *The Copywriter's Handbook: A Step-by-Step Guide to Writing Copy That Sells* (New York: Henry Holt & Co., 1990).
How to write effective copy.

―――. *Getting Started in Speaking, Training, or Seminar Consulting* (New York: John Wiley & Sons, 2000).
How to get speaking and seminar engagements.

―――. *How to Get Your Book Published* (Yonkers, NY: Roblin Press, 2000).
How to write a nonfiction book and get it published.

―――. *Power-Packed Direct Mail* (New York: Henry Holt & Co., 1995).
A guide to planning, writing, designing, and producing direct mail promotions.

―――. *Selling Your Services* (New York: Henry Holt & Co., 1994).
Selling skills for service providers.

―――. *Start and Run a Successful Mail Order Business* (North Vancouver, BC: Self Counsel Press, 1997).
How to sell information products and other goods by mail order.

————. *The Perfect Sales Piece* (New York: John Wiley & Sons, 1993).
Guide to creating effective brochures, catalogs, and other sales literature.

Caples, John. *Tested Advertising Methods* (Englewood Cliffs, NJ: Prentice Hall, 1974).
Secrets of writing effective space ads.

Cates, Bill. *Unlimited Referrals* (Wheaton, MD: Thunder Hill Press, 1996).
How to get lots of referral leads.

Floyd, Elaine. *Marketing with Newsletters* (St. Louis, MO: Newsletter Resources, 1994).
How to create effective promotional newsletters.

Harris, Godfrey, with J. Harris. *Generate Word of Mouth Advertising: 101 Easy and Inexpensive Ways to Promote Your Business* (Los Angeles, CA: The Americas Group, 1995).
Interesting, innovative low-cost promotions for yourself and your clients.

Lant, Jeffrey. *No More Cold Calls* (Cambridge, MA: JLA Publications, 1994).
How to generate leads for your service business.

Muldoon, Katie. *How to Profit Through Catalog Marketing* (Lincolnwood, IL: NTC Business Books, 1996).
Recommended for anyone writing catalog copy.

Ogilvy, David. *Ogilvy on Advertising* (New York: Crown, 1989).
Required for every copywriter writing print ads.

Reeves, Rosser. *Reality in Advertising* (New York: Alfred A. Knopf, 1985).
Excellent book on how to increase advertising effectiveness.

Sayles, Sarah. *Creative Direct Mail Design* (Rockport, MA: Rockport Publishers, 1998).
How to illustrate and design direct mail pieces.

Smith, Terry. *Making Successful Presentations* (New York: John Wiley & Sons, 1984).
Excellent guide to writing and delivering workplace, instructional, and sales and marketing presentations.

Stone, Bob. *Successful Direct Marketing Methods, Seventh Edition* (Chicago, IL: NTC Business Books, 2000).
Everything you need to know about direct marketing.

Vitale, Joe. *CyberWriting: How to Promote Your Product or Service Online* (New York: AMACOM, 1997).
How to write copy for the Internet.

Yaverbaum, Eric. *Public Relations Kit for Dummies* (Indianapolis: Hungry Minds, 2000).
How to get yourself featured in the media.

## Directories

### Bacon's Publicity Checklist
332 S. Michigan Avenue
Chicago, IL 60604
1-800-621-0561
Media lists for mailing press releases.

### The Encyclopedia of Associations
Gale Research
Book Tower
Detroit, MI 48226
313-961-2242
Associations to whose membership lists you can target promotions.

**Exhibitors Resource Directory**
206 S. Broadway, Suite 745
Rochester, MN 55904
507-289-6556
A directory of trade show suppliers.

**The Interactive Multimedia Sourcebook**
R. R. Bowker
121 Chanlon Road
New Providence, NJ 07974
908-464-6800
Sourcebook for marketers interested in Internet promotion.

**National Directory of Mailing Lists**
Oxbridge Communications
150 Fifth Avenue
New York, NY 10114-0235
1-800-955-0231
Directory containing descriptions and contact information for
15,000 mailing lists.

**O'Dwyers Directory of Public Relations Firms**
J. R. O'Dwyer & Company, Inc.
271 Madison Avenue
New York, NY 10016
212-679-2471
Directory of public relations firms.

**Standard Directory of Advertising Agencies**
R. R. Bowker
121 Chanlon Road
New Providence, NJ 07974
908-464-6800
Directory of advertising agencies.

**Standard Rate and Data Service**
1700 Higgins Road
Des Plaines, IL 60018-5605
847-375-5000
Comprehensive directory of publications that accept advertising.

**Writer's Market**
1507 Dana Avenue
Cincinnati, OH 45207
513-531-2222

**Yearbook of Experts, Authorities, and Spokespersons**
2233 Wisconsin Avenue NW
Washington, DC 20007
1-800-932-7266
Sourcebook used by editors and producers to find experts to interview for their publications and feature as guests on their shows. Gurus can purchase listings and ads.

**Web Site**

**Speaking Success**
www.dubinspeak.com
Tips on how to become a successful professional speaker.

# *Appendix B*

# Recommended Vendors

To accomplish some of the tasks outlined in this book, you may want to work with outside vendors or e-business solution providers. This list is by no means comprehensive—it simply lists the vendors I recommend in each category right now. A recommendation doesn't guarantee your satisfaction, so you should check out vendors thoroughly before hiring them. You may find updates to this list on www.bly.com and e-business solution providers at www.evendorsonline.com.

## Audio and Video Duplicating
**Cine Magnetics**
100 Business Park Drive
Armonk, NY 10504-1750
1-800-431-1102 or
914-273-7500

## Audio Taping
**Anthony Cioffi**
Boulevard Productions
280 Boulevard
New Milford, NJ 07646
Phone: 201-262-5202
Fax: 201-262-5216

## Business Plans
**Lisa Hines**
Business Plan Concepts
134 Oklyn Terrace
Lawrenceville, NJ 08648
609-530-0719

## Cartoons
**The Cartoon Bank**
A division of *New Yorker* magazine
382 Warburton Avenue
Hastings on Hudson, NY 10706
1-800-897-8666 or
914-478-5527
www.cartoonbank.com

**Ted Goff**
PO Box 22679
Kansas City, MO 64113
816-822-7370
E-mail: tgoff@tedgoff.com
Web site: www.tedgoff.com

## CD-ROM Duplication and Packaging

**Disc Makers**
7905 N. Route 130
Pennsauken, NJ 08110
1-800-237-6666

## Competitive Intelligence

**Brian Donnelly**
Data Source International
200 Business Park Drive, #304
Armonk, NY 10504
914-273-6100

**Doug House**
Washington Information Group
1350 Connecticut Avenue NW #502
Washington, DC 20036
202-463-3284

## Digital Printing

**Paul Lukas, Account Executive**
Regent Group
20 West 20th Street
New York, NY 10011
212-691-9791

## Feature Syndicates

**Universal Press Syndicate**
45-20 Main Street, Suite 700
Kansas City, MO 64111
816-932-6600

**AP Newsfeatures**
50 Rockefeller Plaza
New York, NY 10020
212-621-1500

**Los Angeles Times Syndicate**
202 W. First Street
Los Angeles, CA 90053
213-237-5000

## Freelance Writer

**Linda Kallman**
402 North Broadway
Upper Nyack, NY 10960
914-358-5202
Web content, editorial, PR, newsletters, marcom, corporate com

## Ghostwriters (Books, Articles)

**Author's, Publisher's, and Writer's Hotline**
7 Putter Lane
Middle Island, NY
516-924-8555

**American Society of Journalists and Authors**
New York, NY
212-997-0947

**David Kohn**
3117 Lake Shore Drive
Deerfield Beach, FL 33442
954-429-9373

**Editorial Freelancers Association**
New York, NY
212-929-5400

**Jerry Gross**
63 Grand Street
Croton on Hudson, NY
10520-2518
914-271-8704

**Scott Michel Literary Services**
80 Broome Avenue
Atlantic Beach, NY 11506
516-239-7092

**Toby Stein**
45 Church Street
Montclair, NJ 07042
201-744-0475

**Joe Vitale**
303 Mill Stream Lane
Houston, TX 77060
713-999-1110

**William Greenleaf**
525 E. Stonebridge Drive
Gilbert, AZ 85234

**New York Editors**
521 Fifth Avenue, 17th Floor
New York, NY 10175

**Free Expressions**
3780 W. Lucas, Suite 239
Beaumont, TX 77706
409-892-3522

**Zebra Communications**
Suite 203 #255
4651 Woodstock Road
Roswell, GA 30075

**Gary Robert Muschia**
Box 172
South River, NJ 08882
908-390-0683

**Irene Frankel**
PO Box 2075
Hoboken, NJ 07030
201-798-0298

## Graphic Design, Brochures

**Mr. Steve Brown**
Brown and Company
138 Joralemon Street, #4R
Brooklyn, NY 11201
718-875-0674
E-mail:
browncompany@yahoo.com
or pubart@yahoo.com

**Leslie Nolan**
Nolan Design
1211 Sixteenth Avenue
Belmar, NJ 07718
Phone: 732-280-7989
Fax: 732-280-7998

## Illustration

**Bob Calleja**
490 Elm Avenue
Bogota, NJ 07603
Phone: 201-488-3028
Fax: 201-488-3527

**David McCoy**
28 Hilltop Terrace
Bloomingdale, NJ 07403
973-283-4323
E-mail: davetoons@aol.com

**Lorraine Garafola Represents**
206 Linda Lane
Edison, NJ 08820
908-756-9254
www.lgrepresents.com

## Letter Shop

**Access Communications Systems**
80 Ruland Road
Melville, NY 11747-6200
1-888-546-8642

**Steve Grech**
Dispatch Letter Service
New York, NY
212-307-5943

**Mitch Hisiger**
Fala Direct Marketing
70 Marcus Drive
Melville, NY 11747
516-694-1919

**Mr. Jerry Lake**
Jerry Lake Mailing Service
Airport Industrial Park
620 Frelinghuysen Avenue
Newark, NJ 07114
973-565-9268

**Mailco**
Woodridge, NJ
973-777-9500

## Library Research

**Bob Concoby**
1675 E. Main, #221
Kent, OH 44240
Phone: 330-498-0921
Fax: 330-966-8055
E-mail: concoby@usa.net

**Mr. John Maddux**
2665 Leda Court
Cincinnati, OH 45211
513-662-9176

## Literary Agents
**Bob Diforio**
D4EO Literary Agency
7 Indian Valley Road
Weston, CT 06883
Phone: 203-544-7180
Fax: 203-544-7160
E-mail: d4eo@home.com

**Faith Hamlin**
Sanford J. Greenburg
Associations
55 Fifth Avenue, 15th Floor
New York, NY 10003
212-206-5607

**BK Nelson**
1500 S. Palm Canyon Drive,
Suite 7
Palm Springs, CA 92264
Phone: 760-318-2773
Fax: 760-318-2774

**Shana Cohen**
Stuart Kershevsky Agency
381 Park Avenue South #819
New York, NY 10016
212-725-5288

**Tim Hays**
Literary Agency
923 Sawmill River Road,
#147
Ardsley, NY 10502
Phone: 914-478-5110
Fax: 914-478-5076
E-mail: Thayslit@aol.com

## Mailing Lists
**Direct Media**
200 Pemberwick Road
Greenwich, CT 06830
203-532-1000

**Mr. Steve Roberts**
Edith Roman Associates
PO Box 1556
Pearl River, NY 10965
1-800-223-2194

## Market Research
**Peter Fondulas**
Taylor Research and
Consulting
6 Glenville Street
Greenwich, CT 06831
203-532-0202

**Terrence J. Pranses**
Pranses Research Services
730 Park Avenue
Hoboken, NJ 07030-4006
201-659-2475

## Media Buying

**David Geller and Associates**
535 Fifth Avenue, 2nd Floor
New York, NY 10017
212-455-0100

**Maryanne Marillo**
Manhattan Media
535 Fifth Avenue, 10th Floor
New York, NY 10017
212-807-4077

**National Mail Order Advertising**
PO Box 5
Sarasota, FL 34230
941-366-3003
E-mail: nmoc@gte.net

**Novus Marketing**
601 Lakeshore Parkway, #900
Minneapolis, MN 55305
612-476-7700

**Linick Media**
7 Putter Lane
Middle Island, NY 11953
516-924-8555

## On-Hold Advertising Messages

**Fred Guarino**
Tikki
186 Glen Cove Avenue
Glen Cove, NY 11542
516-671-4555

## On-Hold Marketing and Communications

4910 Urvandale Avenue
Des Moines, IA 51310
1-800-259-2769

## Phone Number Sourcing

**TeleSource**
1-888-322-9466

## Photographers

**Jonathan Clymer**
Jonathan Clymer
Photography
180-F Central Avenue
Englewood, NJ 07631
201-568-1760

**Phil Degginger**
Degginer Photography
9 Evans Farm Road
Morristown, NJ 07960
201-455-1733

**Bruce Goldsmith**
Bruce Goldsmith
Photography
1 Clayton Court
Park Ridge, NJ 07656
201-391-4946

## Pocket Folders and Binders

**Mr. Jeff Becker**
Clients First
90 Elm Street
Westfield, NJ 07090
908-232-1200

## PowerPoint Presentations

**Joyce Carmeli, Bonnie Blake, Mary Cicitta**
Design On Disk
336 President Street
Saddle Brook, NJ 07663
973-253-2554

**Prime Time Staffing**
1250 E. Ridgewood Avenue
Ridgewood, NJ 07450
201-612-0303

## Premiums and Incentives

**Hanig and Company**
1200 Business Center Drive, #400
Mount Prospect, IL 60056
847-699-9090

**Nelson Marketing**
210 Commerce Street
PO Box 320
Oshkosh, WI 54902-0320
1-800-982-9159

**Perrygraf Slide Charts**
19365 Business Center Drive
Northridge, CA 91324-3552
1-800-423-5329

**Professional Concepts, Inc.**
728 Lafayette Street
Paramus, NJ 07652
201-251-1822
Thomas M. Begg

## Printing

**Joe Pity**
V&L Printing
Dumont, NJ 07628
201-384-9126

**Royal Impressions**
New York, NY
212-944-1133
www.ezroyal.com
Bruce Beyer

**Steve Brody**
Intelligeneer Printing
320 Eden Road
Lancaster, PA 17601
717-291-3100

**Lou Finger**
Omega Printing
201-207 William Street
Bensenville, IL 60106
630-595-6344
www.omegaprinting.com

## Printing, Books

**1st Books Library**
2511 West Third Street
Bloomington, IN 47404
1-800-839-8640
www.1stbooks.com

**Matt Parrott and Sons**
Waterloo, IA
1-800-728-4621
Joe Robert

## Project Management Outsourcing

**Fern Dickey**
Back Burner
9-16 Fourth Street
Fair Lawn, NJ 07410
201-797-9663

## Proofreading

**Debra Godfrey**
Godfrey Editorial Services
3 Rush Court
Plainsboro, NJ 08536
609-936-0753
E-mail: dgodfrey@prodigy.net

**Cynthia L. Shaw**
3300 Neshaminy Boulevard, #566
Bensalem, PA 19020
215-891-5165
E-mail:
Cindy_lynne@msn.com

**Robyn Waage**
164 Roosevelt Avenue
Westwood, NJ 07675
201-358-2817
E-mail: rfwaage@aol.com

## Public Relations Agencies

**Mr. Mark Bruce**
GHB Marketing
Communications
1177 High Ridge Road
Stamford, CT 06905
203-321-1242

**Mr. Don Levin**
Levin Public Relations
30 Glenn Street
White Plains, NY 10603
914-993-0900

**George Whalen**
G. J. Whalen and Company, Inc.
59 Lambert Road
New Rochelle, NY 10804
914-576-6750

## Public Seminar Companies

**American Management Associates**
1601 Broadway
New York, NY 10019
212-903-7915

**Pryor Resources, Inc.—
Division of CareerTrack**
9757 Metcalf Avenue
Overland Park, KS 66212
303-447-2323

**Conference Board**
845 Third Ave.
New York, NY 10022
212-759-0900

**Dun and Bradstreet
Corporation Foundation**
Business Education Service
PO Box 3734
New York, NY 10008-3734
212-312-6880

**Learning International**
225 High Ridge Road
Stamford, CT 06905
203-965-8400

**Padgett Thompson of
American Management
Association**
11221 Row Avenue
Leawood, KS 66211
1-800-255-4141

**Pryor Resources, Inc.**
9757 Metcalf Avenue
Overland Park, KS 66212
913-722-3990

**Publishing on Demand**
**Xlibris**
436 Walnut Street, 11th
Floor
Philadelphia, PA 19106
1-888-795-4274
www.xlibris.com

**ToExcel.com**
37 Scarborough Park
Rochester, NY 14625
617-787-2092
James Bittker

**Radio Commercials**
**Chuck Hengel**
Marketing Architects
14550 Excelsior Boulevard
Minneapolis, MN 55345
612-936-7500

**Self-Promotion Consultant**
**Ilise Benun**
The Art of Self-Promotion
1012 Park Avenue, Suite 6
Hoboken, NJ 07030
201-653-0783

## Stock Illustrations

**Stock Illustration Source**
16 W. 18th Street
New York, NY 10011
212-691-6400
www.sisstock.com

## Telemarketing

**Grace Software Marketing**
3091 Mayfield Road
Cleveland, OH 44118
216-321-2000

**Jody Kelley**
VIP Communications
201-656-3700

**Frank Stetz**
240 E. 82 Street, 20th Floor
New York, NY 10028
212-439-1777

**Mariann Weinstein**
MAW Associates
115 N. 10th Street
New Hyde Park, NY 11040
516-437-0529

## Trademark Searches

**American Trademark and Research Data**
www.trademarkresearch.com

**Thomson and Thomson**
1-800-692-8833

## Translations

**Harvard Translations**
137 Newbury Street
Boston, MA 02116
617-424-9291

## Word and Data Processing

**PCM Data Processing**
13-09 Berdan Avenue
Fair Lawn, NJ 07410
201-703-8860

# Appendix C

# Sample Documents

## Sample Press Release

FROM: Microchip Gardens, 174 Holland Avenue; New Milford, NJ 07646

CONTACT: Bob Bly, phone 201-385-1220

For immediate release

MICROCHIP GARDENS, WORLD'S FIRST "GIGAPET CEMETERY," OPENS IN NORTHERN NJ

When seven-year-old Alex Bly's gigapet died after he dropped it in the toilet, he couldn't find a place to bury it. So his father, NJ-based entrepreneur Bob Bly, created Microchip Gardens—the world's first gigapet cemetery—in the family's suburban backyard.

Now if your child's gigapet dies and can't be revived, instead of unceremoniously tossing it in the trash, you can give it a proper burial in a beautiful, tree-lined resting place.

For fees starting at $5, based on plot location and method of interment (burial, mausoleum, cremation), Bly will give your dearly departed gigapet an eternal resting place in Microchip Gardens, complete with funeral service and burial certificate.

"Even gigapets don't last forever," said Bly. "There are pet cemeteries for dogs and cats; now gigapets have one too."

To help owners get the most pleasure from gigapet ownership, Bly—author of 35 published books including The "I Hate Kathie Lee Gifford" Book (Kensington) and The Ultimate Unauthorized Star Trek Quiz Book (HarperCollins)—has written an informative new booklet, "Raising Your Gigapet." The booklet covers such topics as purchasing your first gigapet; taking the pet home; care and feeding; and play and discipline. Gigapet burial rituals and the origins of Microchip, Gardens are also covered.

To get your copy of "Raising Your Gigapet," which includes complete information on the Microchip Gardens gigapet cemetery, send $4 to: CTC, 22 E. Quackenbush Avenue, Dumont, NJ 07628.

## Sample Article Query Letter

You can promote yourself by publishing how-to and informational articles related to commercial writing in trade and business magazines read by your potential clients. To propose an article to an editor, use a query letter. The sample query below got me an assignment to write an article on letter-writing for Amtrak Express magazine—they even paid me $400!

---

Mr. James A. Frank, Editor
AMTRAK EXPRESS
34 East 51st St.
New York, NY 10022

Dear Mr. Frank:

Is this letter a waste of paper?

Yes—*if* it fails to get the desired result.

In business, most letters and memos are written to generate a specific response: close a sale, set up a meeting, get a job interview, make a contact. Many of these letters fail to do their job.

Part of the problem is that business executives and support staff don't know how to write persuasively. The solution is a formula first discovered by advertising copywriters—a formula called AIDA. AIDA stands for Attention, Interest, Desire, Action.

First, the letter gets attention ... with a hard-hitting lead paragraph that goes straight to the point, or offers an element of intrigue.

Then, the letter hooks the reader's interest. The hook is often a clear statement of the reader's problems, his needs, his concerns. If you are writing to a customer who received damaged goods, state the problem. And then promise a solution.

Next, create desire. You are offering something—a service, a product, an agreement, a contract, a compromise, a consultation. Tell the reader the benefit he'll receive from your offering. Create a desire for your product.

Finally, call for action. Ask for the order, the signature, the check, the assignment.

I'd like to write a 1,500-word article on "How to Write Letters that Get Results." The piece will illustrate the AIDA formula with a variety of actual letters and memos from insurance companies, banks, manufacturers, and other organizations.

This letter, too, was written to get a specific result an article assignment from the editor of AMTRAK EXPRESS.

Did it succeed?

Regards,

Bob Bly

P.S. By way of introduction, I'm an advertising consultant and the author of five books including TECHNICAL WRITING: STRUCTURE, STANDARDS, AND STYLE (McGraw-Hill).

## Sample Pitch Letter

A pitch letter positions an individual (or in this case, a company) as an expert available to the media for interviews on a topic of interest.

August 19, 1999

Dear Editor:

Anxiety, indecision, intimidation and agony are common feelings that surface whenever you begin the process of decorating your home. Do you tackle a big room in the house—the kitchen—or start with something smaller like reorganizing the closets? What simple home accessories can you use to brighten up the look of your living room? What type of storage do you have to keep your space from looking cluttered?

IKEA has quick and simple decoration solutions to all of these questions that are frequently asked when taking on the daunting task of decorating your home.

Enclosed please find examples of before and after visuals with easy and affordable tips on how to reorganize a closet as well as redo a kitchen. Also included is an anxiety fact sheet and an IKEA 2000 Catalog.

An IKEA spokesperson is available to demonstrate simple and quick makeover steps for the kitchen, living room, bathroom, closets and any other room in the home. We will literally create these rooms on your set with "before" and "after" displays that are simple, fun, creative and affordable—and most importantly—will not cause anxiety and fear about decorating a room.

I will follow up with you later this week. In the meantime, if you have any questions or need more information, please feel free to contact me at 212-645-6900, x128.

Regards,

Jeanette Chin

## Sample Book Proposal

### Become an Instant Guru!

### How to Gain a Reputation as a Leading Expert In Your Field—In 60 Days or Less

### By

### Robert W. Bly

### D4EO Literary Agency

Robert G. Diforio
7 Indian Valley Road
Weston, CT 06883
d4eo@home.com
203-544-7180
203-544-7160 fax
203-545-7180 cellular

Marilyn Allen
615 Westover Road
Stamford, CT 06902
ma615@aol.com
203-359-9965
203-357-9909 fax
971-797-9894 cellular

**Overview**

The average professional speaker gets $3,500 for a speech and has to market like crazy to get the engagements, but Tom Peters has more requests than he can handle for speeches at $30,000 a pop. *Why?*

There are thousands of attorneys with better track records than Alan Dershowitz, but when the media wants to interview an expert for an opinion on a hot case, he's the one they call. *Why?*

The world is filled with clinical researchers, family counselors, and psychotherapists, but ask people to name a sex expert, and 99 out of 100 will answer without hesitation, "Dr. Ruth Westheimer." *Why?*

The answer: These people are gurus—recognized authorities in their fields. Because of their guru status, they enjoy greater visibility and reputation than their peers, not to mention more success, income, and wealth.

But they are gurus not because they are more talented or successful, or because their performance and track record are superior. (Lots of attorneys have won more cases than Dershowitz.) Instead, they gained their guru status through self-promotion and publicity. That is, they are gurus not because they are great at what they do, but because they are great at *selling and marketing* themselves and what they do.

*Become an Instant Guru* is the first book to show the average practitioner in any field how, through a deliberate plan of self-promotion, they, too, can quickly elevate themselves to guru status—and enjoy the success, money, fame, and other benefits that go with the position. By becoming a guru, you set yourself above your competitors, become the preferred source of advice and service in your market, and eliminate the need to make cold calls and do the selling ordinary vendors do.

If you have ever looked at the gurus in your field and thought, "How did they become gurus? Why does the media and the public fawn over them? I know more than they do, and I'm better than they are," now you can join their elite ranks—and have others envy and wonder about you in the same way. And they will never be able to match your newfound expert status, unless you take pity on them and give them this book.

**Format**

*Become an Instant Guru* will be a trade paperback of approximately 75,000 words. It consists of a dozen chapters in three parts.

**Part I, "So You Want to Be a Guru,"** examines the guru phenomenon and the benefits of attaining guru status.

**Part II, "The 60-Day Instant Guru Plan,"** tells you what you have to do to become a guru, and provides specific, practical advice for completing each task.

**Part III, "Living the Guru Life,"** tells how to maintain and increase your guru status, while maximizing your profits from it.

The book will be packed with samples of self-promotion materials including brochures, direct mail packages, letters, seminar invitations, and press releases. Many will be from my own self-promotions, where I can discuss the story behind the promotion in detail, including cost, response, and results.

The book will be based both on the author's personal experience in becoming a guru in his niche (direct marketing) as well as case histories of others who have established guru status using the methods outlined in the book. Examples include Roger C. Parker (desktop publishing), Tony Robbins (peak performance), Jay "The Juice Man" Kordich (juicing), Jakob Nielsen (Web usability), Rosabeth Moss Kanter (change), Ed Yourdon (software engineering), Seth Godin (permission marketing), Peter Drucker (management), Martha Stewart (entertaining at home), and Joseph Juran (quality).

Using all the methods described in the book, the author has attained a level of guru status in direct marketing that eliminates the need for him to do any personal selling of his services (including sales calls) of any kind. Steve Roberts, president of Edith Roman Associates, one of the largest mailing list brokers in the United States, says, "Bob Bly is to direct marketing what Mozart is to music."

Bob's guru status brings him regular assignments from virtually every major direct marketer (including Phillips Publishing, Rodale, Boardroom, and KCI). He has won numerous industry awards (including an Echo, the "Oscar" of direct marketing) and has authored a number of classic books on the subject (including *The Copywriter's Handbook,* cited as a "Mini-Class of Direct Marketing" by the Direct Marketing Club of New York). His guru status provides a steady flow of more assignments—than he can possibly handle—giving him an annual gross income of $400,000 a year. This is approximately eight times the average income for freelance copywriters reported by *Creative Business* newsletter.

**Table of Contents**

Preface

**Part I: So You Want to Be a Guru**

Examines the guru phenomenon and the benefits of attaining guru status.

**Chapter 1. What Is a Guru?** Definition. Benefits of becoming a guru. Examples. Why our society is enamored of them, and how you can take advantage of this attitude.

**Chapter 2. How to Join the Guru Elite.** Gurus are not born, they are "manufactured," through self-marketing and promotion. This chapter outlines the philosophy, attitude, and action plan you must implement to elevate yourself to guru status.

**Part II: The 60-Day Instant Guru Plan**

Explains what you have to do to become a guru, with specific, practical advice for completing each task.

**Chapter 3. Articles.** Writing articles for publication is the quickest and easiest way, and usually the first step, in building your guru reputation. This chapter shows how to come up with article ideas, write a winning query letter, research and write a successful article, get it published, use the reprints in self-promotion, and get people to respond to your articles and buy your products and services.

**Chapter 4. Books.** Writing one or more books is crucial to attaining guru status. In an article in *CIO* magazine about the top ten gurus in Information Technology, every one of the ten had written at least one book. In this chapter I share my experience, gained in writing 50 published books, to show the reader how to write a book on your area of expertise and get it published.

**Chapter 5. Information Products.** Gurus are focal points of information on a specific niche topic, and they enhance their reputations as experts by producing and marketing "information products" on these topics. This chapter shows what these products are and how to create and market them. It includes audio tapes, videos, CD-ROMs, software, directories, resource guides, special reports, market research, booklets, pamphlets, and more.

**Chapter 6. Newsletters and E-Zines.** A powerful technique for building your reputation with a defined audience over a period of time is to regularly send them a newsletter, which can either be free or paid subscription. This chapter tells how to produce, distribute, and market traditional print newsletters as well as electronic newsletters delivered via the Internet (e-zines).

**Chapter 7. Speaking.** Giving keynote speeches at meetings and conventions quickly establishes your reputation as expert. This chapter shows how to get these invitations and deliver a memorable talk that positions you as an expert in your topic.

**Chapter 8. Seminars.** Virtually every guru gives seminars, both to reach new prospects as well as solidify his or her position as a leading expert. Speeches are short talks, typically an hour long. Seminars, in comparison, are more comprehensive presentations ranging from a half day to three days. This chapter outlines the various types of seminars, the pros and cons of each, and how to use them effectively to promote yourself, your company, and your services or products.

**Chapter 9. Public Relations.** How to get the print and broadcast media—newspapers, magazines, radio, TV—to interview you and feature you in stories relating to your area of expertise.

**Chapter 10. The Internet.** Another central component of establishing yourself as a guru is building a Web presence, the centerpiece of which is a Web site that is both an information resource and community of interest on a subject relating to your core expertise. This chapter shows how to map out and create a Web site for you as a guru, and covers other Web marketing techniques including e-mail marketing, banner ads, forums, chat rooms, and discussion groups.

**Part III: Living the Guru Life**

How to maintain and increase your guru status, while maximizing your profits from it.

**Chapter 11. Profiting from Your Guru Status.** How to capitalize on your guru status and use it to sell lots of your products and services at higher prices than you charged when you were less well known.

**Chapter 12. Maintaining and Enhancing Your Guru Position.** Strategies for staying current in your field and preventing your expertise from becoming dated and out of vogue. Also covers ways to keep yourself in the forefront of your field, both in the media and your target market's top-of-mind awareness.

**Appendixes**

A. Books

B. Periodicals

C. Web Sites

D. Technology

E. Model Documents

About the Author

Index

**Markets**

*Become an Instant Guru* will appeal to several strong book-buying markets:

- **Consultants.** Consultants can use the methods in this book to promote their consulting businesses as well as generate additional income (guru-building techniques such as writing books or giving seminars can be lucrative profit centers). According to Occupational Outlook Quarterly, there are more than 230,000 management consultants in North America. The best-selling book on consulting, *How to Succeed as an Independent Consultant* by Herman Holtz (John Wiley & Sons), has sold more than 160,000 copies.

- **Authors.** Like consultants, authors (especially nonfiction) can increase their sales if they are perceived as the guru in their subject. There are approximately 250,000 writers in North America.

- **Corporate executives and managers.** In today's corporate environment, workers increasingly specialize in narrow areas—everything from local area networking to cost-based accounting. Becoming a guru in your niche can help you rise to the top of the corporate ladder, earning a salary in six figures or higher. According to the Occupational Outlook Quarterly, more than 3 million workers in North America are classified as "managers and executives."

- **Entrepreneurs and "wanna-be" entrepreneurs.** One of the most effective ways for a small business to grow large and profitable is to position the company or its owner as a guru in its field or industry. Ken Hakuta, known as "Dr. Fad," made millions with his Wacky Wall Walker. Jay "The Juice Man" Kordich once sold 5,000 juicing machines at $395 each after doing a single 20-minute radio interview on the health benefits of drinking fresh juice. In the United States alone, there are more than 10 million small businesses, with 625,000 new businesses starting annually.

- **Opportunity seekers.** There is a core market of people who want to quit their jobs and make money in their own business, and regularly buy books of this type. They are the opportunity-seekers, readers of such magazines as *Entrepreneur* and *Spare-Time Opportunities.* There are more than one million of these eager book buyers available on commercial mailing lists in North America.

- **Speakers and aspiring speakers.** The surest path to a busy speaking schedule and five-figure fee for a professional speaker is to be recognized as a guru in his or her field. The National Speakers

Association, a group for professional and aspiring speakers, has 4,000 members. The number of "wanna-be" speakers may be as high as 5 to 10 times this number, based on nonmember attendance at NSA functions.

## Promotion

The most cost-effective way to promote this book is through press releases and selected review copies to general business magazines, newspapers, and trade publications. Promotion could also take place via sale of second serial rights to business publications.

Other marketing opportunities include advertising in appropriate card decks, offering the book through associations to members, and speaking at appropriate meetings of entrepreneurs, speakers, consultants, and other professionals.

We could run a "Become a Guru" contest where I personally work with a reader to help him become a guru, and we then publicize the results.

## Competition

There are dozens of books on public relations, self-promotion, and publicity, including my own just-published *Public Relations Kit for Dummies* (IDG, co-authored with Eric Yaverbaum). But, almost no books focus on positioning an individual or small firm as the guru in their field.

*Free Agent Nation: How America's New Independent Workers Are Transforming the Way We Live* by Daniel Pink (Warner Books, 2000, hardcover, 288 pages, $24.95) promises to touch on some of the same ground I do. But it is a social issue book focusing on the phenomenon of self-employment, not a how-to guide on positioning yourself at the top of your chosen area of specialization.

*Get Noticed: Self Promotion for Creative Professionals* by Sheree Clark and Kristen Lenner (North Light Books, 2000, paperback, 144 pages, $29.99) focuses on self-promotion, but is limited to "creative professionals"—illustrators, copywriters, designers, photographers—mainly in the advertising field. Similarly, *The Pocket Self Promotion, Marketing, and Advertising Guide* by Ernie Blood (Carmel Publishing, 1997, 233 pages, $29.95) covers self-promotion only for realtors.

There are several new books on "personal branding" as a means of promoting your career, such as *Brand Yourself: How to Create an Identity for a Brilliant Career* by David Andrusia and Rick Haskins (Ballantine Books,

2000, paperback, 272 pages, $14). But *Brand Yourself* and the other personal branding books focus on building an acceptable image rather than differentiating yourself with expertise as a guru, and are written primarily for corporate employees. By comparison, *Become an Instant Guru* is aimed at helping entrepreneurs and self-employed professionals gain a competitive advantage in the marketplace rather than the workplace.

**Author's Bio**

Bob Bly earns a six-figure annual income as an independent copywriter, and became a self-made millionaire, without selling, marketing, or going on prospect meetings, ever. He has achieved this by positioning himself as a guru in a small niche field: direct mail copywriting. The methods he used include writing articles, authoring books, teaching at a university, and giving seminars and speeches.

Mr. Bly is the author of 50 books including *Selling Your Services* (Henry Holt & Co.), *Internet Direct Mail: The Complete Guide to Successful e-mail Marketing Campaigns* (NTC Business Books), *The Six-Figure Consultant* (Dearborn), and *Getting Started as a Speaker, Training, or Seminar Consultant* (John Wiley). His articles have appeared in such publications as *Direct Marketing, Business Marketing, Direct, Writer's Digest, New Jersey Monthly, Cosmopolitan, Amtrak Express, Computer Decisions,* and *Sharing Ideas.* He is the editor of a monthly magazine, *Bits & Pieces for Salespeople,* published by Economics Press.

Bob has given keynote and breakout presentations at many association meetings including the International Tile Exposition, Mail Order Nursery Association, American Chemical Society, and International Laboratory Distributors Association. Organizations that have hired Bob to give in-house training to their employees include Walker Richer & Quinn, Thoroughbred Software, IBM, Arco Chemical, Foxboro, Metrum Instrumentation, Cardiac Pacemakers, the U.S. Army, and Osteonics. In addition, Bob has successfully sponsored his own public seminars including "How to Become a Published Author," aimed at consumers, and "Writing for ISO 9000," aimed at a business audience.

Bob has taught marketing and writing at New York University. He has appeared on dozens of radio and TV shows including CNBC and *Hard Copy.*

## Sample Short-Form Resource Box

> BOB BLY, an independent copywriter and consultant, has written copy for more than 100 companies including IBM, AT&T, Agora Publishing, Hyperion Software, and AlliedSignal. He is the author of over 35 books including The Advertising Manager's Handbook (Prentice Hall), Business-To-Business Direct Marketing (NTC Business Books), and The Copywriter's Handbook (Henry Holt & Co.).
>
> Bob writes sales letters, direct mail packages, ads, brochures, articles, press releases, newsletters, scripts, and other marketing materials clients need to sell their products and services to businesses. He also consults with clients on marketing strategy, mail order selling, and lead generation programs.
>
> For more information contact: Bob Bly, 22 E. Quackenbush Avenue, Dumont, NJ 07628, phone 201-385-1220.

## Sample Long-Form Bio

> ### Business-to-Business/High-Tech/Direct Response
>
> BOB BLY is an independent copywriter and consultant with 20 years of experience in business-to-business, high-tech, industrial, and direct marketing. He is the director of the Center for Technical Communication, a consulting firm in Dumont, NJ.
>
> Bob has written copy for such clients as ITT Fluid Technology, Medical Economics, M&T Chemicals, Brooklyn Union Gas, Sony, Ascom/Timeplex, G.E. Solid State, Graver Chemical, Plato Software, IBM, AT&T, Agora Publishing, McGraw-Hill, CoreStates Financial Corporation, Swiss Bank, Value Rent-a-Car, Hyperion Software, GeorgeTown Publishing, Alloy Technology, EBI Medical Systems, Citrix Systems, AlliedSignal, The BOC Group, John Wiley & Sons, DataFocus, and Graver Chemicals. His work has won several awards, including a Gold Echo from the Direct Marketing Association, an IMMY from the Information Industry Association, two Southstar Awards, an American Corporate Identity Award of Excellence, and the Standard of Excellence award from the Web Marketing Association.

Bob is the author of more than 40 books including *The Advertising Manager's Handbook* (Prentice Hall), *Business-To-Business Direct Marketing* (NTC Business Books), and *The Copywriter's Handbook* (Henry Holt & Co.). Other titles include *Power-Packed Direct Mail And Successful Telephone Selling,* both from Henry Holt & Co., and *Keeping Clients Satisfied,* from Prentice Hall. His articles have appeared in *Business Marketing, Direct, Computer Decisions, New Jersey Monthly, Writer's Digest, Amtrak Express, Web Bound, Science Books & Films,* and *Direct Marketing.* Bob edits *Bits & Pieces for Salespeople,* published monthly by Economics Press.

Bob has presented marketing, sales, writing, and customer service seminars for numerous groups including the Publicity Club of New York, Women in Communications, Direct Marketing Association, Independent Laboratory Distributors Association, American Institute of Chemical Engineers, American Chemical Society, Business Marketing Association, International Tile Exposition, Direct Marketing Creative Guild, Women's Direct Response Group, Direct Media Coop, and American Marketing Association. He also taught business-to-business copywriting and technical writing at New York University.

Bob writes sales letters, direct mail packages, ads, brochures, articles, press releases, newsletters, scripts, and other marketing materials clients need to sell their products and services to businesses. He also consults with clients on marketing strategy, mail order selling, and lead generation programs.

Bob Bly holds a B.S. in chemical engineering from the University of Rochester. He is a member of the American Institute of Chemical Engineers and the Business Marketing Association. For a FREE information kit, or a free, no-obligation cost estimate for your next project, contact:

*Bob Bly*
*22 E. Quackenbush Avenue*
*Dumont, NJ 07628 / phone 201-385-1220 / fax 201-385-1138*

## Sample Pitch Letter to Get Speaking Engagements

Another excellent way to market yourself is by giving talks and speeches to groups of advertising and marketing professionals. Here's a model query letter you can use to generate such engagements:

---

Ms. Jane Smiley
Program Director
Women in Engineering
Big City, USA

Dear Ms. Smiley:

Did you know that, according to a recent survey in *Engineering Today*, the ability to write clearly and concisely can mean $100,000 extra in earnings over the lifetime of an engineer's career?

For this reason, I think your members might enjoy a presentation I have given to several business organizations around town, "10 Ways to Improve Your Technical Writing."

As the director of Plain Language, Inc., a company that specializes in technical documentation, I have worked with hundreds of engineers to help them improve their writing. My presentation highlights the 10 most common writing mistakes engineers make, and gives strategies for self-improvement.

Does this sound like the type of presentation that might fit well into your winter program schedule? I'd be delighted to speak before your group. Please phone or write so we can set a date.

Regards,
Blake Garibaldi, Director
Plain Language, Inc.

---

## Letter Requesting Referrals

One of the best sources of sales leads is referrals from existing clients. If your clients aren't giving you as many referrals as you want, here's a letter you can use to ask for more:

---

Ms. Joan Zipkin
Acme Retail Outlets
Anytown, USA

Dear Joan:

I'm glad you liked the Spring catalog I recently completed for you. Like you, I'm always on the lookout for new business. So I have a favor to ask. Could you jot down, on the back of this letter, the names, addresses, and phone numbers of a few of your colleagues who might benefit from knowing more about my services?

(Naturally, I don't want anyone whose product line competes with your own.)

Then, just mail the letter back to me in the enclosed reply envelope.

I may want to mention your name when contacting these people. Let me know if there's any problem with that.

And thanks for the favor!

Regards,
Sam Tate

---

## Letter for Soliciting Testimonials from Clients

After completing a job successfully, you can use this letter to solicit a testimonial from the client. A sheet of paper filled with testimonials is a very powerful addition to a promotional package and convinces prospects you are good at what you do. I always send a self-addressed stamped envelope and two copies of the letter. This way the recipient doesn't have to make a copy of the letter or address and stamp his own envelope.

Mr. Andrew Specher, President
Hazardous Waste Management, Inc.
Anywhere, USA

Dear Andrew:

I have a favor to ask of you.

I'm in the process of putting together a list of testimonials—a collection of comments about my services from satisfied clients like yourself.

Would you take a few minutes to give me your opinion of my writing services? No need to dictate a letter; just jot your comments on the back of this letter, sign below, and return to me in the enclosed envelope. (The second copy is for your files.) I look forward to learning what you like about my service ... but I also welcome any suggestions or criticisms, too.

Many thanks, Andrew.

Regards,
Bob Bly

YOU HAVE MY PERMISSION TO QUOTE FROM MY COMMENTS, AND USE THESE QUOTATIONS IN ADS, BROCHURES, MAIL, AND OTHER PROMOTIONS USED TO MARKET YOUR FREELANCE WRITING SERVICES.

Signature _____ Date _____

## Letter for Getting Permission to Use Existing Testimonial

Some clients will send you letters of testimonial unsolicited. Before you use them in your promotions, get their permission in writing, using this form letter:

---

Mr. Mike Hernandez
Advertising Manager
Technilogic, Inc.
Anytown, USA

Dear Mike:

I never did get around to thanking you for your letter of 2/15/87 (copy attached). So ... thanks!

I'd like to quote from this letter in the ads, brochures, direct mail packages, and other promotions I use to market my writing services with your permission, of course. If this is okay with you, would you please sign the bottom of this letter and send it back to me in the enclosed envelope. (The second copy is for your files.)

Many thanks, Mike.

Regards,
Bob Bly

YOU HAVE MY PERMISSION TO QUOTE FROM THE ATTACHED LETTER IN ADS, BROCHURES, MAIL, AND OTHER PROMOTIONS USED TO MARKET YOUR FREELANCE WRITING SERVICES.

Signature _____ Date _____

---

## Sample Virus Protection Policy

Explain to new and existing clients in a memo the steps you take to prevent the files you send them from being contaminated with viruses. Here is a sample anti-virus protection policy.

TO: All clients and potential clients
FROM: Bob Bly
RE: Our anti-virus policy
LAST UPDATED: 10-13-97

1. We make every effort to ensure that files sent to our clients via e-mail or disk are virus-free—but we CANNOT guarantee it.

2. We run McAfee 3.5 VirusScan, which is the most widely used anti-virus program worldwide. It is used by 25 million people, 80% of the Fortune 1000, and 40,000 organizations.

3. According to McAfee, VirusScan technology has been shown in lab tests to detect virtually every virus. These include boot, file, multi-parties, stealth, mutating, encrypted, and polymorphic viruses.

4. Since new viruses crop up all the time, we routinely upgrade our VirusScan program by downloading the latest versions from the McAfee BBS (bulletin board). We recommend that clients running VirusScan do likewise.

5. Even running the latest anti-virus software cannot guarantee a virus-free file with absolute certainty, because of the new viruses being launched constantly. Clients should run the most recent version of whatever anti-virus software they use.

6. If you open a file we sent you via e-mail and it contains a virus, that does NOT mean it had a virus when we sent it from our end: Files sent via the Internet can pick up files in transit.

7. The only 100% foolproof protection against receiving a virus is to request that documents be faxed instead of e-mailed. You can't pick up a virus from a hard copy.

8. If you have any problems with a virus in a file we send you, please notify us immediately: 201-385-1220. If you are having a virus problem in general, we can refer you to computer consultants who may be able to help.

**One-Page Course Description for an In-House Corporate Training Seminar**

# Persuasive Presentations Skills for Technical Professionals

Making technical sales presentations is a difficult task. Often the audience is diverse, consisting of listeners at many different levels of technical competence and with different interests and objectives. Your challenge is to deliver the technical "meat" to the hardcore techies while giving less technical listeners the bottom-line information they need to make a decision in your favor. On top of that, many technical professionals are uncomfortable speaking before groups, making the task even tougher.

This seminar shows technical professionals how to make team and customer presentations that get their message across, build their credibility as an authority in the topic, and get the audience to trust them and want to do business with them. You'll discover how to make even the most seemingly boring subjects come alive for listeners by finding and focusing on the "kernel of interest" that connects their needs with the subject matter.

**Contents:**

- Determining the exact topic of your talk
- Researching your subject matter beyond your own knowledge
- Organizing your material for maximum audience interest and appeal
- How to grab and keep your audience's attention
- How to determine—in advance—what the audience needs and wants to hear from you
- Getting the audience to "buy into" your approach, technology, system, or solution

- Creating, finding, and using visual aids that enhance rather than detract from your talk
- What materials should you hand out—and when?
- Positioning the audience to take the next step
- Answering questions—especially when you don't know the answer
- Overcoming stage fright and gaining comfort and confidence when speaking to groups
- Communicating one-on-one with your audience
- Advanced tips to boost your presentation quality to the next level—quickly and easily

**Length of Program:** 1- or 2-day

CTC, 22 E. Quackenbush Avenue, Dumont, NJ 07628, phone 201-385-1220

## Sample Client Satisfaction Survey (Post-Assignment)

TO: Clients
FROM: Bob Bly
RE: Performance evaluation
filename: Survey1

Dear Valued Client:

Would you please take a minute to complete and return this brief questionnaire to me? (Doing so is optional, of course.) It would help me serve you better—and ensure that you get the level of quality and service you want on every job. Thanks!

-----------------------------------------------------------------------------------

1. How would you rate the quality of the presentation I gave to your group?
   ❏ Excellent   ❏ Very good   ❏ Good   ❏ Fair   ❏ Poor

2. What overall rating would you give my services?
   ❏ Excellent   ❏ Very good   ❏ Good   ❏ Fair   ❏ Poor

3. How would you rate the value received compared with the fee you paid?
   ❏ Excellent   ❏ Very good   ❏ Good   ❏ Fair   ❏ Poor

4. What did you like best about my service?   _____

   _____

5. What would you like to see improved?   _____

   _____

Your name (optional):   _____

   _____

Company:   _____

   _____

Please return this form to:

Bob Bly
22 E. Quackenbush Avenue
Dumont, NJ 07628
fax 201-385-1138
phone 201-385-1220
e-mail Rwbly@aol.com

## Sample Promotional Newsletter

---

**Bob Bly's Direct Response Letter**

Resources, ideas, and tip for improving response to business-to-business, high-tech, industrial, and direct marketing.

*Vol. I. No. 1*        *$5*

---

### WELCOME TO THE PREMIERE ISSUE ...

... of Bob Bly's Direct Response Letter—Bob Bly, publisher; Ilise Benun, Editor.

\*\*\*\*\*\*\*\*

### WHY "BOB BLY'S DIRECT RESPONSE LETTER"?

Many of our clients, prospects, colleagues, readers, and friends complain that we don't keep them up-to-date on Bob's latest books, articles, publications, direct mail tips, marketing techniques, clients, projects, and controls. This short newsletter is designed to fill that gap. The retail price is $5 per issue, but you have been chosen to receive a subscription absolutely FREE. If you'd rather not receive it, just let us know (contact information appears at the bottom of the reverse side of this sheet).

Right now, Bly's Direct Response Letter is available only as a hard copy publication. In the future, we plan to offer an e-mail version. We will also post past issues on Bob's new Web site (see below). Any suggestions you have for improvement—or articles you want to contribute—are welcome.

\*\*\*\*\*\*\*\*

### VISIT BOB'S NEW COPYWRITING WEB SITE

Samples of direct mail packages, brochures, and other marketing materials written by Bob Bly can now be viewed at Bob's new copywriting Web site, www.bly.com. You'll also find a ton of useful information including a library of downloadable how-to articles on direct marketing. (You may reprint these in any of your publications as long as you credit Bob as the author and include his Web site address, www.bly.com.)

\*\*\*\*\*\*\*\*

### BECOME A PUBLISHED MARKETING AUTHOR!

Prentice Hall has selected Bob as the editor of its forthcoming reference manual, *The Marketing Manager's Handbook.* If you've written how-to articles on marketing and would like to see them considered for inclusion in the book, please send them along. We'll acknowledge every article received and, if it's selected, let you know when the book (and your article) is published.

\*\*\*\*\*\*\*\*

### BOB APPOINTED EDITOR OF "BITS & PIECES FOR SALESPEOPLE"

Economics Press, publishers of *Bits & Pieces,* has appointed Bob editor of their latest publication, *Bits & Pieces for Salespeople.* This monthly pocket-size mini-magazine provides tips, techniques, and inspiration to salespeople, sales managers, and other sales and marketing professionals. For a FREE sample issue, call Economics Press at 800-526-2554. Or visit their Web site www.epinc.com.

(over, please)

## BOB'S LATEST BOOK!

Bob's latest book, *The Encyclopedia of Business Letters, Fax Memos, and E-Mail,* has just been released by Career Press. According to the cover blurb, the book "features hundreds of model letters, faxes, and e-mails you can pick up and adapt to give your business writing the attention it deserves." The book can be ordered online at www.amazon.com or by calling Career Press at 1-800-CAREER-1. Trade paperback, 286 pages, $18.99.

********

## "HOW TO INCREASE DM RESPONSE" PRESENTED AT DMAW

On July 13, 1999 Bob will give a presentation, "How to Increase Your Direct Mail Response Rates," for the Direct Marketing Association of Washington DC (DMAW). To order an audio cassette of Bob's talk, call DMAW at 703-821-DMAW (3629).

********

## AWARD NEWS

Bob NEVER enters awards contests, but occasionally our clients enter something he's written for them. A Web site Bob helped produce for Edith Roman Associates, a major mailing list and Internet marketing company, recently won a Standard of Excellence Award from the Web Marketing Association. You can check out the site at www.edithroman.com. And if you need mailing lists, Bob recommends Edith Roman highly; call 800-223-2194 for list recommendations or a list catalog.

********

## BOB FOR HIRE

Bob is available on a limited basis for copywriting of direct mail packages, sales letters, brochures, ads, PR materials, and Web pages. We recommend you call for a FREE copy of our updated Copywriting Information Kit. Just let us know your industry and the type of copy you're interested in seeing (ads, mailings, etc.), and we'll tailor a package of recent samples to fit your requirements. Call Ilise Benun at 201-653-0783 or e-mail Ilise@artofselfpromotion.com.

********

## THE VIRTUAL OFFICE BECOMES A REALITY

Lots of articles herald the coming of the "virtual office," but we've been doing it for years. Bob works out of Dumont, NJ—phone 201-385-1220. Ilise, who is Bob's representative for copywriting and consulting services, is based in Hoboken—phone 201-653-0783. Carolyn Mazza, administrative assistant, is in Fair Lawn—phone 201-703-8860. We're in constant touch, so you can reach any of us, at any time, by calling any location; if one of us is out, one of the others will respond right away. This way you don't have to wait to get your need addressed.

| | |
|---|---|
| Bob Bly | 22 E. Quackenbush Ave. |
| Copywriter/consultant | Dumont, NJ 07628 |
| Rwbly@bly.com | phone 201-385-1220 |
| www.bly.com | fax 201-385-1138 |

# Index

## A

Abraham, Jay, *Stealth Marketing*, 85
Abrams, Norm, 4
action plans, 32-34
agents, publishers, compared, 77-78
animation, outside vendors, 253
Armstrong, Richard, 15
*Art of Self Promotion, The,* newsletter, 30
articles
    books, compared, 70-73
    deadlines, 55-57
    editors, contacting, 48-53
    exclusivity, 53-55
    length, 55-57
    magazines, choosing, 44-45
    publishing
        trade journals, 43-44
        Web, 57-60
    writing, 33, 43
    types, 45-47
Atkins, Robert, 4
attitude, gurus, 23-25
attitudinally (jargon words), 32
audience, books, considerations, 69-70
audio, Web sites, 209-210
audio albums, 90
audio duplication, outside vendors, 253
audio tapes, 90
    outside vendors, 253

## B

Bachner, Jane, *Speaking Up*, 134
*Bacon's Publicity Checker*, 44
Baldridge, Letitia, 4
Beckwith, Harry, 6
Bennis, Warren, 5
Benun, Ilise, 29
Birnbaum, Stephen, 6
Blake, Bonnie, *Design on Disk*, 259
Blake, Gary, 70
Blanchard, Ken, 3, 5
Bly, Robert, 47
    *Copywriter's Handbook: A Step-by-Step Guide to Writing Copy That Sells, The,* 247
Bock, Wally, 14
Bogle, Jack, 234
booklets, 87
Bookman, Robert, 40
books, 89
    articles, compared, 70-73
    audience considerations, 69-70
    e-books, 81-82
    market comparisons, 73-75
    pricing, 75
    publishing, 69
        agents, 77-78
        options, 67-68
        self-promotion, 76-77
        self-publishing, 78-81
    selling online, 208-209
    writing, 33, 63-67, 78
Bradbury, Ray, *Zen and the Art of Writing*, 64
Brazelton, T. Berry, 5
Bryant-Quinn, Jane, 5
Buffett, Warren, 6
business plans, outside vendors, 253

## C

calculating earning potential, 228-231
Caples, John, *Tested Advertising Methods*, 248
Carmeli, Joyce, *Design on Disk*, 259
cartoons, outside vendors, 253
case studies
    Davidson, Jeff, 38-41
    Parker, Roger C., 17-18
catalogs, information products, 92-93
Cates, Bill, *Unlimited Referrals*, 248
CD-ROMs, duplication, outside vendors, 254
*Chemical Engineering* magazine, 49
Chopra, Deepak, 6
Cialdini, Robert B., 5
classified ads, information products, 98-104
columns (syndicated), public relations, 183-192
company newsletters, 106-107
competitive intelligence, outside vendors, 254
*Complete Idiot's Guide to Direct Marketing, The,* 47
*Complete Idiot's Guide to Managing Stress, The,* 40
*Complete Idiot's Guide to Managing Your Time, The,* 40
*Copywriter's Handbook: A Step-by-Step Guide to Writing Copy That Sells, The,* 247
cost
    newsletters, considerations, 118-120
    seminars, controlling, 164
Covey, Stephen, 3, 5
*Creative Direct Mail Design*, 249
critical mass, achieving, 35
critical mass phase (guru development), 36
Csikszentmihalyi, Mihaly, 4
*CyberWriting: How to Promote Your Product or Service Online*, 249

## D

data processing, outside vendors, 262
Davidson, Jeff, case study, 38-41
deadlines, articles, 55-57
DeBono, Edward, 4

deductions, taxes, 240-242
Delefamina, Jerry, 3
DeMarco, Tom, 4
demassification, 32
Dershowitz, Alan, 1, 3, 5
designing newsletters, 111-112
developmental phases, gurus, 35-36
digital printing, outside vendors, 254
direct marketing, information products, 94-98
disability insurance, 245
domain names, Web sites, 198-199
Drucker, Peter, 2-5, 22
Duke, James, 5
Dunn, Rick, 47
Dutka, Alan, 4

# E

e-books, 81-82, 207-208
e-lists, building, 202-203
e-mail promotions, 203-204
e-zines, 105-106, 122-124
    articles, publishing in, 57-60
    cost considerations, 118-120
    designing, 111-112
    free-of-charge e-zines, 120-122
    promoting, 110-111
    publishing, 33
    subscriber lists, building, 108-110
    subscription fees, charging, 113
    Web sites, 205-206
earning potential, calculating, 228-231
Ebert, Roger, 4
editors, contacting, 48-53
*Effective Communication of Ideas,* 126
ending speeches, 137-138
ethics, gurus, 25-26
exclusivity, articles, 53-55
*Expanding Your Consulting Practice with Seminars,* 147

# F–G

feature syndicates, outside vendors, 254
fees
    newsletters, charging, 113
    seminars, 159-161
fit-a-category strategy, invented term strategy, compared, 30-32
Floyd, Elaine, *Marketing with Newsletters,* 248
free tutorial seminars, 151-154
free-of-charge newsletters, 120-122
freelance writers, outside vendors, 254

Garafola, Lorraine, *Lorraine Garafola Represents,* 256
Gates, Bill, 5
*Generate Word of Mouth Advertising: 101 Easy and Inexpensive Ways to Promote Your Business,* 248
*Getting Started in Speaking, Training, or Seminar Consulting,* 247
ghostwriters, outside vendors, 255
Gilbert, Rob, SWL + SWL = SW formula, 8
Godin, Seth, 5

graphic design, outside vendors, 256
Gray, John, 22
    *Men Are from Mars, Women Are from Venus,* 14
growth phase (guru development), 35
guru-focused Web sites, topic-focused Web sites, compared, 199-202
gurus, 1-6
    action plans, 32-34
    attitude, 23-25
    benefits of, 11-13
    case study, 17-18
    development, phases, 35-36
    ethics, 25-26
    hatred of, 6-8
    knowledge base, 27-28
    list of today's top gurus, 3-6
    love of, 19
    market niches, 28-30
    methodology, 26-27
    mini-gurus, compared, 22-23
    philosophy, 21-22
    popularity of, 6-8
    qualifications, 13-15
    veracity of, 8-11

# H

Hakuta, Ken, 4
Hammer, Michael, 31
handouts, speeches, 139-143
*Harvard Business Review,* 47
Hawkins, Stephen, 5
health insurance, 243
Holtz, Herman, 4
    *Expanding Your Consulting Practice with Seminars,* 147
hooks, public relations, developing, 170-173
Hopkins, Tom, 6
*How to Advertise and Promote Your Small Business,* 74
*How to Create and Market a Successful Seminar or Workshop,* 161
*How to Get Your Book Published,* 77, 247
*How to Profit Through Catalog Marketing,* 248
*How to Promote Your Own Business,* 70
Huntsinger, Jerry, 11

# I–J

illustrations, outside vendors, 256
incentives, outside vendors, 259
income, investing, 228, 232-235
information products, 33, 84-85
    audio albums, 90
    audio tapes, 90
    booklets, 87
    books, 89
    catalogs, 92-93
    direct marketing, 94-98
    manuals, 89
    monographs, 88
    newsletters, 91
    pamphlets, 87
    power packs, 91

reasons for, 86-87
resource guides, 89
selling, profitably, 93-94
small ads, 98-104
software, 92
special reports, 88
tip sheets, 87
types, 87-92
videotapes, 91
insurance
disability insurance, 245
health insurance, 243
life insurance, 244
Internet, 197
articles, publishing for, 57-60
e-lists, building, 202-203
networking, 216-218
search engines, 218-222
using, 34
Web sites
audio, 209-210
book sales, 208-209
domain names, 198-199
e-mail promotions, 203-204
guru-focused Web sites, 199-202
marketing, 212-215
need for, 197-198
surveys, 210-211
video, 209-210
invented term strategy, fit-a-category strategy,
 compared, 30-32
investing, 232-235
income, 228
Investment Act of 1940, 233
Irwin, Steve, 6

Janal, Dan, 5
jargon, avoidance of, 32
Javed, Naseem, 5
Jessel, George, 138
*Joy of Simple Living, The*, 40

**K–L**

Kanter, Rosabeth Moss, 4
Kay, Alan, 26
Kehoe, Joseph E., 240
King, Stephen, *Secret Windows*, 2
Klinghoffer, Steve, 108
knowledge base, gurus, 27-28
Kolb, Wayne, 230
Kordich, Jay, 5

Lagasse, Emeril, 4
Landers, Ann, 5
Lant, Jeffrey, 94
 *No More Cold Calls*, 248
 *Rule of Seven*, 36-37
Lanyi, Andrew, 11
Leeds, Dorothy, *PowerSpeak*, 137
Leider, Richard J., *Power of Purpose*, 237
length
articles, considerations, 55-57
speeches, 138-139
letter shops, outside vendors, 256

letters to the editor, public relations, 173-174
Libey, Don, 26
library research, outside vendors, 256-257
life insurance, 244
Limbaugh, Rush, 4
literary agents, outside vendors, 257
Lukas, Paul, Regent Group, 254

**M**

Mackenzie, Alex, 6
magazines
articles, exclusivity, 53-55
choosing, articles, 44-45
editors, contacting, 48-53
researching, 47-48
mailing lists
outside vendors, 257
seminars, obtaining, 162-163
maintenance phase (guru development), 36
*Making Successful Presentations*, 133, 249
Mandino, Og, 6
manuals, 89
market comparisons, books, 73-75
market data research, SRDS (Standard Rate and
 Data Service), 70
market niches, 28-30
market research, outside vendors, 257
marketing, Web sites, 212-215
*Marketing with Newsletters*, 248
*Marketing Your Consulting and Professional
 Services*, 40
McFee, Travis, 22
McKenna, Regis, 5
media buying, outside vendors, 258
*Men Are from Mars, Woman Are from Venus*, 14
Metcalfe, Bob, 5
methodology, gurus, 26-27
Mickelthwait, John, *Witch Doctors, The*, 7,
 63, 83
mini-gurus and gurus, compared, 22-23
*Modern Materials Handling* magazine, 49
monographs, 88
Moore, Geoffrey, 6
Muldoon, Katie, *How to Profit Through Catalog
 Marketing*, 248
multimedia Web sites, 209-210
Murdoch, Rupert, 7

**N**

Naisbitt, John, 26
names, Web sites, 198-199
Negroponte, Nicholas, 4
Nelson, Bob, 4
networking, Internet, 216-218
newsletters, 91, 105-106
company newsletters, 106-107
cost considerations, 118-120
designing, 111-112
free-of-charge newsletters, 120-122
frequency, 107-108
promoting, 110-111
publishing, 33
size, 107-108

subscriber lists, building, 108-110
subscription fees, charging, 113
  writing, 114-118
niches, 28-30
Nicholas, Ted, 228
Nielsen, Jakob, 6
Nierenberg, Gerald, 5
*No More Cold Calls,* 248
North, Gary, 13, 27

## O

*Ogilvy on Advertising,* 248
Ogilvy, David
  *Ogilvy on Advertising,* 248
  *Unpublished Ogilvy, The,* 32
Oldenburg, Don, 40
*On the Air: How to Get on Radio and TV Talk Shows and What to Do When You Get There,* 193
on-hold advertising messages, outside vendors, 258
online polls, 210-211
online surveys, 210-211
outside vendors
  animation, 253
  audio duplication, 253
  audio taping, 253
  business plans, 253
  CD-ROM duplication and packaging, 254
  competitive intelligence, 254
  data processing, 262
  digital printing, 254
  feature syndicates, 254
  freelance writers, 254
  ghostwriters, 255
  graphic design, 256
  illustration, 256
  letter shops, 256
  library research, 256-257
  literary agents, 257
  mailing lists, 257
  market research, 257
  media buying, 258
  on-hold advertising messages, 258
  phone number sourcing, 258
  photographers, 258
  pocket folders and binders, 259
  PowerPoint presentations, 259
  premiums and incentives, 259
  printing, 259-260
  project management outsourcing, 260
  proofreading, 260
  public relations agencies, 260
  public seminar companies, 260-261
  publishing on demand, 261
  radio spots, 261
  self-promotion consultants, 261
  stock illustrations, 262
  telemarketing, 262
  trademark searches, 262
  translations, 262
  video duplication, 253
  word processing, 262

## P–Q

*Packaging* magazine, 47
paid-subscription newsletters, 91
pamphlets, 87
Parinello, Al, *On the Air: How to Get on Radio and TV Talk Shows and What to Do When You Get There,* 193
Parker, Roger, 4
  case study, 17-18
  parts, speeches, 136-137
Peppers, Don, 5
*Perfect Sales Piece, The,* 248
periodicals
  articles, exclusivity, 53-55
  choosing, articles, 44-45
  editors, contacting, 48-53
  researching, 47-48
Peters, Tom, 1, 3-4, 31
phases, development, gurus, 35-36
phone number sourcing, outside vendors, 258
photographers, outside vendors, 258
pitch letters, public relations, 182-183
*Plant Engineering* magazine, 47
pocket folders and binders, outside vendors, 259
polls, online polls, 210-211
Popcorn, Faith, 4, 26
Porter, Michael, 4
*Power of Purpose, The,* 237
power packs, 91
*Power-Packed Direct Mail,* 247
PowerPoint presentations
  outside vendors, 259
  speeches, 143-146
*PowerSpeak,* 137
Poynter, Dan, 6
  *Self-Publishing Manual, The,* 15
PR (public relations). *See* public relations
premiums and incentives, outside vendors, 259
presentations, speeches, planning, 133-135
press releases, public relations, 174-182
pricing, books, 75
printing, outside vendors, 259-260
producing information products, 33
project management outsourcing, outside vendors, 260
promoting newsletters, 110-111
proofreading, outside vendors, 260
public relations, 169-170
  agencies, outside vendors, 260
  campaigns, conducting, 34
  hooks, developing, 170-173
  letters to the editor, 173-174
  pitch letters, 182-183
  press releases, 174-182
  radio talk shows, 192-193
  syndicated columns, 183-192
  TV appearances, 193-195
public seminar companies, outside vendors, 260-261
publications
  articles, exclusivity, 53-55
  editors, contacting, 48-53
  researching, 47-48

*Publicity Handbook, The,* 169
publishers, agents, compared, 77-78
publishing
    articles, 43-44
    books, 63-69
        options, 67-68
        self-promotion, 76-77
        self-publishing, 78-81
    e-books, Web sites, 207-208
    e-zines, 33
        Web sites, 205-206
    newsletters, 33
    reports, Web sites, 207-208
publishing houses, ideas, selling to, 69
publishing on demand, outside vendors, 261

### R

radio commercials, outside vendors, 261
radio talk shows, public relations, 192-193
Raphel, Murray, 6
*Reader's Guide to Periodical Literature,* 198
*Reality in Advertising,* 248
reconceptualize, 32
Reeves, Rosser, *Reality in Advertising,* 248
reference manuals, 89
referrals, 223-225
repeat orders, 225-227
reports, Web sites, 207-208
resales, 227-228
resource guides, 89
retirement plans, 240
Robbins, Tony, 5
Roberts, Ken, 5
*Rogue of Publishers Row, The,* 87
Romano, Frank, 4
Rosenzweig, Mark, 49
Rukeyser, Louis, 5
Rule of Seven, 36-37
Russo, Jim, 47
Rutherford, Emelie, 8, 31

### S

Safire, William, 4
Sagan, Carl, 3
saving
    money, 231-232, 235-237
    time-savings, 237-240
Sayles, Sarah, *Creative Direct Mail Design,*
    249
scheduling seminars, 160-161
Schonberger, Richard, 5
search engines, Internet, 218-222
*Secret Windows,* 2
Seidman, Dan, Web usage, 201
self-promotion, 2
    seminars, 165-168
self-promotion consultants, outside vendors,
    261
self-publishing books, 78-81
*Self-Publishing Manual, The,* 15
self-sponsored fee-paid public seminar,
    154-157
selling information products, 33
    profitably, 93-94

*Selling Your Services,* 247
seminars, 147-149
    considerations, 149-151
    costs, controlling, 164
    fees, 159-161
        setting, 159-160
    free tutorial seminars, 151-154
    giving, 34
    mailing lists, obtaining, 162-163
    positive aspects, 158-159
    scheduling, 160-161
    self-promotion, 165-168
    self-sponsored fee-paid public seminars, 154-
    157
    titles, choosing, 161
Shenson, Howard, 86
    *How to Create and Market a Successful*
        *Seminar or Workshop,* 161
Siegel, Connie McClung, *How to Advertise and*
    *Promote Your Small Business,* 74
Simmons, Richard, 4
Simpson, O.J., 3
Sixty-Day "Become a Guru" action plan, 33
Skills, Interests, Aptitudes, and Experiences
    Inventory Worksheet, 14
small ads, information products, 98-104
Smith, Terry, *Making Successful Presentations,*
    133, 249
software, information products, 92
*Speaking Up,* 134
special reports, 88
*Speech Writing Guide, The,* 138
speeches, 125-126
    ending, 137-138
    giving, 34
    handouts, 139-143
    length, 138-139
    opportunities
        choosing, 129-130
        finding, 127-129
    parts, 136-137
    PowerPoint presentations, 143-146
    presentations, planning, 133-135
    promotional deals, negotiating, 130-132
    timing, 138-139
Spencer, Barbara, 49
SRDS (Standard Rate and Data Service) market
    data, 70
*Start and Run a Successful Mail Order Business,*
    247
start-up phase (guru development), 35
*Stealth Marketing,* 85
Stewart, Martha, 4
stock illustrations, outside vendors, 262
Stone, Bob, *Successful Direct Marketing Methods,*
    249
Stone, Janet, *Speaking Up,* 134
strategies
    fit-a-category strategy, 30-32
    invented term strategy, 30-32
subscriber lists, newsletters, building, 108-110
subscription fees, newsletters, charging, 113
*Successful Direct Marketing Methods,* 249
Sugarman, Joseph, 4
surveys, online, 210-211
SWL + SWL = SW formula, 8
syndicated columns, public relations, 183-192

## T–U

talk shows
    radio, public relations, 192-193
    television, public relations, 193-195
taping audio, outside vendors, 253
taxes, deductions, 240-242
telemarketing, outside vendors, 262
television talk shows, public relations, 193-195
*Tested Advertising Methods,* 248
third-party endorsement postings, Web sites, 215-216
time-savings, 237-240
timing, speeches, 138-139
tip sheets, 87
titles, seminars, choosing, 161
Toffler, Alvin, 4
trade journals, articles, publishing in, 43-44
trademark searches, outside vendors, 262
*Trading for a Living,* 12
translations, outside vendors, 262
Trout, Jack, 5
Trump, Donald, 4
Tufte, Edward, 6
tutorial seminars, 151-154

Uhlan, Edward, *Rogue of Publishers Row, The,* 87
*Unlimited Referrals,* 248
*Unpublished Ogilvy, The,* 32
Usborne, Nick, 61
Usheroff, Roz, 21

## V

Vardaman, George, *Effective Communication of Ideas,* 126
vendors
    animation, 253
    audio duplication, 253
    audio taping, 253
    business plans, 253
    CD-ROM duplication and packaging, 254
    competitive intelligence, 254
    data processing, 262
    digital printing, 254
    feature syndicates, 254
    freelance writers, 254
    ghostwriters, 255
    graphic design, 256
    illustration, 256
    letter shops, 256
    library research, 256
    literary agents, 257
    mailing lists, 257
    market research, 257
    media buying, 258
    on-hold advertising messages, 258
    phone number sourcing, 258
    photographers, 258
    pocket folders and binders, 259
    PowerPoint presentations, 259
    premiums and incentives, 259
    printing, 259-260
    project management outsourcing, 260
    proofreading, 260
    public relations agencies, 260
    public seminar companies, 260-261
    publishing on demand, 261
    radio spots, 261
    self-promotion consultants, 261
    stock illustrations, 262
    telemarketing, 262
    trademark searches, 262
    translations, 262
    video duplication, 253
    word processing, 262
video, Web sites, 209-210
video duplication, outside vendors, 253
videotapes, 91
Vitale, Joe, *CyberWriting: How to Promote Your Product or Service Online,* 249

## W–X–Y–Z

Web sites
    articles, publishing for, 57-60
    audio, 209-210
    books, selling, 208-209
    domain names, 198-199
    e-books, 207-208
    e-lists, building, 202-203
    e-mail promotions, 203-204
    e-zines, 205-206
    guru-focused Web sites, 199-202
    marketing, 212-215
    need for, 197-198
    networking, 216-218
    polls, conducting, 210-211
    reports, 207-208
    search engines, 218-222
    surveys, conducting, 210-211
    third-party endorsement postings, 215-216
    topic-focused Web sites, compared, 199-202
    video, 209-210
Welch, James, *Speech Writing Guide, The,* 138
Westheimer, Ruth, 1, 6
White, Alexander, *Trading for a Living,* 12
Winston, Stephanie, 5
*Witch Doctors, The,* 7, 63, 83
Wooldridge, Adrian, *Witch Doctors, The,* 7, 63, 83
*Writer's Market,* 44
writing
    articles, 33, 43
        deadlines, 55-57
        length, 55-57
        types, 45-47
    books, 33, 63-67, 78
    newsletters, 114-118

Yale, David, *Publicity Handbook, The,* 169
Yaverbaum, Eric, 3

*Zen and the Art of Writing,* 64

# About the Author

Although far from a household name, **Bob Bly** has made a successful career establishing himself as a "mini-guru" in the niche field of direct mail copywriting, where he has worked for more than 20 years.

He is the author of 50 books, many of which are on marketing, direct mail, writing, and business communication. Titles include *The Complete Idiot's Guide to Direct Marketing* (Alpha Books) and *The Copywriter's Handbook* (Henry Holt & Co.).

Bob's articles have appeared in such publications as *Direct, DM News, Business Marketing, Amtrak Express, Cosmopolitan, New Jersey Monthly, Computer Decisions, Newsletter on Newsletters,* and *Chemical Engineering Progress.*

Bob has written copy for over 100 clients, including Lucent Technologies, IBM, Phillips, Agora Publishing, Medical Economics, Boardroom, Chemical Bank, PSE&G, and Alloy Technology.

He has presented seminars for such organizations as Arco Chemical, Thoroughbred Software, American Chemical Society, International Tile Exposition, Haht Software, Cambridge Technology Partners, the U.S. Army, and the Publicity Club of New York.

Bob is a member of the Business Marketing Association, Newsletter and Electronic Publishers Association, and the American Institute of Chemical Engineers. He holds a B.S. in chemical engineering from the University of Rochester.

Bob was a columnist for *Direct Marketing* magazine and editor of a monthly newsletter for Economics Press, *Bits & Pieces for Salespeople.*

Prior to becoming a freelance direct mail copywriter, Bob was a staff writer for Westinghouse and advertising manager for Koch Engineering, a manufacturer of process equipment.

Questions and comments on *Become a Recognized Authority in Your Field* may be sent to:

Bob Bly
22 East Quackenbush Avenue
Dumont, NJ 07628
Phone: 201-385-1220
Fax: 201-385-1138
E-mail: rwbly@bly.com
www.bly.com